THE UNIVERSITY OF MICHIGAN
CENTER FOR CHINESE STUDIES

MICHIGAN PAPERS IN CHINESE STUDIES
NO. 19

CHINESE AND JAPANESE
MUSIC-DRAMAS

Edited by

J. I. Crump
and
William P. Malm

Ann Arbor

Center for Chinese Studies
The University of Michigan

1975

ISBN 0-89264-019-7

Copyright © 1975

by

Center for Chinese Studies
The University of Michigan

Printed in the United States of America

Cover illustration by Elleanor H. Crown.

CONTENTS

PREFACE

This book is the result of a conference on the relations between Chinese and Japanese music-drama held at The University of Michigan (Ann Arbor), October 1-4, 1971, under the auspices of the Association for Asian Studies and the Center for Japanese Studies, the Center for Chinese Studies, the School of Music, and the Speech Department of The University of Michigan. One important inspiration for the creation of such an interdisciplinary conference was the fact that each participant had found, after years of individual research on music-drama in East Asia, consistent frustration caused by attempts to deal by himself with multiple cultural and technical problems. Another motivating force was an awareness among many members of the four disciplines involved (Chinese, Japanese, music, and drama) that the topic is in fact one of the largest untouched fields of scholarly endeavor in both Asian and theatrical studies.

The conference was founded on the assumption that no one scholar could be an expert in all the topics. Thus, each member delivered to the others copies of a draft chapter on one aspect of one area of the subject in advance of the meeting. The four days were then spent helping each other with comments and added information from each individual's area of expertise, which took on new significance in the context of the studies of others. With the aid of a rapporteur (Dale R. Johnson of Oberlin) all this was put together into the collection which forms this book. The subject is by no means closed; on the contrary, it is now opened in a scholarly "multimedia" direction that we hope will stimulate further efforts in this exciting field.

William P. Malm
J. I. Crump
Ann Arbor 1975

vii

Abbreviations Used

HK	Hsi-hsüeh Hui-k'ao
Huo-yeh	Chung-hua Huo-yeh Wen-hsüan
Sixty	Liu-shih-chung Ch'ü
YCH	Yüan-ch'ü Hsüan
ZJBS	Zeami jūroku-bu shū hyōshaku

Giants in the Earth: Yüan Drama as Seen by Ming Critics

J. I. Crump

"There were giants in the earth in those days
and . . . mighty men which were of old,
men of renown."

Genesis 6:4

I   Introduction: The Formularies

Early Ming dynasty literature was devoted to forms and criteria belonging to the T'ang and Sung dynasties (probably as a reaction to the "foreign" Yüan), but as the dynasty matured and drama became more and more a proper medium for serious writers, men began to comment on and appreciate the older Yüan drama and to evaluate, criticize, and admire those mighty men which were of old, and who lived in Yüan times.   Possibly because the lingering orthodox view was that all good things had to have come from the great <u>Chinese</u> dynasties of the past, Ming critics of the Yüan giants often comment that "of course, these <u>ch'ü</u> were heavily influenced by northern border music" and so were not to be considered in the same universe, for example, as the Sung <u>tz'u</u> (lyrics).   But having got past this <u>pro forma</u> preamble, they then subject classical Yüan musical drama to what is often searching and honest criticism.

There is a saying which reveals a part of the healthy irreverence the Chinese have toward literary criticism: <u>Hsīen yǔ wén; hòu yǔ tsé</u>, "First someone must write literature; others will find rules for it later."   It is more than a truism, it is an injunction: the author <u>should</u> be so busied with his creation that he has little time or taste for criticizing the product.   If our only alternatives were the literature <u>or</u> the criticism there would be no contest, but happily we have, in the case of Yüan musical drama, both the <u>wen</u> created during the Mongol era and the <u>tse</u> applied to it during the Ming dynasty.

We often find it useful to make some of the same observations about historical periods that we do about humans, and certainly the

1

last part of the Yüan dynasty (ca. 1264-1370) was an age characterized
by immense dramatic creativity--an age seemingly absorbed in creating,
the way an author should be--and one which left us almost no criticism
of the musical drama called tsa-chü or pei-ch'ü which was its chief
legacy.   There exists, to be sure, a brief set of do's-and-don't's
(called Tso-tz'u Shih-fa) which Chou Te-ch'ing appended to his Chung-
yüan Yin-yün (Rhymes of the Central Provinces) published in 1323, but
even these strictures were addressed to the lyric poet rather than to
the poet-dramatist--to the writers of san-ch'ü rather than hsi-ch'ü. [1]
There is also the Cho-keng Lu of T'ao Tsung-yi (fl. 1360), which contains anecdotes about dramas and dramatists and is informed more by
relish for a good story than a desire to evaluate artistic creations and
creators. [2]   Other than these, however, there is nothing which seriously
concerns itself with passing artistic judgment on the tsa-chü musical
drama during its most flourishing age.

But almost as soon as the Ming government was well established
(let us say by 1390), we begin to get publication of the so-called "ch'ü
formularies" (ch'ü-p'u) which not only gave examples of great lyrics
from dramatic ch'ü (arias) on which to pattern one's own efforts, but
also included much evaluative, critical and appreciative comment on
Yüan drama, dramatic theory, and the requirements of composing to
music and for performance--all done in an age when the Yüan dramatic form was almost extinct.   Almost without exception these critics show admiration (often amounting to reverence) for Yüan tsa-chü
and the men who wrote them even though it was, by the time all but
the earliest formularies were written, an art form which could no
longer be staged, for the simple but crucial reason that no one living
knew the music.

This considerable body of critical literature[3] is valuable for in-
sights it provides both on the tsa-chü and on Ming tastes.   The ch'ü
formularies are without doubt our best sources of information, but
they must be used with the following considerations in mind:

(1)   Many of the best known among the Ming treatises deal indiscriminately with both the longer Ming ch'uan ch'i drama form and the
Yüan tsa-chü in such a fashion that one is not always sure which genre
is being evaluated.   This shortcoming is often informative, however,
since the critics (who are frequently composers as well) are trying
to synthesize their requirements for Chinese drama in general, rather
than for either of the two forms in particular.

(2) Blind chance seems to dictate the contents of many of the
formularies and the order in which topics are treated. For example,
Chu Ch'üan († 1448) in his <u>T'ai-ho Cheng-yin P'u</u>,[4] the earliest and
in some ways the most important of the formularies, begins the book
with his own classification of musical verse (according to both topic
and style), continues with a list of nine types of parallelism, a list
of 187 Yüan poets (whose verse he tries to characterize in a sentence
or two), 150 others of second rank, sixteen gifted playwrights of the
Ming era, general comment, the traditional twelve divisions of Yüan
dramatic subject matter, and concludes the whole first section with
these interesting but <u>non-sequitur</u> observations:

> . . . Chao Tzu-ang [a Yüan dramatist] said: "When a
> youth from a good family plays in a <u>tsa-chü</u> it is called
> 'living a life of the troupe,' (<u>hang-chia sheng-huo</u>) but
> when entertainers (<u>ch'ang-yu</u>) act in it it is called a
> 'slave play' (<u>li-chia pa-hsi</u>). Men of good family always
> felt that the shame of acting cost them so dear that there
> never were very many; and there are fewer today than
> ever. Therefore, to call acting by entertainers 'life of
> the troupe' is to be very wide of the mark."
>
> Someone asked him why [these terms were used] and
> he replied, "Tsa-chü come from the pens of scholar-
> officials and poets or writers who are all freemen.
> If our class did not write them, how could actors act
> in them? If one pursues the root of the matter, it
> becomes clear that actors are truly our 'slaves'."

Much of the rest of this work and several others resembles a literary magpie nest.

(3) As one reads <u>T'ai-ho Cheng-yin P'u</u>, for example, he discovers that even it (near as it was in time to the Yüan) draws heavily
upon the Yüan dynasty <u>Chung-yüan Yin-yün</u>. This points up another
weakness of the formularies: they are derivative of each other (see
note 3 above) so that despite their number the total information they
contain is less than one would expect because they are so often
repetitious.

(4) Lastly, some of the statements found in the formularies are
simply wrong. It is possible, however, to isolate certain clusters of
misinformation (for example, the use of the <u>ch'ü</u> in the Yüan exami-

nation system, which will be treated at length in Section IV) and by discounting them make the bulk of the remaining commentary usable.

FOOTNOTES

1. See Yoshikawa Kojirō, Gen Zatsugeki Kenkyū. Tr. Cheng Ch'ing-mao. (Taipei: 1960), p. 252.

2. It does contain, however, the raw materials for criticism; for example, the valuable complete list of ch'ü-p'ai by modes which is still appended to several modern editions of Yüan-ch'ü Hsüan (hereafter, YCH).

3. It will serve the purpose of those who want to go further into the subject of Ming criticism to append an abbreviated list of the important formularies:

    1. Chu Ch'üan, T'ai-ho Cheng-yin P'u (pub. 1398) (written under the pseudonym Tan-ch'iu Hsien-sheng, Han-hsü-tzu).

    2. Hsü Wei (1521-1593), Nan-tz'u Hsü-lu (although it concentrates on Southern drama it contains much general information on earlier ch'ü).

    3. Ho Liang-chün (fl. 1566), Ch'ü-lun (very short but very influential).

    4. Wang Shih-chen (1526-1590), Ch'ü-tsao (short, derivative from the above).

    5. Wang Chi-te (Po-liang), Ch'ü-lü (pub. 1624) (longest and most informative.)

    6. Shen Te-fu, Ku-ch'ü Tsa-yen (pub. 1618) (very short but influential).

    7. Hsü Fu-tso (1560-1630), Ch'ü-lun (mostly derivative).

    All of these may be found in the ten-volume set published 1959-60 known as Chung-kuo Ku-tien Hsi-ch'ü Lun-chu Chi-ch'eng (Peking, 1960), (Vols. I-X), which is incomparably the best edition for all of them. All page citations of these works given below refer to this set.

4.   Compiled by the sixteenth son of the founder of the Ming, a man of quite remarkable talents who wrote on subjects as diverse as Taoist alchemy and the art of ch'in playing and composed some twenty tsa-chü of which two are extant. His knowledge of Yüan music, drama, and verse would have been impressive in a professional and is amazing in a prince of the royal house (he is generally known as Ning-hsien Wang) who was enfeoffed in T'aining in 1403.

The first section of his Cheng-yin P'u is usually included as prefatory matter in editions of YCH where it is attributed to one Han-hsü Tzu (Master of Emptiness), a soubriquet of Chu Ch'üan's.

II Tsang Mou-hsün and his Anthology

There is another Ming dynasty compilation quite distinct from the
formularies which in its way is vastly more important for evaluation
and criticism of Yüan drama than all of the formularies taken together. I refer, of course, to the Yüan-ch'ü Hsüan (Anthology of Yüan
Drama) (YCH) which has been more widely read and reprinted than any
other similar collection, and through which successive generations of
students and scholars gained an appreciation of the genre. The prefaces to the YCH constitute an epitome--albeit a biased one--of Ming
knowledge of and attitudes toward Yüan music and drama which will
repay careful reading. The remainder of this paper will consist of
a brief introduction to Tsang Mou-hsün, the editor of YCH (Section II),
a translation of his prefaces (Section III), and finally, an analysis of
some of the questions the prefaces pose and some of the information
to be had from them. In the process of discussing what Tsang's prefaces tell us about Yüan drama and Ming criticism of it, I will draw
upon information from most of the important formularies in order to
point up or make contrasts with Tsang's statements (Section IV).

Tsang Mou-hsün (T. Chin-shu, known also as Tsang of Wu-hsing)
got his chin-shih degree in 1580 and died in 1621. He was an icono-
clast with antiquarian literary tastes, unorthodox interests, and was
accused of impropriety by his stuffier contemporaries. He began to
publish his collection of 100 Yüan and early Ming tsa-chü in 1615.
"The First Collection" (Ch'ien-chi) of fifty appeared that year with its
own preface. He did only the first half because he "found it more
difficult to collect them" than he had at first thought, and he had run
out of money. In his case, the latter reason was important for he had
already quit his office and had no means of support--visible from this
distance, at any rate. However, the very next year he published the
remaining fifty together with a second preface. The two parts and two
prefaces are now generally published together. There is no doubt that
Tsang was one of the most informed men of his time on matters of
earlier drama, and his selection includes the very best of Yüan tsa-
chü. This was recognized by Wang Chi-te (Po-liang) in his Ch'ü-lü
(p. 170) at a time when Tsang's anthology could not yet have been a
decade old. Wang says:

The literatus of Wu-hsing, Tsang Chin-shu, has recently
edited and published 100 Yüan dramas in two sets. There
has never been a richer collection than this since the form
originated. . . . Among the hundred, he has included eight

out of ten of those excellent dramas which have always
satisfied the tastes of men. On the whole, his selection of a hundred has included three of every four worth-
while examples. Of course, some "confusion of fish-eyes
with pearls" is inevitable.

In other words, not all of us would have selected all[1] the things
Tsang chose, but every student of drama must be grateful for his
taste, skill and passionate love for Yüan theater.

This great affection for the tsa-chü form and the products of its
golden age two centuries before Tsang's time led him into somewhat
intemperate criticism of the then contemporary ch'üan-ch'i drama
which was written to southern music and the otiose nature of which
suffers badly in comparison with the tight, orderly musical suites
and unitary plots of tsa-chü. Tsang looks upon the Ming ch'uan-ch'i
with their innumerable acts and patrician appeals as little more than
decadent tsa-chü. In fact, in his prefaces Tsang, who is very astute
about other literary matters, comes perilously close to flaying one
genre because it does not have the characteristics of another. He
has been taken to task for this love-blindness by many men, the earliest being Meng Ch'eng-shun, editor of the Ku-chin Ming-chü Ho-
hsüan (1633),[2] who quite properly notes that not all ages nor places
must be expected to sing the same air. Tsang's strong preference
for tsa-chü over the southern ch'üan-chi works to the advantage of
the modern student of drama, for in the process of berating the faults
of Ming drama he makes quite clear his critical judgments on what
constitutes a good Yüan play. His use of the word ch'ü (arias) to
mean Yüan drama (tsa-chü) makes his prefaces at first glance appear
to deal mostly with the musical requirements of the genre, but, as
you will see, he also pays critical attention to spoken passages, plot,
characterization, and even to the use of dialects. It is my opinion
that this fondness of his for Yüan drama impelled him to believe
(though he claims in the first of the prefaces that "others" say this
while he reserves judgment) that the Yüan dynasty government used
the composition of Yüan dramas as a means of examining and selecting some of its civil servants. He should have known better, and
perhaps he did, but could not resist discovering for the general public
yet one more remarkable fact about his beloved Yüan ch'ü. However,
more of that later.

Tsang's anthology was originally called "One Hundred Ch'ü by Yüan
Authors" (Yüan-jen Pai-chung Ch'ü) and because Tsang's studio was

called the Tiao-ch'ung Kuan, the book was also known as "One Hundred Examples from the Tiao-ch'ung Hall". Cheng Ch'ien points out[3]
that it was not until the Commercial Press printed its 1918 edition
under the title of Yüan-ch'ü Hsüan that the book came to be known by
that name. It was the largest of the Ming collections, well edited and
printed; it represented the most authors and has been the most popular
anthology of Yüan drama for several centuries. Praise for Tsang's
work must be somewhat qualified: "There is no question," says Cheng
Ch'ien, "that Tsang was a very diligent editor. However, he altered
the text of both the spoken and sung sections too often and was too
quick to add to or subtract from the number of songs in a t'ao-shu
or the mechanisms of the plot; every time he changed the original he
ran great risk of converting gold into iron."

Cheng continues:

There are those who criticize his alterations and
claim they "concealed the true nature of things and
hid important evidence." I have been thinking carefully about this for several years and have concluded
that it is an overly harsh accusation. In the first
place...there are so many variorums that it makes
one's head swim to read them [by this Cheng means
Tsang himself used texts which had already been altered in many little ways for which he was not res-
ponsible], so criticism of Tsang on this score is
somewhat unrealistic. Secondly, adding beautifying
phrases is something like a face lifting. (Whether
the face was ugly and coarse to begin with and
whether face lifting improved it or made it still
more ugly is another matter entirely.) But there
certainly is no sense giving a face a handsome nose
and luxuriant hair and then hanging signs upon it
saying "this nose used to be smashed," or "this
part used to be bald." No, what I criticize Tsang
for has nothing to do with this kind of thing. His
alteration of Yüan texts showed a certain arrogance
toward what was simple and unadorned and at times
did lead him to transmute gold into iron by mistake,
but . . . accusing him of "hiding the true nature" and
"concealing important evidence" is in no way just.
In his age other editions were still in circulation
and persons wanting to see earlier texts were free

to do so. Tsang could never have guessed that two
hundred years later his publication would be everywhere and would have displaced all other versions. [4]

In addition to this temperate and intelligent judgment on Tsang's
motives and editorial activities, Cheng Ch'ien (and others) has always
cautioned the student of drama to keep uppermost in his mind when
criticizing texts and editions that <u>there never were</u> authorized editions
of anything in the drama field. Unlike the situation pertaining with
classical and canonical texts, piety for received editions and scholarly
collections of variants was to the Chinese literatus simply inconceiv-
able in something so frivolous as entertainment.

Tsang's altering of the texts, which we find utterly unconscionable
today, was actually quite common among connoisseurs of his day and
often was an expression of deep love for the objects of this kind of
editorial interference. Chin Wei (+ 1661), better known as Chin Sheng-
t'an, meddled with the text of <u>Shui-hu Chuan</u> in a manner and to a degree undreamed of by Tsang, yet only the most simplistic view would
miss the fact that Chin not only admired <u>Shui-hu</u> greatly but gave it
the most serious consideration any piece of fiction had ever had. Tsang's
text emendations (and, to be perfectly fair one must add, improvements)
were undertaken in a similar spirit of admiration and desire to have
others share his enthusiasm for the "One Hundred Ch'ü by Yüan Authors"; his efforts succeeded beyond his fondest hopes.

With this brief preamble concerning Tsang's unique qualifications
and crotchets, let me turn to the two prefaces he wrote for <u>YCH</u>.
Though they are obscure in some places (and downright wrong in others),
they contain some of the most explicit critical judgment ever brought to
bear on Yüan drama and by implication they raise many of the questions
about artisitc and technical values with which the Ming critics were
concerned. Even though Tsang was collecting and writing during the
earliest years of the seventeenth century, and <u>tsa-chü</u> had not been a
part of living theater for well over a hundred years, he could view the
earlier form in the light (the strong and revealing light) of Ming <u>ch'uan-
ch'i</u> practices and tastes. This comparison leads Tsang to underrate
the theatrical potentials of <u>ch'uan-ch'i</u>, but the compactness and dramatic power of the earlier <u>tsa-chü</u> form stand forth vividly by contrast.

Because Tsang was writing for a contemporary audience of connois-
suers and alludes tersely to things well understood by that fashionable

"we group," many more explanatory notes than suit my usual taste have been appended to the translation in Section III; this is not as great a loss as it might be, however, for though his periods are balanced and his rhythm is acceptable, the prefaces are important more for their critical content than for their literary appeal. Since Tsang uses the term ch'ü to mean either "aria," "drama," or "song" and since his ch'ü often means tsa-chü or ch'uan-ch'i (Ming drama), I have added in brackets the particular meaning I feel Tsang had in mind when he used the term. The most helpful edition for the translator (although not without its faults) is that found in the so-called "Chung-hua Looseleaf Anthology" (Chung-hua Huo-yeh Wen-hsüan, hereafter, Huo-yeh).[5]

FOOTNOTES

1. For example, Hsiao Shu-lan (YCH 88) was undoubtedly chosen for its virtuoso use of the four "difficult rhymes" (hsien-yün) in each of its acts. It is certainly a "fish-eye"; a wearisome thing at best.

2. Usually referred to as the Liu-chih and Lei-chiang Chi.

3. "Tsang Mou-hsün K'ao-ting Yüan Tsa-chü P'ing-yi," Bulletin of the College of Arts, National Taiwan University, #3, 1961, pp. 3-14. See also Tsing Hua Journal of Chinese Studies, New Series #7, 2 (1969), pp. 145-55.

4. Tsing Hua Journal, New Series #7, 2 (1969), p. 150.

5. (Shanghai, 1965), Vol. V, pp. 241-51.

III Translation of the Prefaces

Preface to the First Collection

The world speaks of the "lyrics" (tz'u) of the Sung dynasty and the "songs" (ch'ü) of the Yüan, but the fact is that "lyrics" were already superbly written in T'ang times by such men as Li Po and Ch'en [Li] Hou-chu,[1] so why should the Sung dynasty be given credit for their genesis? Ch'ü [dramas] however, were entirely the creation of the Yüan dynasty. Both the northern and the southern dramas of the Yüan times had music in seventeen modes,[2] but there are, in addition to Hsi-hsiang Chi, several hundred and more northern ch'ü [tsa-chü] while southern ch'ü [dramas] are represented by only two examples--the Yu-kuei Chi and the P'i-pa Chi.[3] It is said that Yüan civil service examinations required the composition of dramatic verse (t'ien-tz'u) the way we require the writing of essays, and since men were chosen for what they could accomplish "under the windy eaves" of the examination hall and within the "inch of time" afforded them by the tests, even the most renowned scholars of the age, such as Ma Chih-yän and Ch'iao Meng-fu, when they reach the fourth act of their dramatic verse, have lost their impetus. They also say that only the topic, the song titles, and the rhyme were selected by the examiner. The dialogue of these plays, they say, wasn't written until actors supplied it for the stage--which accounts for its crudity and dependence upon cliche. Still others say that everything in all five books of Hsi-hsiang Chi was written by a single hand and not a word can be removed or added to [either dialogue or verse], for which reason it is the crown of Yüan drama--I don't pretend to be able to choose among these statements. But I do take exception to those who write ch'ü [dramas] today, for the music of the south and the north may differ, but the requirements of modes and rhymes remain the same. Ever since Kao Ming's (fl. 1354) line in P'i-pa Chi, "search not for modes here nor number the tunes"[4]--which he actually wrote to cover up his own weakness--modern writers have cited the statement as evidence that rules for ch'ü composition in the northern style are rigorous but for the southern style they are loose: this is absurd!

In general terms, the marvel of Yüan dynasty ch'ü [tsa-chü] is their seeming effortlessness. The more elegant draw [easily] upon all yüeh-fu[5] for their diction and the cruder could include colloquialisms [with grace]. But after Cheng Jo-yung's Yü-chüeh Chi with its

encyclopedic style[6] came Chang Po-ch'i with Hung-fu Chi and his
disciples with still other thesaurus endeavors beyond counting.

Dialogue should never be excessive. However, a tsa-chü has
to tell its whole story in four acts--if you look at the twenty-one
acts[7] of Hsi-hsiang Chi, you will see that the dialogue [in one act]
scarely amounts to a thousand words and it will become evident that
dialogue here is somewhat too scanty. A thing desired even less in
dialogue is using too many parallel phrases: the "huang-men"[8] section and other parts of P'i-pa Chi were early offenders in this respect.

At the other extreme, in T'u Lung's T'an-hua Chi there are
acts which contain not a single aria [but are all in dialogue] while
the dialogue in Liang Ch'en-yü's Huan-sha Chi and Mei Ting-tso's
Yü-ho Chi does not contain a single unadorned expression[10]--these
are much more serious transgressions!

T'ang Hsien-tsu's four works, including the Tzu-ch'ai Chi, [11]
contain a number of northern songs; in fact, he all but gallops across
the border. But the tenor of the lyrics does not fit the tunes. [By
using northern songs] he has fallen into the error of sweetly singing
"East flows the Long River" to the sound of the clanging iron. [12]
But why are his southern ch'ü so lacking in talent that they seem to
come from another hand completely?[13] Ho Liang-chün praised Shih
Hui's (fl. 1295) Yu-kuei Chi as far better than the P'i-pa Chi. [14]
Wang Shih-chen (T. Yüan-mei) dismisses this are merely a "statement for sensational effect." However, Yu-kuei Chi now contains
much which is forgery and I wonder if Ho Liang-chün is aware of
this?

Wang Shih-chen is a very superior scholar but once when I
was taking wine with him I remarked that the aria-sets "Liang-chou
Hsü" and "Nien Nu-chiao Hsü" in P'i-pa Chi were so totally unlike
[the rest of] Kao Ming's work in tone[15] that they were likely the
insertions of a later writer. He agreed and praised [my observations].
[Since this is so with P'i-pa Chi] I wonder what one can say about Yu-
kuei Chi?

I have a great many rare editions of tsa-chü in my library.
Recently, passing through Huang-chou Fu, I borrowed some two hundred scripts from Liu Yen-po which he said he had copied from the

files of the Imperial Academy: they differ from the texts on the open market, I collated and edited them, therefore, and selected the best from among them; these I carefully edited into two parts both divided into ten sections, one for each of the cyclical signs.[16] I publish[17] this so that it may have currency in all cities, including the capital itself, for there must be some, like Ho Liang-chün, who can appreciate it. I hasten to deny that I have made any unjustifiable alterations in the text or that I have hoped to add anything to the geniuses of Yüan times.

> The third of the third month
> in the forty-third year of Wan-li
> (1615) written in the monastery
> on West Lake.

Preface to the Second Collection

Today the southern ch'ü [drama] is in the ascendancy. Everyone proclaims himself a playwright but no one seems to realize how far he falls short of his Yüan predecessors! In Yüan times officials were selected[18] by their ch'ü [drama or aria] compositions--there were in all twelve categories of these--and even men of the stature of Kuan Han-ch'ing had to test their skill to the utmost in order to make their names. As for those who actually took part in performances (who put on the grease paint, consorted with actors and lived with singing girls permanently), it may be that they did it for the same reasons the Seven Sages of the Bamboo Grove abandoned themselves to wine during the Western Chin era[19]--I do not really know.

They say that shih poetry changed and became tz'u lyrics and these in turn changed into ch'ü; though all came from the same source, the further the change progressed the more difficult it was to become skilled in the form. Why? Tz'u not only developed from shih forms but even used the same subject matter. The only real excellence of tz'u was to take the issue of another womb and raise it successfully as its own offspring. Though ch'ü [drama] arose from tz'u it was never limited to the subject matter of tz'u; the Six Classics, the Buddhist and Taoist canons, as well as unorthodox histories and fiction all became material upon which the ch'ü [drama] could draw.

In general terms, ch'ü must select the best passages from their sources,[20] extract their pith and combine the elegant and vulgar in such a way that no scars are visible and the results delight the ear of the audience--this is the task called "balancing the emotion required with the diction used."

Because nobility and ignominy, beauty and ugliness, obscurity and clarity in the world at large meet and fuse in so many ways, we cannot hope that the forms they assume are limited to hundreds or even thousands. Yet the composer must write arias that ring with authentic dialect and situations that have the true look of reality (pen-se)[21]; he must have nothing extraneous in his mise-en-scène and nothing false in his dialogue--this is the task called "tight control over details of the plot."

There are seventeen modes (kung-tiao) in northern music and nine--slightly more than half the number--in southern. The insertion of up to ten "additional verses" into an aria and a score or more "padding words" into a line is something totally unknown to southern music but often used simply to demonstrate virtuosity in northern arias. Naturally, then, one must be completely conversant with the yin and yang classes of words and the level and oblique types of language tones or he will be hard put to write even inferior arias. (Should we not, therefore, accuse these drawlers of southern dialect pronouns of being impossible braggarts[22] when they claim to sing as sweetly as our old northern rascals of the past?) This is the task called "matching music and lyrics both in language tone and contour."

To sum up, ch'ü [dramas] are well written by either renowned scholars[23] (ming-chia) or actor-playwrights (hang-chia). The great scholar is so conversant with musical verse (yüeh-fu) and his literary style is so rich that all men of vast and broad learning have been excellent writers of ch'ü [dramas]. The actor-playwright will have put on the paint and performed every place until he knows every twist to each drama, until he acts as though he were truly present at the reality instead of performing in a scene. (The one who can make an audience stroke its whiskers in sheer happiness, wring its hands in agitation, hide its tears in sadness and quicken its desires in admiration must be a true inheritor of Yu-meng's mantle.) That is why when ch'ü [tsa-chü?] are praised, the first class is always called "of the troupe" (tang-hang).[24] If this were not so why would the Yüan government use the "twelve categories"[25] for examinations to select scholars of national stature, and why would scholars of such stature have chosen one of them to be examined in? Was it not because men of the widest accomplishment were hard to find and even the actor-playwright found it difficult to master his craft?[26]

I have read the comment made by Wang Shih-chen in his Yi-yüan Chih-yen where he speaks of the ch'ü [arias] and says, "Northern ch'ü run to a large number of words per line so the music is sparse; the sinew of this type of ch'ü lies in the strings. The southern ch'ü has fewer words per line so the tunes are dense; the force of this music lies in the percussion." However, the use of string accompaniment in northern ch'ü (and the same is true for the use of the woodwinds in the southern arias) produces a restrained and sorrowful kind of music which is quite moving. (The voice fluctuates and floats with the instruments as though the singer had no control over it.) But this is a variant and not the authentic ch'ü. If percussion is used to punctuate the aria, then it is equally important to either northern or southern ch'ü. If one says that the "sinew of northern ch'ü lies in the strings", would it not be equally correct to say that in southern ch'ü the force is in the woodwinds? But would anyone accept that statement? It is a pity that Wang Shih-chen knew so little of tsa-chü!

For all these reasons when I criticize Wang Tao-k'un's (fl. 1561) late southern ch'ü [tsa-chü] about Mount Kao-t'ang and the Lo River, [27] it is not that they lack beauty--but since they are composed almost entirely to elegant language their defect is extravagance. Hsü Wei's (1521-1593) late northern ch'ü [tsa-chü] of Ni Heng[28] and the monk Yü-t'ung[29] on the other hand, are perspicuous enough but include so many vulgarisms that their defect is coarseness. T'ang Hsien-tsu's work comes close to the ideal, but his knowledge falls short of a true "comprehension of the mysteries" (t'ung-fang) and his studies have given him little skill with harmonizing word-tones[30] (hsieh-lü). He uses words and phrases in many places which are crabbed and ill-conceived--his defect is carelessness. The rest (of the later composers), no matter how they strain their talents and sensibilities, fall shorter still of the mark: those who sing their works cannot produce the kind of magic that makes "music wreathe the rafters and forces clouds to stop and listen"; those who hear them no longer "forget their hunger and fatigue". Ch'ü [dramas] of this quality Yüan playwrights would spit upon, but the "amateurs" of today give them their most solemn attention.

This is why I have selected 100 tsa-chü to show the marvels of the Yüan dynasty ch'ü [dramas] and to furnish those who work with the southern products something they can use as models.

Written on this first yi day of spring
in the forty-fourth year of Wan-li (1616)
by Tsang Chin-shu of Hsia-jo Village[31]

FOOTNOTES

1. It is hardly possible that Ch'en Shu-pao (553-604), last sovereign of the Ch'en dynasty, is meant here; more likely, the surname is a mistake for Li. Li Hou-chu (Yü) was the best known of the early writers of "lyrics."

2. "In T'ang music there were seven [mode] variations based on the note kung and three other notes [a total of twenty-one]. . . Subsequent ages discarded some of these possibilities until by Chin and Yüan times . . . there were only six kung and eleven tiao or seventeen kung-tiao." See Chung-wen Ta Tz'u-tien.

3. It is not clear why Tsang excludes Sha-kuo, Ching-ch'ai and Pai-t'u Chi, all of which had been written by early Ming times. Yu-kuei Chi is also known as Pai-yüeh T'ing.

4. A citation, somewhat wrenched out of context, from the Prologue (Act 1) of P'i-pa Chi reprise of "Shui-tiao Ko-t'ou." After the fu-mo has sung of the many kinds of fiction there are, he concludes:
   > Now let us speak of ch'uan-ch'i plays:
   > To pleasure men is easy,
   > To move men is hard.
   > My lord who knows his music
   > Please watch this with a lenient eye.
   > We will not cram in japes nor obscene jokes
   > Nor search overhard for modes and sequences of tunes. . .

   Liu-shih-chung Ch'ü (hereafter Sixty). Ed. Mao Chin. Shanghai: Chung-hua, 1958, Vol. I.

5. Yüeh-fu here means "musical verse" and certainly not "Han and Wei yüeh-fu poetry" as the Huo-yeh edition has it. In Chu Ch'üan's T'ai-ho Cheng-yin P'u, p. 15, it says: "If the [verse] was literary and elegant they called it yüeh-fu; if it lacked literary adornment they called it a 'rustic song'." Chu Ch'üan also lists 335 ch'ü-p'ai and tz'u under their mode headings and calls them "335 examples of yüeh-fu" (p. 54ff). All citations are to the pages of Chung-kuo Ku-tien Hsi-ch'ü Lun-chu Chi-ch'eng edition, (Peking, 1959, unless otherwise cited.

6. Cheng spent twenty years compiling an encyclopedic work, Lei-chün, on the model of Yi-wen Lei-chü. Some of this preoccupation was liable to have rubbed off onto his ch'ü writing. Tsang

is accusing him (and his followers) of strained and pedantic elegance--not without justification.

7.   There are twenty by my count: five "books" of four acts apiece, but some Ming editions take the large hsieh-tzu preceding Book II, Act 2, to be an act. It is a curious observation, but quite true, that the dialogue in Hsi-hsiang Chi averages about a thousand words per act as it does in a great many of the less chatty tsa-chü in Tsang's anthology.

8.   "Huang-men section", i.e., Act 16 (not 15 as it says in the Huo-yeh edition), Sixty edition, Vol. I, p. 59, where the character who identifies himself as the hsiao-huang-men, "usher," declaims some twenty lines of parallel or balanced prose mostly in six-four rhythm. It does become annoying but the "usher" often had the dramatic duty to create verbally scenes inside the imperial court, and this takes well to somewhat florid phraseology, cf. Act. 3 of Yu-kuei Chi. Ch'ü-lü says in P'i-pa Chi it is actually "true speech threaded in pairs but comprehensible to all." (p. 141. See Sec. IV, 2) The scene-setting by a court usher has old and genuine storytelling credentials. This was often the place where "set-pieces" of parallel prose were inserted. Cf. Hsüan-ho Yi-shih, (Ch. 2, p. 45, in the Sung-jen P'ing-hua Ssu-chung).

9.   To wit: 3, 7, 13, 30, 31, and 34. See Sixty #53.

10.   This is not literally true but near enough to be a proper bill of indictment. The various ching roles speak with much less mannered diction, but this only serves to emphasize the precious and precocious locutions of other characters the more. Huan-sha, the first of the k'un-ch'ü, is Sixty #4 and Yü-ho is Sixty #28.

11.   Tzu-ch'ai Ssu-chi that is; the so-called Yü-ming T'ang Ssu-meng [The four dreams from Yü-ming Hall]. The Yü-ming T'ang was the name of T'ang Hsien-tsu's studio, and the "four dreams" are the Han-tan Chi, Tzu-ch'ai Chi, Nan-k'o Chi and Mu-tan T'ing (Huan-hun Chi). Tsang wrote an introduction (yin) to his own "stage versions" of the Yü-ming T'ang Ssu-meng called Yü-ming T'ang Ch'uan-ch'i in which he damns T'ang's knowledge of music (though they were friends) with very faint praise indeed, saying:
        This is a desk-top book; these are not dramas
        (ch'ü) meant to be given in a hall. But if

they are called <u>ch'ü</u> and yet cannot be performed
why should we give them the rame of "dramas"
at all?

12. "Eastward flows the Long River" is the opening line of Su Tung-
p'o's "Nien Nu-chiao," and it was said of Su's <u>tz'u</u> that they sang
with a "brazen lute and iron clapper," meaning that they had a
strong, masculine quality. Here Tsang seems to imply that the
dramas' delicate subject matter set to the stronger northern music was liable to have been overwhelmed. See Sec. IV, 4, below.

13. The <u>Huo-yeh</u> text begins a new paragraph with "But why are the
southern songs so lacking in talent" etc. This requires that one
add "nowadays" or "today" to give sense to the next section which
otherwise would become a <u>non</u> <u>sequitur</u>. I believe <u>Huo-yeh</u> is
wrong and that this still refers to T'ang Hsien-tsu (Lin-ch'uan)
because that is how Wang Po-liang in his <u>Ch'ü-lü</u> (p. 170) reads
it. He has:
> Tsang also says that Lin-ch'uan's "southern songs
> lack talent" (<u>nan-ch'ü chüeh wu ts'ai-ch'ing</u>), but
> Lin-ch'uan was only clumsy about the rules [of
> prosody]; it is precisely his talent which sur-
> passes all others and this statement of Tsang's
> is unfair.

Yagizawa Gen, <u>Mindai Gekisakka Kenkyū</u>. Trans. Lo Chin-t'ang.
(Hong Kong: 1966), p. 461, also construes the remark as I do.

14. It is not now generally believed that <u>Yu-kuei Chi</u> as we have it
today was written by any one author; like three of the other First
Five <u>ch'uan-ch'i</u> it seems to have evolved rather than having been
composed all at once.

15. Literally, "so unlike Yung-chia" which is the district from which
Kao Ming came and which is generally cited as the birthplace of
the <u>nan-hsi</u> [southern drama]. Tsang does not mean "unlike Yung-
chia dialect" for the songs contain literary phrases that were
never spoken by anyone in any dialect. One of these two "unre-
lieved" <u>ch'ü</u> ("Liang-chou" has one brief interjection) is also
criticized by Ho Liang-chün for its cloying quality and its poor
exploitation of the <u>ch'ü's</u> genre characteristics; see below, Sec.
IV, 5.

16. I.e., part one was divided into ten sections of five plays each, each section designated by a cyclical sign. The same was true of part two. In older editions when the two parts are published together the two sets of five plays under each sign are brought together so you get "chia set, upper" followed by the five plays in "chia set, lower" etc. (See Yoshikawa, Gen Zatsugeki Kenkyu, pp. 28-37.

17. Literally, "deposit them on famous mountains." We are told that the ancients, for fear their books might not survive, "encased them in stone containers and placed them on famous mountains." The phrase later became used to mean one's important publications.

18. What was a suggestion in the first preface is now stated as a fact: officials were selected on the basis of their ability to write ch'ü. History is in conflict with Tsang's partisan enthusiasm; there is no evidence ch'ü were ever a part of Yüan civil service examinations. The chih-ch'iung . . . che is an "as for those" beginning, I'm sure: note line 4, p. 249: chih yü yi ch'ü . . . che.

19. Tsang is implying that those poets who actually took to the stage did so as a kind of protest against their age and to give themselves such low visibility that their high talents would not attract the unwanted attention of officialdom.

20. Yoshikawa, Gen Zatsugeki Kenkyū, p. 251, takes this to mean: "the language of these works," but I'm certain the context forces something like my version: we are still talking about ts'ai "raw material."

21. For the critical extensions and nuances of pen-se, see Sec. IV, 6, below.

22. Literally, "as overflowing (in praise for themselves) as the Yellow River and the Han."

23. He calls Ma Chih-yüan and Ch'iao Meng-fu "scholars of repute" in Preface I, doubtless distinguishing them from someone like Kuan Han-ch'ing, who was probably a stage professional and who may even have put on the greasepaint himself.

24. Tang-hang meant superior in quality but always in the sense of
     "stageworthy" or "genuine." Ch'ü-lü (p. 131) equates "not tang-
     hang" with "too literary." Wang P'ei-lun's Hsi-ch'ü Tz'u-tien
     gives examples showing its force as "esoteric" in the sense of
     a guild or trade secret.

25. It is probable that these "twelve categories" referred to the old
     division of tsa-chü dramas into twelve classes of subject matter:
     "Gods and Immortals," "reunions and separations," "court robes
     and scepters," etc. See Crump, "Elements of Yüan Opera,"
     JAS 17-23 (1951), p. 420. The T'ai-ho Cheng-yin P'u, p. 24,
     of Chu Ch'üan, which has a preface dated 1398, lists shih-erh-
     k'o, but Tsang may have conceived of them as delineating twelve
     categories in which Yüan aspirants wrote their examinations.
     The Yüan history (cf. K'ai-ming Erh-shih-wu Shih 6754. 1-3)
     neither states nor implies anything of the sort.

26. There is some obscurity to this passage and the final "If this
     were not so . . . etc." seems, in part at least, to be a non
     sequitur. I feel, nevertheless, that the way I have construed
     it is nearer the mark than Prušek's translation (Origins and
     Authors of Hua-pen (Prague, 1967), p. 54, n. 1) because above
     all else Tsang is trying to make the point the real ch'ü (and here
     he must mean dramatic verse) was difficult to write even for the
     Yüan dynasty experts of two types, literary and professional.

27. Wang Tao-k'un (Po-yü), fl. 1561, wrote Ta-ya T'ang Tsa-chü
     Ssu-chung, a group of four one act tsa-chü to southern music.
     Tsang is referring to the first and the fourth. See Sheng-ming
     Tsa-chü, Ch. 1 and 4.

28. Chief character of Hsü's "tsa-chü" called K'uang Ku-shih. Also
     see his biography in Hou Han Shu.

29. The monk in Act 1 of Hsü's Yü Ch'an-shih; both these plays are
     from his Ssu-sheng Yüan (Four Cries of the Ape). See Ch'ü-hai
     Tsung-mu T'i-yao, Ch. 5, items 12 and 13.

30. T'ang Hsien-tsu once wrote of his own dramas that as long as
     his meaning reached others, "it doesn't matter if half the empire
     breaks its throat (on my music)." See T'ang Hsien-tsu Chi.
     Peking: Chung-hua, 1962, p. 1299.

31. At the beginning of <u>YCH</u>, the author is given as Tsang Chin-shu of "Jo-hsia Village."

IV Tsang's Critical Assumptions and
Comparisons with the Formularies

1. "It is said that Yüan civil service examinations required the composition of dramatic verse."

Although this statement is not concerned with literary criticism,
it does bear directly on Tsang's disposition to view the Yüan drama
in a particularly favorable light. He seems really to know that the
Yüan court did not use ch'ü when they restored the examination system in 1313--and here in the first preface he acknowledges that "it is
said" they did--but his enthusiasm for Yüan drama finally overcomes
his better judgment and in the second preface he treats their presence
in Yüan official examinations as a fact. Chinese scholars as early as
Liang Yü-sheng (1745-1819)[1] noted that there is nothing in the Yüan
records to substantiate the use of Yüan drama forms when the examinations were reinstituted. As long ago as 1912 Japanese scholars
pointed out that Ming critics had consistently and mistakenly insisted
that ch'ü were so employed. That Tsang was not the only man of the
times who indulged in such assertions can be made clear from the following, written by Shen Te-fu, a contemporary of Tsang, who took his
degree only two years after the publication of YCH (1618):

Before the Yüan destroyed Southern Sung they used
[tsa-chü] to distinguish grades of officials. They gave
each [candidate] a topic on which he was to compose a
tsa-chü (t'ien-tz'u). This was the same principle used
in the Sung during the Hsüan-ho period when students of
painting were made to write a piece of verse in the
T'ang manner on their pictures to make the painting
stand out. The ones who showed the best taste in
things beyond simply their graphic creation were given
the highest grades. It is precisely for this reason that
the paintings of Sung and the dramas of Yüan have been
incomparable throughout the ages. (Ku-ch'ü Tsa-yen,
p. 214-215)[2]

2. "The dialogues of these plays, they say, [weren't] written
until actors supplied [them] for the stage."

Tsang all but refutes this in the next sentence ("every word of
all five books of Hsi-hsiang Chi was written by the poet") and again
two paragraphs later where he begins, "Dialogue should never be

excessive." Granted the eventual subject of this last statement is P'i-pa Chi, there is still little doubt that important Ming critics thought of dialogue as one of the prime concerns of any playwright-- witness the following from Wang Chi-te's Ch'ü-lü (p. 140):

Pin-pai (speech) is also called shuo-pai. There are entrance speeches which are done in six-four and orna- mental style, and there is normal dialogue which is the plain speaking done by all characters. In entrance speeches one should reveal a bit of his talent but the lines cannot be obscure: all of the speech in Tzu-hsiao (Sixty #43) is extremely good six-four prose--unhappily the audience cannot understand it. In P'i-pa Chi the monologue by the court usher (huang-men) is just ord- inary speech that has been balanced, and everyone can understand it, which is why it is played even today.

Dialogue must be clearly spoken and simple in character-- one cannot afford to make it excessively literary. The use of chih, hu, che, yeh is not professionally acceptable (tang-chia). Huan-sha (Sixty #4) is pure six-four and it all but bores a person to death! (Che is only used in northern tsa-chü;[3] anyone who uses it in the dialogue of a southern drama is violating [the integrity of] its style.) The length of sentences and their tonal balance must be reconciled so well that their sense will be persuasive and their sound resonant--although the dialogue is not as important as the arias it must please the ear. There are good composers whose treatment of dialogue is not skillful--dialogue in its own way is as hard to do as the songs. All the forms of dialogue in Yü-chüeh Chi (Sixty #45) are clean, elegant, and yet not obscure. They dif- fer from the songs only in the dashing (po-lan) effect of the latter. Generally speaking, if one does more than [is done in Yü-chüeh] the audience will find it wearisome, if he does less, he will not have achieved the best effects dialogue is capable of. . .

Granted again that the above deals specifically with Ming ch'uan ch'i form, the implication is quite clear that these strictures apply to all drama, and since Wang almost always shows himself to be an admirer of Yüan tsa-chü, the further implication is that he takes it

for granted that the Yüan composer was responsible for the artistry
of his dialogue as well.

Modern scholarship has found that assuming the arias and the
dialogue of Yüan drama had two different authors raises more problems than it solves. Yoshikawa[4] argues a fortiori that the relationship between the songs and the pin-pai is so close in many instances
that arguments for separate sources collapse in absurdity. Scholars
have noted the intricacy with which spoken lines are used to move
dramatic action along right in the midst of song[5] and careful reading
of Yüan drama shows the interdependency of speech and song to be
one of the chief characteristics of the metrical form which we call
the dramatic ch'ü. It is not impossible that there was collaboration
between the literatus and the actor--indeed it would be surprising if
there were not--but all evidence indicates that each of the collabo-
rators would have thought of the final product as an amalgam in which
song, verse, and dialogue were integrated.

3. ". . . for the music of the south and the north may differ, but
the requirements of modes and rhymes remain the same."

Unhappily, the situation is much more complicated than Tsang
suspected and the subject is largely overlooked in early texts. There
seems to be no doubt that the earliest form of southern style drama
(nan-hsi) did not, in fact, concern itself with grouping its songs by
modes. Hsü Wei's Nan-tz'u Hsü-lu gives the most information on
the matter--even though much of what Hsü says about music demonstrates that his knowledge of it was unsophisticated by modern measurements.

In order to put the bulk of his statements into the proper perspective, one should start with a quote that reveals both Hsü Wei's
feet of xenophobic clay and his worshipful attitude toward the past:

> . . . There are those who have the greatest faith in the
> [perfection of] northern songs (so much so that they
> act as though a singing girl performing a southern tune
> were committing a crime). Here is stupidity indeed!
> Is northern music the true offspring of the famous poets
> of T'ang and Sung? No; the tunes are simply specious
> products of border areas and half barbarian people.
> (p. 241)

The implication behind this is a very Chinese one: insofar as the music (or customs, speech, habits, etc.) of today differs from the more glorious periods of the past, it is degenerate. That is to say, all change is for the worse. I include this to warn the reader that in what follows Hsü Wei is not being descriptive but prescriptive:

> The northern music of today is probably from the Liao and the Chin; it is vigorous, powerful, cruel and savage-- the songs of warriors on horseback--but when it got as far as the central plains it had become the day-to- day music of the common folk. Since the Chinese could no longer play the music of Sung tz'u on their instru- ments, the people to the south [of the barbarians] wel- comed this new music. It became so faddish among both high and low that soon made them look ridiculously vulgar. (p. 241)

> The nine kung and the twenty-one tiao came from T'ang and Sung times but the [language of the northern Chinese] had only three language tones left after the four tones were destroyed. Now the southern ch'ü are one step removed from northern songs. I cannot imagine why one would wish to encompass (hsien) them with a [mere] nine kung. (p. 241)

His statements on the origins of his music may be very nearly what actually took place, but he would have us understand that such a state of affairs is to be considered lamentable because the Chinese "became faddishly addicted." In the final paragraph Hsü seems to indicate that since the ancients needed nine kung and twenty-one tiao to classify their music, surely describing southern music in only nine kung is, in some way, presumptuous.[6] The sad state of Chinese (Han) music is spelled out in the following:

> In the central plains, ever since the invasion of the Chin and the Yüan, foreign ch'ü have flourished mightily until today only the ch'in repertory perserves ancient [Chinese] music. Instrumental repertories for the p'i-pa, the cheng, the ti, the juan-hsien [yüeh-ch'in], the hsiang-chan [?][7] and others of that sort only in- clude ch'ü like "Ying Hsien-k'o" and "Ch'ao T'ien-tzu"; not one of them can recapture an old piece of music. (p. 241-2)

Since the author of these passages has the reputation of being an accomplished musician and since he was a native of Chekiang (as well as having some kind of student-teacher relationship with Chi Pen, a renowned musical theorist),[8] one has to take his major implications seriously. We need hardly subscribe to his T'ang-is-transcendent-Sung-is-superlative attitude, but when he insists that a linguistic change in tone classes of the language has some effect on musical structure we must not only pay heed, we should probably consider it one more piece of evidence that the relationship between linguistic phenomena and ch'ü (aria) structure must have been of a totally different order than the relationship between lyrics and melody in the traditional Western sense.[9] When one has this fact firmly in mind, he is in a better position to see why Tsang's assumption that "common basic requirements existed for both northern and southern lyrics" must be wrong. The close ties between language and music also seem to imply that the music of a certain dramatic form might have many devotees yet be impossible to mount on the stage in another dialect area. This is not simply a matter of the difference between the five-tone scale which southern ch'ü seem to have preferred and the seven-tone which the north used. I think we are dealing with a complex musical-linguistic situation which is, in fact, the nexus of the problem of Chinese dramatic music.

All evidence indicates that one of the greatest differences between northern and southern music from late Sung onward was the increasingly greater interest northerners showed in organizing their music around modal concepts. Hsü Wei has some curious things to say about the subject:

> I really don't know who produced the present "nine modes" for southern music (I imagine it was done by some musician attached to the Imperial Academy during the early years of the [Ming] dynasty), but they are badly researched and ridiculous . . .

> By the end of Sung everything from "modern prose" to an angry cry was put into some kind of mode (kung-tiao) and it became more and more contrived. When composition of Sung tsa-chü began at Yung-chia [i.e., the Wen-chou tsa-chü], their music came from the little songs sung in village and hamlet; not only did they lack modes (pen wu kung-tiao) but even a measured beat was rare. The music consisted of what came easily to the lips of

the farmer in his field or the women at the market.
(Perhaps the "song of the heart," as the proverb calls
it, is what gave them their skill.) Perhaps one or
two observed tonal rules but they were not examples
for the rest. (p. 241)

His implication is clear (and certainly mistaken): the music of southern ch'ü was somehow free and unstructured until academic types got
hold of it and imposed modal and other rules upon it. This would be
akin to a situation in which a people's language was one thing before
grammarians analyzed it and never the same thereafter. Linguists
and musicologists would certainly become unbearably self-important
if such things did occur; fortunately for the modesty of these pro-
fessions, however, the likelihood never was great.

Hsü is of two minds about the lack of modal specification in
southern music. He is self-conscious and defensive:

Certainly southern [music] is not the equal of the
northern in the matter of modes, but southern music
has a superiority, too--it has four language tones.
Northern music, while it accords [well] with the
rules, can only do so with three tones and is incapable of restoring the correct central plains [music]
of past ages. (p. 241)

He also realizes that there are, nevertheless, internal consis-
tencies to be found in southern drama:

Though southern ch'ü [dramas] assuredly do not have
modes, there is an order to the sequence of songs and
one must make a suite out of neighboring sounds. And
among the songs there are classes which cannot be confused: the aria "Huang Ying-erh," for example, must
be followed by "Tsu Yü-lin"; "Hua-mei Hsü" is followed
by "Ti-liu Tzu." Each has a fixed place and for this reason a composer would do well to read the older dramas
with respect. (p. 241)

Confusing and contradictory as Hsü's statements may be, they do contain a grain of truth: once an influential literatus devises rules for
composition, others will compose according to them and, eventually,
clever exploitation of rules will become more important than musi-
cality and taste. More will be said about this subject below.

4. "T'ang Hsien-tsu's four works . . . contain a number of northern songs . . . but the tenor of the lyrics does not fit the tunes."

It is not entirely clear what Tsang is saying here. If I have understood the phrase yin-yün shao hsieh correctly and Tsang means that the yün "rhymes," (i.e., lyrics) do not harmonize with the yin, (i.e., tune) then the next statement is not a non sequitur (see Sec. III, note 12), but the two statements together are a complaint that T'ang Hsien-tsu has used northern songs in places where they should not be used because their subject matter does not take well to the more masculine northern music. [10]

Assuming I am right in my translation, there are still difficulties to resolve when the statement is confronted with the facts. It appears to me that in the Nan-k'o, Han-tan, and Tzu-ch'ai Chi, T'ang Hsientsu used northern songs no more frequently than had many other playwrights. Several important acts he sets (quite skillfully, I feel) into combined northern and southern t'ao (song suites). In Han-tan Chi, for example, (which is a reworking of the T'ang dynasty tale usually known as the Yellow Millet Dream) Act 20 consists of a combined northern and southern t'ao which runs completely through this lively unit. In it the male lead, soldiers, and the executioner all sing to northern music while the wife--pleading again and again for her husband's life to be spared--sings all her arias in southern music. A similar matching of role-types and musical styles is to be found in the Nan-k'o Chi. In Mu-tan T'ing alone no dramatic purpose seems to be served by the way the composer parcels out the northern and southern music among the roles. The female lead in the last act sings mostly northern arias and I imagine this did not enhance nuances of feminity. One wonders, however, why Tsang did not single out Mu-tan T'ing, then, instead of implying the fault was common to all four "dreams."

Tsang could not have pressed his objections very far along this line (and indeed all the critics who insist that northern music had a martial or masculine cast to it are on equally shaky ground), for he would soon have had to conclude that no Yüan dynasty tsa-chü should ever have been written around a love story because the character of northern music is incompatible with tender sentiments: this he would certainly not have contended. I suspect he is objecting here to northern music used in a largely southern music environment where, by contrast, it appears to be more muscular and so accords ill with a

feminine role. However the following statement from Wang Po-liang's
Ch'ü-lü (p. 56) may indicate an aspect of the compatibility between
lyrics and music types which at this stage in our knowledge we do not
comprehend at all:

> Southern lyrics are concerned with provoking and stirring
> [emotions] and are transformed into "flowing beauty"
> (liu-li); northern lyrics concern themselves with noble
> and energetic [subjects] and are transformed into "gen-
> uine simplicity" (p'u-shih). But to achieve this simpli-
> city the sounds of the latter must adhere strictly to the
> rules and cannot be blurred; to achieve flowing beauty
> the former must be sung in a sinuous manner which
> blends easily.

We now arrive at the point where a general observation should
be made. With Tsang Chin-shu as a representative of one side and
T'ang Hsien-tsu a model for the other, we can discern dimly what has
happened by 1618 to the Ming musical drama, its critics, and its prac-
titioners. It would appear that composition of ch'uan-ch'i had taken two
paths: one led in the direction of music and the other in the direction
of literature. On the side of musical considerations, Tsang Chin-shu's
position is supported by many who wrote ch'uan-ch'i by simply filling
in sets of prosodic requirements with lyrics which then were easily
sung to the tune formulae indicated. These men, a number of whom
wrote formularies, often had very little literary taste; their creations
were lifeless; but they could be sung, that is, staged. These men
merely did what third-rate Chinese poets had always done--with "regulated verse," with Sung lyrics, with Yüan dynasty san-ch'ü: they
created linguistic anagrams in the fond belief that they were writing
literature. I am certain Tsang, who had a sound taste for literature
as well as a musical sense, would have objected to being classed with
these men whom literary historians contemptuously call the "rule
school" (ko-lü p'ai), but he would have agreed that the writers of
closet dramas were sacrificing theatrical and musical (i.e., performing)
values which he, I am sure, set great store by. At the end of his second preface he remarks (and I detect a sigh of despair) that "T'ang
Hsien-tsu's work comes close to the ideal but . . . he has little skill
with harmonizing word tones," by which he certainly mean T'ang's plays
were unsingable.

Tsang and others tried to adapt T'ang Hsien-tsu's works to music
to make them performable but it is common enough for literary men

to have no musical talent at all and T'ang, who had a tin ear, I suspect, was as infuriated as any modern playwright coming upon others
meddling with his hard-won phrases:

> You must follow my original of <u>Mu-tan T'ing</u> and have
> nothing to do with the Lü version. I don't care if he
> only changes a word or two to make it easier to sing,
> it still becomes something different from what I in-
> tended![11]

Unhappily, the "rule school" and the drama-for-literature school
seldom reconciled themselves to each other and in the end, as always,
the insects triumphed again. The chirpers of tone patterns and the
diligent polishers of meaningless (but balanced) phrases (<u>shih-wen p'ai</u>)
dominate the later years of the Ming dynasty.

5. "The aria-sets "Liang-chou Hsü" and "Nien Nu-chiao Hsü" in
<u>P'i-pa Chi</u> <u>were . . . likely the insertions of a later writer.</u> "

Whether or not these long, florid passages were done by a later
hand is not as interesting to the student of Ming dramatic criticism as
the fact that these same aria-sets are also singled out by critics other
than Tsang as poor examples of the <u>ch'ü</u> (aria) genre. In the process
of describing why they are poor specimens, critics make their prime
criteria for <u>ch'ü</u> quite clear. Ho Liang-chün in the <u>Ssu-yu Chai Ch'ü-
shuo</u> says, for example:

> Kao Ming's style is [sometimes] heavy with elegance:
> in Act 28 of [<u>P'i-pa Chi</u>] the "Ch'ang-k'ung Wan-li"[12]
> is one long splendid lyric flight (<u>fu</u>). But should one
> ever expect to encompass such a thing in the <u>ch'ü</u> form?
> By its very nature a <u>ch'ü</u> demands the occasional addi-
> tion of pungent garlic or a little thin gruel--things which
> this most elegant confection of lyrics lacks completely.
> It is as though a wealthy table had been overloaded with
> rich and fatty dishes--camel's hump, panda paws--and
> unrelieved by so much as a single bland vegetable or
> piquant relish dish: one rapidly loses his taste for the
> delicacies there. (<u>Hsin Ch'ü-yüan</u> edition, p. 8)

Thus, the <u>ch'ü</u> form--that is to say, all the arias of musical
dramas--by definition incorporates elements of spoken (or near spoken)
language and would not be <u>ch'ü</u> if purged of these elements.

This opinion was shared by Ch'ing critics like Hsü Ta-ch'un (1693-1771) in his Yüeh-fu Ch'uan Sheng, Sec. 2:

> What people of today don't understand is that the nature
> of [the ch'ü] is entirely different from either the tz'u
> or the shih. The ch'ü will choose the direct over the
> circuitous, the ordinary over the elegant, and the clear
> over the obscure. If ch'ü were used to transmit the
> words of the ancients, the most ignorant man and
> woman would see and understand everything about these
> words and they would not remain only works to be in-
> toned by the learned or elegant in their studies. (Ku-
> tien Hsi-ch'ü Sheng-yüeh Lun-chu Ts'ung-pien edition,
> 1957)

The language of the ch'ü is by definition more clear than allusive, more direct than circuitous: in a word, the ch'ü should be more narrative. Jen Na (1894-) in a note on Chou Te-ch'ing's Tso-ch'ü Shih-fa warns that this requirement carries its own dangers:

> Since the nature of the ch'ü is to adjust diction so that
> it will accommodate spoken forms and since ch'ü subject
> matter can be so vast, the writer, if he be incautious,
> will find it only too easy to create lyrics which tend
> toward the simply vulgar or trite.

From very early times, then, the ch'ü form was expected to contain elegant phraseology mixed tastefully with spoken forms and simpler diction. [13] It is entirely probable that these strictures re-flect the demands made upon the form by its performing history: early and late ch'ü were always supposed to be comprehensible when sung (though what degree of comprehensibility was required and how well tutored the audience was supposed to be is always unclear). In any case, critics agree that to be either top-lofty with elegance or bottom-heavy with vulgarity damages just the effects in which the form should excel. This becomes important to keep in mind when the term pen-se is discussed in the next section.

6. Yet the composer must write arias that ring with authentic dialect and situations that have the true look of reality (pen-se).

Here Tsang uses the important critical term pen-se in one of its more obvious meanings. There can be very little doubt that it here

means "verisimilitude" in exactly the same way the Ch'ing critic Hsü
Ta-ch'un uses it in the following:

> One must also take into account what kind of a story he
> is narrating. If it concern the court or the literati as
> a class, then there is little harm in becoming more ele-
> gant of phrase--the proper tone will not be destroyed
> thereby; if one is doing a tale of city streets or village
> lanes it is proper for the narrative to contain even dia-
> lect phrases. To sum up: you must work from a know-
> ledge of the men you describe and if the tone you use is
> very evocative of them, you will have created what is
> called "perfected pen-se" . . . (Yüeh-fu Ch'uan Sheng)

But there are many times when Ming critics use pen-se to mean
a kind of genuineness which has nothing to do with the illusion of real
life on the stage. The most common usage seems to be "early simplicity" of language, as in Ho Liang-chün's Ssu-yu Chai Ch'ü-shuo:[14]

> In sum, Hsi-hsiang Chi wears make-up everywhere and
> P'i-pa Chi devotes itself to the display of learning. The
> early simplicity of language (pen-se yü) is seldom found.
> And yet it is precisely this simple language one should
> use to write ch'ü [arias] if one lays any claim to being
> a real composer. (p. 2a)

And in Hsü Wei's Nan-tz'u Hsü-lu:

> P'i-pa is the best of them . . . Ching-ch'ai, Pai-yüeh
> and others contain a few readable passages but the arias
> of all the rest are quite rustic--there is one great aspect
> to them, however: every sentence is in unadorned lang-
> uage (pen-se) and there is nothing of the pa-ku-wen
> flavor we get from modern composers. (p. 243)

It is certainly this meaning of pen-se (coupled with knowledge of
the dates of reputed authors) which Aoki uses to classify Yüan drama
into early pen-se and early wen-ts'ai (elegant) schools, though he goes
on to characterize further the diction of the arias by their tone and
subject matter.[15] However, the term had a number of other nuances
which the student of Ming criticism and the Chinese musical drama
may find useful to keep in mind.

Most dictionary definitions of <u>pen-se</u> can be summed up under three main categories: 1. "undyed," and, one suspects, this also includes the sense of <u>crudus</u>, i.e., ecru, unbleached, as well; 2. "original, basic"; 3. "in kind" which seems to have been a usage known only in Ming times. The "Shih-huo Chih" of the <u>Ming shih</u> informs us, " 'It is ordered that citizens wishing to substitute silver, currency or woven goods . . . shall be allowed to.' Thereafter the rice and wheat which were used to pay the grain tax were designated '<u>pen-se</u>,' payment in kind." More literally, payment with the original article. Meanings one and two were used in literary criticism very early on, but one must add the third definition as part of the constellation of meanings that a Ming writer could have had in mind when he used the term. [16]

To this information should be added a very interesting letter from T'ang Shun-chih (1507-60) to Mao K'un (Lu-men) (1512-1601) on the requirements of great writing. Since T'ang Shun-chih at the time was the dean of Ming dynasty <u>ku-wen</u> writers and the younger Mao later became famous in his own right, we can hope to learn from their correspondence more about the values the term <u>pen-se</u> could have had in Ming times to the literatus who used it to characterize Yüan and Ming drama:

> . . . now let us say we have two men: One of them
> has a very superior nature (<u>hsin ti ch'ao-jan</u>), a man
> of whom we would say "he can visualize all the past
> has to offer in his own eye." He has never set pen
> to paper nor has he intoned and recited rules of com-
> position, but his hand writes directly what he feels
> inside himself as though he were composing a letter
> home. It may be a bit careless, but since it contains
> no trace of the sour, bloated practice essay, it will
> stand as an excellent piece of writing anywhere in the
> world.

> The other man is of a very common cut: He may have
> studied writing diligently, he may be equipped with every
> rule of composition and rhetoric; nevertheless, though he
> write and rewrite it, his product will have as much value
> as something from the tongue of a garrulous granny. He
> may have been seeking that vital essence (<u>chen ching-shen</u>)
> which stays undimmed throughout all time, but his writing

will not contain it. Let him be as skilled in composition as you wish, but his writing will always be low-grade.

This is a matter of pen-se in writing.

Let me take poetry, for example: T'ao [Ch'ien] P'eng-tse never in his life tried various kinds of phonology, never embellished his lines, but what came from his hand direct will always be a poem anywhere in the world. Why? His was a towering pen-se.

In the history of poetry no one was more acute about faults of phonology or more punctilious about rules for the embellishment of lines than Shen Yüeh. He spent a lifetime of energy on it, but when you read his verse you find it merely stultified and narrow. In the entire accumulation of his correspondence hardly a single good sentence strikes the eye. Why? His pen-se was inferior. If a man's pen-se is inferior his writing will not succeed--how much less can be expected when pen-se is not present at all?[17]

So it would seem that there could also lie behind the Ming critic's use of the term pen-se a sense of "talent" or "natural genius" and that the Yüan dramas which were characterized as being pen-se were those which the critic felt to have had this elusive quality, dramas which somehow combined simple yet striking use of language and music in such a way that "the events were perfectly matched with the tunes to make the listener glad he had come and the watcher forget his troubles."[18]

FOOTNOTES

1. In his P'ieh-chi, Ch. 7. See Yoshikawa, Gen Zatsugeki Kenkyū, p. 203.

2. Ssu-k'u editors take him to task for this statement also. One always hopes that the gains of scholarship will be cumulative, that the same mistakes will not continue to be made. Unhappily, when Marxian dogma runs head on into historic facts, the latter come out second best. Comrade Chih Sun writing in Chin-pu Jih-Pao in 1950 has learned his lesson so well (that "ruling circles" are always wicked) that he discovers yet another act of perfidy: "They appropriated this new form [Yüan drama] which had come from the people and used it to entrap the intellectuals by introducing it into the examinations." He gives the second preface of YCH as his source (see Yüan, Ming, Ch'ing Hsi-ch'ü Yen-chiu-lun-wen Chi (Peking: 1957), p. 236). Our same Comrade Chih also "proves" that tsa-chü were written by "the people" by pointing to Tsang's statement about dialogue, conveniently forgetting that Tsang's words are prefaced by "they say."

3. And then, as Wang should point out, only as a homophone for cho or tse.

4. See Yoshikawa, Gen Zatsugeki Kenkyū, pp. 201-203.

5. See Crump, "The Conventions and Craft of Yüan Drama," in Journal of the American Oriental Society, vol. 91, #1, Jan.-Mar., 1971, p. 27.

6. Also, note that in some unspecified fashion the number of language tone classes (san-sheng, ssu-sheng) affects the description by kung-tiao.

7. Hapax. The only entry to be found in dictionaries refers to this same passage.

8. "Nan-tz'u Hsü-lu T'i-yao," p. 236.

9. There is no a priori reason to expect ch'ü musical structure to be directly reflected in the linguistic patterns of its lyrics (certainly Western lyrics and melodies are not so closely related),

but the work of Cheng Ch'ien and Johnson is very convincing
(see especially Johnson, T'oung Pao, LVI, 1-3 (1970), pp. 124-5).

10. Yin-yün shao hsieh could simply be another rap on the knuckles
     because T'ang Hsien-tsu's compositions slighted the rules of
     tonal euphony (and many other technical musical considerations
     which Tsang thought important) in favor of literary satisfactions.
     But if it were translated that way (e.g., "his tonal and musical
     qualities seldom mesh"), then the allusion to the clapper of iron
     and the lute of brass is left with no referent.

11. See Chung-kuo Wen-hsüeh Fa-ta Shih, Taipei: Chung-hua, 1970,
     p. 929.

12. The opening words of the aria-set "Nien Nu-chiao Hsü."

13. A modern critic, C. T. Hsia maintains exactly the same view
     as the Ming writers:
         "Arias are unlike tz'u poems in their greater hospi-
         tality to colloquial expressions. While many of these,
         the so-called ch'en-tzu . . . serve little poetic func-
         tion . . . many are an integral part of the aria and
         they blend with more literary phrases to produce . . .
         effects not realizable in the tz'u."

14. Hsin Ch'ü-yüan edition. Edited by Jen Na. (K'un-ming, 1940).

15. Chūgoku Bangaku Gaisetsu, trans. Sui Shu-sen (Taipei, 1968),
     pp. 116-170 and Gennin Zatsugeki Josetsu, trans. Sui Shu-sen,
     (Shanghai, 1941), pp. 66 ff. and 99 ff.

16. A rarer and older meaning of pen-se was something like "pri-
     mary colors," i.e., colors from which all others were derivative.

17. See Ching-ch'uan Hsien-sheng Wen-chi, Ssu-pu Ts'ung-k'an edi-
     tion. Ch. 7, 9a-10b.

18. Fu-pao T'ang Chi. Shanghai: Ku-tien, 1958, p. 62, from Tsang's
     introduction to his edition of the "four dreams" of T'ang Hsien-tsu.

BIBLIOGRAPHY

Cheng, Ch'ien. "Significant Facts about Nine Extant Collections of
Yüan Drama Handcopied or Printed in the Yüan-Ming Period."
Tsing Hua Journal of Chinese Studies. New Series no. 7, 2,
1969, pp. 145-155.

Ch'i, Piao-chia. Chung-kuo Ku-tien Hsi-ch'ü Lun-chu Chi-ch'eng.
Peking, vols. I-X, 1959.

Chugoku Bungaku Gaisetsu, trans. by Sui Shu-sen. Taipei, 1968.

Chung-hua Huo-yeh Wen-hsüan [Chung-hua looseleaf anthology]
(abbreviated Huo-yeh). Shanghai, 1965.

Chung-kuo Wen-hsüeh Fa-ta Shih. Taipei: Chung-hua, 1970.

Crump, J. I. "The Conventions and Craft of Yüan Drama." Journal
of the American Oriental Society. Vol. 91, no. 1 (Jan.-Mar.),
1971.

Gennin Zatsugeki Josetsu, trans. by Sui Shu-sen. Shanghai, 1941.

Hsiung, S. I. Romance of the Western Chamber. New York: Columbia
(reissue), 1968.

Hsü, Ta-ch'un. Yüeh-fu Ch'uan Sheng, sec. 2. Peking, 1959.

Huang, Wen-yang. Ch'ü-hai Tsung-mu T'i-yao. Peking, 1959.

Johnson, Dale. "The Prosody of Yüan Drama." T'oung Pao. Vol.
LVI, no. 1-3, 1970.

Liu, James J.Y. The Chinese Knight-errant. Chicago: University
of Chicago Press, 1967.

Liu-shih-chung Ch'ü (Sixty), ed. by Mao Chin. Shanghai: Chung-hua,
1958.

Pian, R.C. "Rewriting of an Act of the Yüan Drama Lii Kwei Fuh
Jing in the Style of the Peking Opera: A Fieldworker's Experiment." CHINOPERL NEWS. No. 2, December 1970.

38

Průšek, Jaroslav. Origins and Authors of Hua-pen. Prague, 1967.

Shen, Tai. Sheng-ming Tsa-chü. Peking, 1958.

Ssu-yu Chai Ch'ü-shuo, ed. by Jen Na. K'un-ming: Hsin Ch'ü-yüan edition, 1940.

T'ang, Hsien-tsu. T'ang Hsien-tsu Chi. Peking: Chung-hua, 1962.

Tsang, Mou-hsün. Fu-pao T'ang Chi. Shanghai: Ku-tien, 1958.

"Tsang Mou-hsün Kai-ting Yüan Tsa-chü P'ing-yi." Bulletin of the College of Arts. National Taiwan University, no. 3, 1961.

Yagizawa, Gen. Mindai Gekisakka Kenkyū, trans. by Lo Chin-t'ang. Hong Kong, 1966.

Yoshikawa, Kojirō. Gen Zatsugeki Kenkyū, trans. by Cheng Ch'ing-mao. Taipei, 1960.

Yüan-ch'ü Hsüan, ed. by Tsang Mou-hsün. Taipei, 1962.

Yüan, Ming, Ch'ing Hsi-ch'ü Yen-chiu-lun-wen Chi. Peking, 1957.

DISCUSSION SECTION ON J. I. CRUMP'S PAPER

Crump: It's a matter of politesse to let the author say why he wrote what he wrote, and being nearly a musical moron I welcome all comments from those who know something about music, especially Eastern music. It will help me over the terribly rough spots. I picked this topic because I've been reading Ming critics of Yüan drama for a long time, and I found myself understanding only half of what they say. Nor is it much comfort to find that few others have understood them. But I thought that the state of the arts had advanced far enough that if I put things down-- right or wrong--some of you could help me understand what they're saying. Central to this issue is to try and comprehend in some way how the words of the lyrics affect the music and the music affects the lyrics and to shed light on their relationships to theatrical form, be- cause there seems to be an unbelievably intimate connec- tion between the two. I haven't unraveled it, and I don't think we will here, but at least I have assembled a num- ber of statements by Ming critics on the subject of dra- matic music and its relationship to lyrics.

Pian: At first, when I looked at all your papers and all your titles, I thought: "My goodness, three papers on Noh and one on Yüan drama, and these are all sophisticated art forms, so what is Peking Opera doing here?" But as I read your papers and saw that you have brought out many fundamental questions, my paper seemed more compatible. After reading your paper, Jim, I said: "Oh, great! That's exactly the way I feel about it!" You asked whether the dialogue was written by the playwright who wrote the lyrics. Was the playwright responsible for both? Were they conceived together?

Crump: Or did each of these men as they collaborated think of the product as a unit--that is, song plus speech?

Pian: Yes, but as a unit for what? A unit for performance or for a reading public?

39

Crump: I should clarify my view: I consider that all except the very late tsa-chü were intended for performance.

Pian: I can only give you an analogy in Peking Opera. There are all kinds. Mentioned in my paper are pieces which are aria centered: arias are followed by the singing of a few rudimentary fragments of dialogue just to clear up the situation and then the singing resumes. When you go to hear Mei Lan-fang you don't go to hear him get involved in intrigue of some kind, you go to hear him sing. But in Peking Opera there are also obvious mixtures of the two--speech and singing--and the speech is just as musical, as artistic, as anything else.

Crump: I wanted to ask when you were discussing with Yang Hsi-mei the setting of the text to music if you were taking into account dialogue.[1]

Pian: But that was such a small section!

Crump: Did he take the dialogue into account though?

Pian: I don't remember. Anyway, in that part we didn't really deal with dialogue at all. Another point is musical formula, stereotyped musical formulae that can be used by musicians almost mechanically. The opposite extreme is creating purely literary works that are enjoyable without action, without music, without anything except the text itself, in fact to be enjoyed preferably sitting in an armchair at home. Both extremes are possible. One need not exclude the other.

Crump: I imagine that this was so, but when you reach the Ming types they break down clearly into two groups, and one group constantly snarls at the other group.

Pian: You mean people . . .

Crump: Yes, performing types, and the most famous example is Tsang Chin-shu's resetting of T'ang Hsien-tsu's Four Dreams.[2] On one side everyone says, "He has ruined this beautiful thing." On the other they say, "He finally made this beautiful thing presentable for the stage."

Pian: I think that is still a literary man's argument. If you
         can prove that it was actually performed and the proprietor
         actually made money on it from an appreciative audience,
         then you can speak of the artisic criterion. The issue is
         valid, but don't try to think of one without the other. And
         what about things in between? There are those who use
         formulae very skillfully, but there are also those who make
         delightful pieces not only for the general public but for the
         literary man as well.

Crump: Here's how it seems to me: Ming critics have a sense of
         inferiority about Yüan tsa-chü. They say, "Here they man-
         aged to succeed; this is pen-se, and it was all performed.
         Why can't we do that?"

Pian: I have several major points: you ask about the use of
         melody (p'ai-tzu) in the southern drama. Of course, I'm
         trying to pit my unknowns against your unknowns. However,
         from your description I think the question will prove to re-
         volve around the two basic types of melodic organization
         that still exist today: one is a series of melodies (differ-
         ent melodies sung in succession) and the other is repeti-
         tions of the same melody but transformed often by melodic
         ornamentation making a very elaborate, very florid, long
         melody--like the man-pan[3] in Peking Opera, the lyric aria.
         This is important because it is what Tsang Mou-hsün (T.
         Chin-shu) was talking about when he referred to the simi-
         larity between the northern and southern drama. Basically
         there are two types: one is the "medley" type like the chu-
         kung-tiao[4]--the sequence of melodies still seen in k'un-ch'ü.
         I know of one type of narrative performance still in exis-
         tence . . . I'd better write it down . . . the sequence I'm
         speaking about is A B C D E (different melodies); the other
         is A, A', A'', A'''.

Crump: The effect, textually, is that A B C D E all bear different
         names but the text is the same each time?

Pian: The text? I'm speaking now of melody!

Crump: Yes, but in the text I would see a song labeled A, and the
         next aria would again be labeled "song A," and I'm talking

now about A', A'', A'''. If it were a variation on the
same melody, wouldn't the text contain the words t'ung-
ch'iang, "same tune"?

Pian: T'ung-ch'iang[5] occurs when you have a combination of the
two, for example: A, A', B, B', C, C'.

Crump: That sort of thing would show up in the text, wouldn't it?

Pian: In the text you would have ch'ien-ch'iang or t'ung-ch'iang.

Crump: So if ch'ü-p'ai appeared in the text followed by "same tune,
same tune," it might be indicated by A', A'', A''', might
it not?

Pian: In Yüan Drama I don't know; in Peking Opera all these
would belong to the hsi-p'i and the erh-huang categories.

Crump: That not only rings a gong, it ends the round because I'm
lost.

Malm: I must confess, I actually called this conference to carry
out one secret mission--to find the difference between hsi-
p'i and erh-huang. (laughter)

Pian: I'm not going to tell you. (laughter) Anyway, this idea
is clear, is it not? And today the Tan-hsien P'ai-tzu Ch'ü
still contains it. Kay Stevens has one beautiful example, a
story told with a series of melodies, each one different.
In technical writings on the mainland, they call it chi-ch'ü.[6]
The same melody, with variations in rhythm and ornamentation, belongs more or less to the same category. And
that it belongs to the same category is also very interesting.
It isn't necessarily recognizable if measured from a musical
point of view, i.e., cadencing notes, most frequent notes,
etc. A little melody from the hsi-p'i category belongs there
simply because everyone knows it belongs there.

Crump: Do you mean that the sequence itself dictates what comes
next?

Pian: Not necessarily the sequence. In Peking Opera the sequence
doesn't always work anymore. Melodies are freely drawn
from a family.

Crump: Do they belong to a family in the same way they might belong to a mode?

Pian: No, I'm trying to avoid using the word mode. Can you think of these melodies as brothers and sisters who happen to belong to the same family, some of whom were adopted and some of whom were naturally born siblings? They all have the same surname, but their friends know them as individuals. They all, however, belong to the same family.

Crump: The analogy doesn't work for me because . . .

Pian: I'm not attempting to provide a musical explanation; I'm not going to give you a logical explanation. I'm trying to show you what they might mean to a Chinese audience. These melodies are individual melodies.

Crump: Do the Chinese recognize them as members of the same family?

Pian: Well, if you ask someone, he won't be able to tell you why.

Crump: If you throw a hsi-p'i melody into a group of erh-huang melodies will it sound strange to him?

Pian: Well, if you tell him that you are playing a hsi-p'i melody and you are, in fact, playing an erh-huang melody, he will know you are wrong.

Crump: O.K.! Erh-huang and hsi-p'i then are two separate families.

Malm: That means that they are totally different?

Pian: Yes, you can analyze it, but then you get involved in musicological details which will interest only the musician or the musicologist but not the average Chinese audience.

Crump: Well, just one thing then: do we have instruments today with moveable bridges?

Pian: Yes, the ku-cheng.

Crump: Good. Now would you arrange all your movable bridges in the same place for all tunes in the same family?

Pian: I can't tell at this point. Anyway, that's another question. There is another term in contrast to this one. It is called pan-ch'iang. And I think a German scholar has already given this a very dignified title--the pan principe. He means the A, A', A'', A''' series, the related melodies; and you have already helped me suggest that these two kinds are not mutually exclusive. Even in k'un-ch'ü today, A can be repeated before it goes on to B. It is interesting because you talk about this kind of melodic organization in Yüan ch'ü. The northern people criticized the southerners for using melodies indiscriminately. Then k'un-ch'ü, which succeeds southern drama, takes over this kind of melody principle. K'un-ch'ü maintained a lofty stature, but Peking Opera uses the opposite principle. I don't mean to suggest that the Peking Opera melody principle is the same as what you suggest for Yüan ch'ü, but it is useful to think along these lines.

Crump: But what bothers me is related to Hsü Wei's marvelous statement that "It became a habit among northerners to fit even an angry cry into a mode." But the southern drama did not speak about modes. Hsü admits they did have certain sequences however, so can he say that they had no modes at all?

Pian: Well, mode means a measure, a yardstick by which you measure something that already exists. You measure it or you don't measure it; northern tunes have been measured and southern tunes have not.

Crump: This is what I perceived to be so. In other words, modes do exist but the southern composer of Yüan and Ming does not care to use them as measurements.

Pian: That's right.

Malm: The research person may measure it, however, in a tonal system.

Pian: Yes.

Malm: The scholar sees there are tones and they tend to fall
          into a hierarchy. Whether the musican knows it or not
          is totally irrelevant. But there is still something wrong.
          All those people in the unsophisticated Chinese audience
          can distinguish between hsi-p'i and erh-huang, and I have
          a Ph.D. and I can't tell the difference. There is some-
          thing wrong somewhere. (laughter)

Pian: Yes, but the Ph.D. is different, you see. If you were in
          China, you would observe that no one among Peking Opera
          lovers asks these questions. Only a Ph.D. would think to
          ask such things.

Crump: Don't knock it. We make a living out of it. (laughter)

Malm: This is interesting. Take the case of the Westerner who
          is watching TV. If you turn down the sound and ask him
          what is taking place on the screen, he may simply remark
          that the picture shows a man walking down the street. But
          if, when you turn up the volume, he hears a double-dimin-
          ished seventh chord, he will automatically say: "Ah-ha!
          Dirty Dalton is just around the corner." If you ask him
          how he knows, he won't be able to tell you. He knows
          nothing about diminished seventh chords, but he does re-
          act correctly. By the same token, I'm convinced that the
          Chinese opera audience does react correctly to certain mu-
          sical signals; his inability to analyze them is quite irrele-
          vant. He understands what makes it work. I'm convinced
          that with hsi-p'i and erh-huang there is something similar
          to my Westerner and his diminished seventh, but I don't
          know what it is.

Pian: Yes, but that involves deep psychological reasoning.

Crump: But it's also cultural.

Malm: Of course; it's cultural conditioning! There is nothing
          dangerous about a diminished chord (laughter), but if you
          play it enough times in a dangerous situation it becomes
          dangerous. By the same token, there is nothing inherently

plaintive about the minor key; it depends on a cultural reaction to it.

Pian: I'm not saying it isn't important; in fact, I think some universals will come out of what we are saying. Convention and tradition are important basic grammar.

Malm: It's hard for the outsider to react to the conventions of a strange culture. He can only discover things through events.

Sesar: I feel we have to keep listening more and more until we can begin to absorb and be able to predict moments for ourselves. Once such a base is established we can begin to pin down formulae.

Crump: This is all right for you who have modern interests, but what about the historian of forms that are dead. I could listen for a lifetime and nothing would happen. I have to judge how much of it is hogwash, how much is idiosyncratic, and how much is an attempt to express an overall feeling about the quality of southern tunes.

Pian: Yes, but you are still using an outside standard.

Crump: No, I'm listening to the critic. He knows what he is saying and why he is saying it.

Sesar: I'm sure that music must have changed considerably by the time this critic started to write anyway. I also feel you would probably get a better clue from reports of the actual performers themselves. I found the few scattered references in these papers to the actual performers the most interesting. It is clear that the literati established the vocabulary for discussing this material because they were interested in the texts; the actors and the musicians simply didn't bother with it.

I also found it fascinating in the second preface that Tsang couldn't understand the motives of those who chose to consort with actors, who were perhaps similar to the Sages of the Bamboo Grove. Zeami was a professional actor; it was because of Zeami's beauty and Yoshimitsu's patronage that actors were elevated to court status. Once they partook of this particular atmosphere, Zeami, who was very brilliant, began to write in that vein for the intelligentsia of his day. Out of it came some good theory. He was a practitioner and was able to present this theory using the intellectual vocabulary of the day.

Crump: The supposed father of Yüan drama, Kuan Han-ch'ing, was also, we think, an actor, and his plays are thought to be the most successful because he was a combination of the literatus and the practitioner. Unfortunately, we know almost nothing about these people.

Sesar: Didn't you say that there were a lot of biographies, at least anecdotes, about actors?

Crump: Not many. There is the <u>Cho-keng Lu</u>[7] and the <u>Register of Ghosts</u>,[8] which lists playwrights and actors, but these seldom go beyond lists of names.

Sesar: Waley in his book of Yüan Mei also translated a few anecdotes about actors and singing girls, and I can see that they were all very remarkable people. I don't think they wanted anything to do with the intelligentsia. Yüan Mei himself was probably the most famous dropout of his day. (laughter) Such things must be lying around somewhere; they would make fascinating reading.

Crump: You are much better off on the Japanese side for biographical material on actors and musicians. On the other hand, we might expect something to turn up in the future. Chinese literati, although outwardly scorning the theatre as vulgar literature, can't be kept out of the theatre.

Pian: There are good parallels today, and I mean those who are still writing <u>tsa-chü</u>. They are not performed but are written for the personal literary enjoyment of the authors. This is an entirely different world from that of actual performance. Look how people are writing Peking Opera nowadays and how the words and music are adjusted to each other. In the second issue of <u>CHINOPERL NEWS</u> you can see where

we tried to rewrite a <u>tsa-chü</u> act as a Peking Opera.
We showed that the music is quite independent. [9]

Crump: It was practically arrogant. (laughter)

Pian: Let's get on to another question. I'm puzzled about one
of Hsü Wei's comments on word tones and the changes in
them. You mentioned tone class. You meant tone shape,
didn't you?

Crump: No.

Pian: Actual tone classes? [10]

Crump: Yes. Because his statements are coupled with the fact
that whatever was wrong with southern drama . . .

Pian: Was due to the language?

Crump: He says that even though southern drama is inferior to
northern drama, it doesn't have the modes; you see, he
is self-conscious about it. But one thing it does have is
<u>ssu-sheng</u>, the four tones.

Malm: What is your word for mode?

Crump: There are two of them: <u>kung</u> and <u>tiao</u>. [11] I wanted Iris
to explain the difference between them. (writes <u>kung-tiao</u>
on the board)

Malm: That's one mode only.

Pian: It has many meanings. It is a messy topic in any culture.

Crump: In ancient texts, in <u>chu-kung-tiao</u> for example, we may
find an aria written in <u>nan-lü-kung</u> and another in <u>nan-lü-
tiao</u>. Anyway, Iris, Hsü Wei was speaking of tone classes
because by this time the north had already dropped the <u>ju-
sheng</u> or entering tone. He added that in the south at least
they had retained that.

Pian: I can only say from observing present-day examples that
different dialects don't really affect music that much. The

music of a region is the way it is because of the style in that area.

Crump: Isn't it true that if you move a music out of its native locale into the region of another dialect, the music and the lyrics are no longer compatible?

Pian: Text setting is another issue. One can set texts to music with different degrees of fidelity. You can imitate the actual tone shape itself, or you can go by basic tone classification (the even and the oblique classes), which change very little from dialect to dialect. Basic tone classes don't change, even after centuries. Scholars, no matter what they write, think in these very abstract classes.

Crump: What does it mean, then, when they say the text is not good because it doesn't fit with the yin-lü?

Malm: What does it mean? Your paper reads: "[Texts] contain a number of northern songs; in fact, he all but gallops across the border. But the tenor of the lyrics does not fit the tunes. By using northern songs he has fallen into the error of sweetly singing 'East flows the Long River' to the sound of clanging iron." (p.) Boy! The guy is upset about something there!

Pian: These are very difficult source materials to use, that's all. Present day practice shows that word tones don't influence music that way.

Crump: In the CHINOPERL text Yang Hsi-mei and Iris were setting a text to music and she said: "That's a rising tone word; don't you want another word there?" Yang agreed that another kind would be better. Then Iris suggested a whole host of words and he finally replied, "No, we'll make do with this one." What he did next was to diddle his music around. [12]

Pian: Well, you can diddle both.

Crump: What Iris and Yang were both up against is the wrong word tone for the music. He finally changed the music because they couldn't agree on a change of text that suited them.

Johnson: I think he said, "The words you are suggesting are all in the rising tone, aren't they? Can't we find one that isn't?" In the end when you couldn't think of one he said, "Well then, we can fix up the music a bit to make it fit."

Pian: Yes. That happens when you care enough to fix it up. You don't always bother with that. Sometimes in a whole melodic line you may want to draw attention to just one or two words, or you may not care about any of them. It all depends.

Crump: You see how dreadful that becomes for the non-musician and the non-performing student of theatre.

Pian: Yes, there are so many variables working together. It makes the task of the composer much easier too, you see.

Crump: And it makes it impossible for the scholar.

Malm: It seems to me, if I understand it, that Mr. Yang is picking the pitches of his melody partially on the basis of the word tones in the lyrics; but how does he decide to use hsi-p'i or erh-huang? Is it the mood or the meaning of the text he is setting?

Pian: You can follow a very, very vague convention which is broken all the time. Fan-hsi-p'i man-pan is often used by a singer who is unhappy. But many examples can be found where a composer deliberately avoids using it, or where he does not use it simply because he doesn't stop to consider it. This is a case of obeying or disobeying convention more or less at will.

Crump: Here you have an example of something really not open to investigation as far as I'm concerned. The artist has his own internalized aesthetic rules and regulations which he doesn't even express. How can you put these personal whims into charts or even words which others can study?

Teele: Perhaps there is an analogy in the Noh play where you have a shifting from tsuyo gin to yowa gin (strong and weak styles) or vice versa. One feels usually that the choice is made on the basis of content or a particular style of poetry. Is it comparable to this?

Crump: In one dimension it is. But do you find as many trans- gressions in Noh as you do conformities?

Teele: And you find something I want to investigate (which my singing teacher told me didn't exist), that is, sometimes there is a shifting from one style to the other producing very special effects. In an old man role, for example, in the play about Komachi[13] where the ghost enters, there is a rapid shifting from strong to weak style.

Crump: From my reading I think it is like the Ming critics who say that when a text dictates something soft and pliant and flowing, southern tunes should be used; northern tunes are reserved for things martial. But in the end, Tsang would never say a thing like that because, after all, how then could you have a love story done to northern style music?

Malm: You were discussing the great frustration of the historian working where he has no real music; again I keep hoping that since we have the world's experts assembled here, terms common to both literatures (Chinese and Japanese) can be identified in terms of their actual usage today, and we can discuss them in relation to what they meant cen- turies ago in Chinese music.

Crump: Apropos, I meant to ask Iris whether or not there is any- thing similar to what I found in your paper, Bill, about movements of a melodic line which, in the course of its movement from this pitch to that pitch, must pass first through an intermediary pitch?

Pian: I don't know of any, but then I haven't investigated Ming dynasty treatises at all, and there may be things there.

Crump: But the other day, Iris, when you were discussing Peking Opera, Dale and I were sitting there with our ears flap- ping because you said you would show us a place where a melody had been altered to take pitch contour into consideration. I thought you were talking about something like this.

Pian: Yes, but that is simply selecting one segment over another segment to fit the same slot when there is a need to match the word tones. I didn't mean to imply that an abstract rule was being followed.

Malm: There are singers the world over who wouldn't recognize an abstract rule if you hit them over the head with a banjo. Whether it be bluegrass or Tibetan chant, the native singer will never transgress the rules of the tradition in which he is performing. He doesn't recognize the rules. He follows a certain procedure within the cultural context.

Pian: But Bill, are those rules in your paper about the movement of melodies based on a treatise, or on your own analysis, or are they products of a modern writer's analysis?

Malm: That particular section is based on a modern treatise.

Pian: Are there any historical treatises on this kind of singing? The only person I know who does this with Chinese music is Laurence Picken. He has analyzed the T'ang dynasty ritual songs. This is the sort of thing we need more of.

Malm: No one sings chaotically. One sings in a given tradition. One may announce, "I am now going to sing an Appalachian folksong; I am now going to sing a song from Alabama; I am now singing a Texas cowboy song." All these traditions may be different and he would be unable to explain them to you, yet he knows exactly what he is doing.

Pian: But you are talking about descriptive rules, and Jim is talking about prescriptive rules.

Crump: Nonetheless, I can't deal with a set of prescribed rules that fluctuate all the time. Our critic is taking a text which everyone admits is a closet drama, only to be read, and then someone else emerges who decides to set it for the stage. Tsang himself does set it for the stage

and it becomes quite a different thing. Those who have
enjoyed it as pure literature say Tsang's effort is terrible.
Those interested in theatre and music say Tsang's effort
is great. Now! what did he do? . . . May I throw in
something I came upon after I wrote the paper? It's from
Wu Mei's <u>Ku-ch'ü Ch'en-t'an</u>. Wu is speaking of what
Tsang did with the plays. "Tsang looked only at the prosody (<u>ch'ü-lü</u>). He paid no heed to literary values but was
always working for the performable aria, not closet drama
poetry. And, when he wrote his own lyrics in, he inevi-
tably transformed gold into iron. His alternations are
criticized as crude, and in fact they are crude. I have
no idea how many alterations he made in the four plays,
but in matters affecting the distribution of dramatis personae in the acts, in the structure of the play, and in the
balance and mix of dialogue and song, he proves himself
most effective." In other words, he improved the plays,
made them performable. He seems to have made these
plays more singable than they were before. Now what
did <u>he</u> do?

Sesar: It's clear that he dispensed with the rules. Regardless
of the rules which had been in application, the actors who
were hired to perform the plays either refused to conform
to the rules, or the rules were already old and stale and
had to be discounted. I'm in total sympathy with those
who speak contemptuously of the "rules school."

Crump: But the "rules school" is precisely the side in which you
would find favor, because the "rules school" maintained
that it couldn't be sung the way it was written. What
they might have been saying was that it just didn't sound
right.

Malm: I had a question about text setting in the first draft of
your paper. Page 15 reads: "The northern <u>ch'ü</u> run to
a larger number of words per line so the music moves
slowly; the sinew of this type of <u>ch'ü</u> lies in the strings.
The southern form of <u>ch'ü</u> has fewer words per line so
the tunes are rapid; the force of this music lies in the
percussion." Is this important and significant with regard
to later practices?

Crump: All I'm doing here is translating, and I confess that I don't understand it.

Pian: Well, one kind is more melismatic than the other.

Crump: The northern?

Pian: No, the southern.

Malm: If there are more words per line, the music moves slowly?

Pian: It means that from note to note the song is more syllabic.

Malm: It could move faster, couldn't it?

Pian: This is very impressionistic writing, I must admit.

Malm: And if there are fewer words per line, the music moves rapidly. Do you mean Oh-o-o-o-o-o-? (sings melismatically) Is that what is meant by slowly?

Pian: It depends on your point of view, doesn't it?

Malm: I thought it might have meant (singing syllabically but very slowly and ponderously) "Na-mu-a-mi-da-bu-tsu" with lots of words. See? Conversely, with lots of words, Oh-o-o-o-o-o-o- (singing fast and melismatically), it might move the musical line much faster. See? This needs clarification in a footnote.

Crump: Johnson used it in his dissertation, and it needed clarification then to me too!

Malm: All right, Mr. Rapporteur will have to make the clarification here![14]

Teele: To what do the yin and yang refer? You were speaking of yin and yang classes of words.

Crump: He may mean one of two things: the least likely explanation is that by that time the northern dialect had dropped the ju-sheng. In this case the first tone had already split and become both first and second tones. It took on two different contours. One was the yin contour, the other was yang. This is not the same as p'ing and tse because they are tone classes. The other explanation is that certain words were thought to be (and I am speaking mostly out of ignorance here) yin or yang insofar as they are ch'ing and cho, "clear" or "muddy" in sound. Phonologically, that generally means voiceless or voiced initials. Pa would be ch'ing and bha (voiced initial) would be cho. The meaning really doesn't matter, however, because the writer needs a balanced sentence in his text, and he is balancing p'ing and tse with yin and yang.

Sesar: This is very much like Zeami when he explains that the writing of a play requires that the author first find a good story. Your translation mentions the Six Classics, the Buddhist and Taoist Canons, as well as unorthodox histories, which are the kinds of sources that Zeami would have sanctioned as fitting material upon which plays could be based. "Ch'ü must select the best passages from their sources, extract the pith and combine the elegant and the vulgar in such a way that no scars are visible and the results delight the ear of the audience--this is . . . called balancing the emotion required with the diction used . . . we cannot hope that the forms they assume are limited to hundreds or even thousands. Yet the composer must write arias that ring with authentic dialect and situations that have the look of true reality (pen-se)." (pp. 13-14) They must fit the person, the setting and the plot. Zeami also quotes general methods for fitting words to lyrics; they are very general, however, not formal.

Pian: Do you have a suggestion for the word pen-se that Jim is translating here?

Sesar: I think you simply call it a "naturalness."

Pian: "True to style."

Sesar: The character se from Buddhism simply means reality or illusion, depending on how you look at it. "The true look of things" seems to serve best here. The true look of things is the natural.

Pian: He also says that it isn't necessarily realism.

Crump: Zeami wouldn't have said it was realism either. Zeami knows, and our preface writer knows too, that people don't walk around singing in "real life."

Pian: So it means something convincing.

Sesar: If you have a deeply moved audience and one not necessarily concerned with the style represented, unless it is composed of connoisseurs, this is the quality that moves them. It rings true to any type of audience.

Crump: That certainly is the primary meaning of pen-se, but many critics used it in a number of curious ways. Sometimes it seems to mean "early simplicity."

Sesar: I'll give you an example. Hank Williams has pen-se in his songs. He is an early country-western singer.

Pian: How about "sincerity?"

Sesar: It definitely is connected to the simplicity of language, basic and direct.

Crump: How about this passage where we have two men, one of whom has a very superior nature but can't write. He has never striven to learn the art of writing, but when he writes, his pen-se is enough to produce something good.

Sesar: "Artless simplicity," or something.

Crump: It has a whole constellation of meanings.

Teele: You mean "artful simplicity." (laughter)

All: Of course! . . . Question?

Addiss: Yes, I wondered what was meant by something unperformable. In Vietnamese music there are three types of musical theatre; one type is based on Yüan drama. As it stands today, it contains a certain number of aria types. Word tones are so important that if you have a high rising tone where the melody drops down, the text will almost certainly be misunderstood. A melody must follow the word tones. If the melody should rise in pitch it might be acceptable, but if it drops in pitch you are in bad trouble. In Vietnam the tonal system changes in different parts of the country. Whereas in both the north and the south the tones are fairly similar, in the central part of the country, a tone that used to be a high rising tone has become a falling tone. This means that local drama of the central region has been fairly well confined to that area. Let us assume that a Vietnamese playwright composes a music-drama and someone declares it unperformable. The question is what is unperformable about it? Word tones are not the issue because the melody types are flexible enough that they can be altered to fit. In a melody that moves upward from SOL to DO, if you need to you can expand it to <u>SOL</u> SOL MI DO <u>TI</u> RE <u>SOL</u> <u>TI</u> DO.[15] In other words, a melody can be altered to suit word tones but still conform to a melody type, so the problem has nothing to do with melody tones being out of order. And it also means that every melody must be different, which is quite marvelous. With each set of new lyrics the melody has to change.

Crump: This must be exactly the case with Yüan drama. Someone once remarked to me that if he knew he was going to hear exactly the same melodies every time he went to the theatre, he would stop going to the theatre; melodies must have been variable. Johnson's work certainly shows this. Even in a normal sequence of five syllables followed by seven syllables, changes could take place. You might find ten syllables, for example, in a slot where the five syllable pattern is expected, so even when the playwright uses "the same melodies" over and over in his plays, the melodies must have been different in some way.

Addiss: What then is unperformable about it? It is very unlikely that stage action was unperformable unless hundreds of years had elapsed since performance. A Vietnamese once wrote a cycle of one hundred of these music dramas. That's unperformable in another sense. (laughter) But

I'm still confused about the unperformableness of these dramas. Had the language become so formal, so stilted, that people wouldn't understand it? It wouldn't be the case in Vietnam, because that happened many times and people still performed them. One other thought: I have a friend who is tone deaf and speaks Chinese in a dead monotone, yet he is consistently understood by his wife and other Chinese people.

Crump: I don't know what they thought was unperformable, I confess.

Pian: Is your tone deaf friend Chinese?

Addiss: He is not Chinese, but his wife is. In Vietnamese he would not have been understood by his wife. Perhaps word tones are more important in Vietnam than in China.

Crump: But do Vietnamese ever whisper to each other?

Addiss: Yes, but they whisper in tones. (demonstrates)

Crump: Exactly! You get cavity resonance or contextual relationships which force the person to hear the tones, and I assure you that Chinese husbands and wives (and other kinds of couples too) do whisper to each other. (laughter)

Addiss: I suggest there are other rules in Yüan dramas (yet to be put forth) which were disobeyed by people writing plays as literature. Is that true?

Crump: Something which is probably unclear to the audience here is that these are the comments of Ming dynasty critics writing about Yüan dramas. First of all, they admit that no one knows how to play Yüan music, so they can't play it. Second, we have statements which say that Yüan playwrights knew how to combine lyrics and yin-lü[16] perfectly. How they know Yüan dramatists knew this, we don't know. Thirdly, Tsang Chin-shu says that if only people knew as much about Yüan music as he does, they wouldn't make these horrible mistakes. The mistakes he refers to are found in popular closet dramas written by T'ang Hsien-tsu, which critics branded unperformable. T'ang himself knows that. He writes in a letter to a friend: "I don't care if every singer in the empire cracks his throat on my plays; what I'm interested in is getting across my emotions."

Addiss: That implies something unsingable about the words.

Crump: Absolutely! Then along comes Tsang who actually knows nothing about Yüan music. He rewrites plays and a sharp split occurs! The "rules school" say it is a great boon to mankind because he has made the plays performable; others say that he has ruined great works because as literature they no longer have the flavor they once had.

Sesar: It seems obvious that they couldn't be performed because he wanted them to be written in a style that would conform to practise?

Crump: This I don't know. He was talking out of two sides of his mouth at the same time. Tsang Chin-shu claimed to know all about Yüan music, but he couldn't have. He also knew the music of his day, and he belonged to the "rules school" (yin-lü p'ai). These rules did fit contemporary music and T'ang Hsien-tsu was writing plays for contemporaries to perform. T'ang didn't claim to know anything about Yüan music, nor did he think a knowledge of Yüan music essential to perform his works--and of course it wasn't.

Addiss: Somehow what made them performable also ruined them as good literature.

Crump: That's Wu Mei's statement! I think he resents any change in a masterpiece.

Pian: Western operatic arias are usually condemned as poor literature, but something makes them good arias.

Crump: What must be involved, I feel, is certainly musical. I have a feeling that Tsang did know good music. He was bragging, I think, to claim he understood Yüan music, but he was a musician and he knew when a song was unsingable. He knew what was musically inferior; he knew this and didn't fill in the "whys."

Malm: I'm curious: does Chinese opera ever have texts where a segment of the lyrics is repeated over and over in a spot where the music changes? This is standard in Neapolitan opera: "Wherefore art thou, -fore art thou, art thou dearest, thou dearest, dearest, dearest. . ."

Pian: Yes! Many examples.

Crump: These are musical elaborations on very simple lyrics. We also have verbal elaborations on lyrics, for example: "Where-fiddledy-ere, -fore fiddledy-ore . . ." (laughter)

Pian: In Peking Opera the technical term for it is kun-pan (rolling).

Crump: Give us an example.

Pian: Well, it occurs in sad songs, where a singer sings "wo-wo-wo-wo" and then can't continue; or "che-che-che . . .," or "ni, ni, ni, ni . . ."

Johnson: One other item! The description of these rules of Yüan music is suspect, I feel, because regardless of the text you read, all tend to be the same. All of them mention the same rules and make the same comments on them. I always suspected that none of the writers really understood what he was writing about. (laughter)

Malm: It sounds like jo-ha-kyū: whenever you get into trouble with Japanese music you simply refer to jo-ha-kyū. (laughter) The whole world gets divided into jo-ha-kyū. It is like the Westerner who boils everything down to sonata-allegro form. (laughter)

Pian: In other words, you are writing a treatise formulaically.

Malm: I feel that by examining the music, regardless of what the critics say, you can go to the music texts and actually determine what is happening. This is what musicology is all about. Music is, after all, a language. Although a speaker cannot identify nouns and verbs in his utterances, he can nonetheless speak sensibly. Likewise, music must contain the basic sonic utterances.

Crump: Of course, some of us wish we had the music around for you to analyze!

From the Floor: Are there elements of Peking Opera that could possibly be traced back to the Yüan? For instance, in the passage that refers to the strings in the northern drama being the sinew of the music, could that be said of Peking Opera as well?

Pian: Again, I think this is a very impressionistic account, but we try to apply it to something we do know. I would refer you to the fact that when one sings, no matter what is sung, rhythm is needed. In drama there are always many dance-like gestures. These are the necessary bones of the song. What provides them? In the north it is the plucking strings, which are not only melodic but rhythmic. In the south flutes cannot provide that, so drums are used in addition to flutes. That passage, in my opinion, refers precisely to this problem, although you can't find it stated in just this way.

Addiss: Are there passages in Peking Opera that use both strings and percussion?

Pian: Yes, there are.

Crump: Let me point out one other feature which Johnson and I have discussed many times. If you look at Yüan drama texts, in any line there are certain words that are considered basic to the line; there are other words in the line which can be regarded as grammatically less important, and therefore extraneous to the line. In a line of five base words, for instance, there might be as many as ten padding words. In southern music we are told this is unheard of. This might be a feature of northern music which could be described as "fast"; perhaps the music moved thus: tum-tum-tum-tum DO, tum-tum-tum-tum RE,[17] and so forth. This should be kept in mind as a possible explanation.

FOOTNOTES

1. The reference is to an article which appeared in CHINOPERL
   NEWS No. 2, pp. 19-39, published by the China Program,
   Cornell University, Ithaca, New York, in December 1970,
   entitled: "Rewriting of an Act of the Yüan Drama, Lii Kwei
   Fuh Jing, in the style of the Peking Opera; A Fieldworker's
   Experiment." It was presented at the CHINOPERL Conference
   on April 5, 1970, at Berkeley, California.

2. T'ang Hsien-tzu (1550-1616) is remembered as perhaps the
   greatest of Ming dramatists. His four famous dream plays
   were the Huan-hun Chi, Han-tan Chi, Nan-k'o Chi, and Tzu-
   ch'ai Chi.

3. The lyric aria (man-pan) in Peking Opera can be characterized
   as a slow, ornate melody in regular duple meter, rarely over
   four textual lines in length. The meter can be compared to
   4/4 time, one heavy beat followed by three lighter beats.

4. Chu-kung-tiao: the dramatic narrative form of the Chin dynasty
   (1115-1234), the most famous of which is Romance of the Western
   Chamber [Hsi-hsiang Chi] by Tung Chieh-yüan. See also
   Dolezelova and Crump, Ballad of the Hidden Dragon, Oxford,
   1971.

5. T'ung-ch'iang or ch'ien-ch'iang: a melody repeated, sometimes
   with variation.

6. Chi-ch'ü: this class should not be confused with the chi-ch'ü
   of Yüan times which indicates an aria constructed by selecting
   phrases from several well-known arias and arranging them into
   new patterns, producing a hybrid aria.

7. The Cho-keng Lu by T'ao Tsung-yi (ca. 1330-1400).

8. The Lu-kuei Pu by Chung Ssu-ch'eng (fl. 1321).

9. See footnote 1.

10. Level tones (p'ing) and oblique tones (tse).

11. <u>Kung</u> and <u>tiao</u>: for a lengthy explanation of the origins and significance of these terms applied to musical keys, see: James J. Y. Liu, <u>The Chinese Knight-errant</u>. Chicago: University of Chicago Press, 1967, Additional Notes #18, p. 213.

12. See note 1.

13. <u>Kayoi Komachi</u> [The nightly courting of Komachi].

14. Fast and slow, although true to the Chinese text, are poor descriptive choices because they lack a stable point of reference. The distinction being made is on the basis of the text and its synchronization with a melodic line. Speaking very generally, the northern drama tends toward syllabic setting of texts to music, whereas the southern drama betrays a penchant for melismatic singing and sparseness of text. If we shift our focal point to the text, one might view the syllabic nature of the northern drama text setting as ponderous, simply because to each melody note a syllable is attached. The melismatic tendencies of the southern drama might be viewed as melody racing far ahead of text. (Johnson)

15. Underlined syllables indicate tones pitched below DO.

16. <u>Yin-lü</u>: music and word tone rules.

17. DO and RE represent base words; "tum" represents padding words.

Aria Structural Patterns in the Peking Opera
(For Lee Hye-ku on his sixty-third birthday)[1]

Rulan Chao Pian

Peking Opera has generally been accepted as a form of drama.
It is on this premise that it has been criticized for lacking structure,
for its readiness to forget plot in favor of a chance to show off the
performers' virtuosity. In fact, there are many kinds of Peking
Opera. It includes well-constructed stories, many of which are
based on classical literary works, and at the other extreme it en-
compasses pieces that are indeed little more than a potpourri of
mime, song and dance numbers.

Nevertheless, neither plot-centeredness nor "play"-centeredness
alone is sufficient to distinguish the Peking Opera as an art form:
Why is it not simply a spoken play with incidental music? What is
the difference between a dramatic aria and a ballad song? I believe
that a closer analysis of the structure of some of the operas can
give us some clues; it is especially relevant to look at the portions
that contain arias. In my previous investigations[2] of the function of
rhythm, the employment of the percussion orchestra, and the setting
of texts in Peking Opera, it was possible to ignore such fundamental
problems as genre definition, form and texture, the role of the music,
etcetera. While it is not my intention to deal with these problems
directly, it is inevitable that the topics touched upon in this paper
will make us conscious of these issues.

The present study is based on a selection of the librettos of
some seventy pieces and on the music, in various forms, of some
of them. I have depended a great deal upon the collection of librettos in the work, Hsi-hsüeh Hui-k'ao[3] (A Compendium on Peking
Opera Dramaturgy) published in 1925. That was a time when many
male-role actors, such as Wang Feng-ch'ing, Yü Shu-yen, Ma Lien-
liang, T'an Fu-ying, and the female-role actors, such as Mei Lan-
fang, Hsün Hui-sheng and Ch'eng Yen-ch'iu,[4] were still in their
heyday and when most of the major operatic pieces still current
today achieved definitive shape in the hands of these artists.

Most of the larger compilations of librettos today have between one hundred and two hundred titles,[5] which always include indications of aria types. The earliest published librettos with musical notation for their main arias also date from the early years of the Republic, although there exist fragmentary manuscripts of Peking Opera music dating from the latter part of the nineteenth century.[6] Full scores of complete operas did not exist until the days of tape recording. Even today full scores of the traditional versions of Peking Opera are very scarce.

To begin with a few words on the formal details of the arias, by musical criteria there are several different kinds of arias; the verse form of all the major aria types, however, is the same. Basically, it is the rhymed couplet, i.e., two lines of seven or ten syllables each. The first line usually ends on an Oblique Tone word and the second line on an Even Tone word. The couplet as a unit, which musically may be called a stanza or strain, is repeated as many times as dramatically necessary. Thus a long aria is simply an indefinite number of repetitions of the couplet and the strain.[7]

The musical scheme, in addition to the tonal scheme, regularly indicates which is line 1 and which is line 2. This is accomplished by the prescribed cadential notes of each line. However, because of the frequent temporary modulation, there are more than just two possible cadential notes.[8] Although from time to time there are exceptions to these rules both in the text and music, on the whole the couplet structure is a fundamental feature not only in the Peking Opera but also in many forms of Chinese popular performing literature.[9] It is this structural expectation of the audience that the Peking Opera composers have capitalized on to create a feeling of suspense in line 1 and a sense of repose in line 2. Over and over again, the two lines of a couplet are split between two singers when they are arguing, quarreling, questioning and answering. In order to maintain a sense of continuity, the couplet may be split between two aria types that are sung in succession. When there is speech in between, a sense of interruption is obtained, especially if line 2 is never resumed.[10]

This device is so simple that it is not at all surprising to find that it has simply become a formula used for many similar situations. The typical pattern in singing, for example, two couplets (or four lines) is to sing three lines in succession, then one line, with speech or at least an interjection (My friend! You villain!) or action in between. The combinations of one line plus three or one plus two plus one (in fact, one line plus any number plus one) are also extremely common. In the last case the typical dramatic situation would be a farewell scene. After a tearful leave-taking or after instructions given to a messenger, as one person walks away the other will change his mind and say, "Come back here!" (Hui-lai!) Then this interruption is followed by the last line, either with further instructions or with the departing person saying something like, "Hurry up and say what you have to say!" In Ssu Lang's leave-taking from his wife when he wants to visit his mother, this device leads to a tearful farewell aria. [11] On the other hand, in Hung-yang Tung (Hung-yang Cave) (HK 5 p. 9b) when a messenger is called back merely to be told to be careful and come back soon, the line seems to serve no other purpose than to fill a musical pattern.

I have already on previous occasions enumerated and described the different kinds of arias used in the Peking Opera. [12] Briefly, they are distinguished from each other most sharply in rhythmic features, and I have given them English labels that vaguely suggest their most common dramatic functions; for example, the Lyric Aria (man-pan), the Narrative Aria (yüan-pan), the Animated Aria (liu-shui and k'uai-pan), the Declamatory Aria (san-pan), the Interjective Aria (tao-pan), and the Dramatic Aria (yao-pan). There are also some melodies that have a distinct proper name, such as Erh-liu, Nan-pang-tzu, Ssu-p'ing-tiao; these on the whole are rather lyric in spirit but not so ornate in melodic contour as the Lyric Aria. I shall deal with each in more detail later; it is only necessary to note that the application of these aria types is by no means absolutely rigid.

Our problem in listening to Peking Opera music is in many ways similar to our problem in listening to most music outside the Western art music tradition. We are not only faced with unfamiliar sounds, new vocabulary and new syntax, but we have to ask fundamental aesthetic questions that we are not used to asking: What holds the music together? What makes it pleasant to the listener? What keeps it going without becoming boring? This is not to say that we can always answer these questions about Western music. We simply are used to Western music and take it for granted. In the case of Peking Operas we also have to ask if it is fair to compare them with Western operas in the expectation that the relationship between words and music and the dramatic requirements pose similar problems to the composer.

I shall try to begin with the musical stuff of the Peking Opera. There is a limited number of melodies used for all the operas.[13] In fact, one possible way of defining the Peking Opera is simply by its specific set of melodies.[14] For convenience I have called them all arias. These arias can be sung one after another in succession; most can be sung individually with any amount of repetition. The choice of aria type depends upon many factors, the dramatic situation certainly being one of the most important. Some scenes or whole operas are sung practically all the way through; others are mixed with speech in any kind of proportion.

Most of the arias have two lines of melody, which fit the couplet form of the text. The feeling of suspense and repose in the two lines of the text is reinforced by the regularly different melodic cadencing for the two lines. Each aria melody can vary in details without losing its identity. The alternate forms of most of these arias are so well-established that it is impossible to determine which is the basic version and which the secondary. Thus each aria melody is highly versatile when used to set the text according to the meaning or the general mood.[15] Multiform melody is commonly found in traditional and folk music of many cultures. The Peking Opera composer simply has explored and developed more fully and more consciously the variant forms of each aria melody.

This does not mean that Peking Opera music is a closed system. In fact, many melodies adopted for special situations are not fully integrated into the Peking Opera system. These are borrowed from k'un-ch'ü, popular ballads, folksongs, and other regional operas.[16] The process of absorption into the Peking Opera has been slow. This is understandable since the dramatic effectiveness in this case depends much upon the manipulation of conventions. Too many new materials introduced at one time will defeat the dramatic purpose.

Coming back to the question of tune identity. Does this mean that a Peking Opera aria melody is amorphous? Not really. One recognizes such a tune by its totality, which includes such aspects as the few notes most emphasized, the balancing of phrases, the rhythmic patterns, and some characteristic turns of the melody. In identifying such a melody as a Peking Opera aria, one has to include all the variant forms. It is true that we could say of the so-called Hsi-p'i melodies as sung by the female roles, that the diagnostic tones of most of them tend to rest on what seems to be the third and sixth degrees of the diatonic scale, and that most of the so-called Erh-huang melodies tend to rest on the fifth and eighth degrees.[17] However, whatever interest this kind of analysis may have for musicologists, it does not mean much to the average Peking Opera goer.

There has been much discussion on the emotional connotations of the two major categories of melodies, the Hsi-p'i and the Erh-huang. It is best to remember the melodies as individual pieces, some of which have vague conventional associations; for example, the Erh-huang Lyric Aria is often used for singing a moody song by an unhappy character. These conventions, however, are constantly broken.[18]

Without counting the incidental tunes for dances, pantomine and occasional songs, there are about a dozen aria melodies with different names within each of the two major categories. With the so-called Fan Erh-huang and the more rarely used Fan Hsi-p'i melodies,[19] which I shall not take time to explain here, the total is about thirty. This seemingly small number is multiplied if we consider the arias of the same generic name sung by the male and female roles to be different melodies. As a matter of fact, they do sound quite different: the male melody constantly occupies the lower portion of the scale, about a fourth or fifth lower than the female melody.[20] However, the difference between the male and female melodies is not a simple matter of shifting registers. Each gender also has its own melodic characteristics.

On the basis of this distinction of the male and female melodies, the dramatist can play with mixtures of the two. Thus an immature or lovesick young man is usually given the female melody, but here and there a touch of the male quality will be added, either by certain melodic turns or voice production. A stoic old matriarch sings essentially the male melody with occasional female melodic flourishes.[21] The role of a clownish elderly woman, which is always played by a man, attempts no disguise in singing a completely male melody in the actor's natural voice. In the comedy Feng Huan Ch'ao[22] (The Phoenix Returns to Roost) the ugly older sister tries to seduce her younger sister's fiance but falls into a similar trap set by a homely man who has an eye for the prettier sister. The only time she (or he?) sings the female melody is when she decides that to marry someone is after all better than not to marry, and she coyly tries to persuade the disappointed man to accept her.

Melodic development in the Peking Opera is not always due to dramatic requirements. There is the interesting case of the male-role performer Liu Hung-sheng, who has an unusually brilliant voice. In order to display his high voice register, as he sings the Animated Aria for the line T'ien tso pao lai ti tso pao "May Heaven and Earth bear witness" in Chan Huang-p'ao (Executing the Royal Robe), he has added segments of the female melody to his ordinary male melody. However, this practice has been regarded by the critics more as an idiosyncracy than a common procedure.[23]

In the following I would like to discuss the use of the arias from the point of view of certain structural features in the Peking Opera. It is possible to discern several types of structural units in which aria singing is involved to some extent. An extensive passage of the Lyric Aria or the Narrative Aria, together with the dialogue that leads up to it, forms an obvious structural unit. It may constitute an entire scene or a portion of a scene. Even without being able to sing a note, a librettist can easily make the decision that the Lyric Aria with its slow, ornate melody in regular duple metre is what he wants for an introspective lyric song. Since even two or four lines of the Lyric Aria with instrumental interludes can take a long time, when more needs to be said the music frequently shifts to the Narrative Aria, which is the same melody with less ornamentation and two instead of four beats to the measure. The Narrative Aria by itself also has a much broader use. As my translated term tries to suggest, it is used for a more straightforward statement of facts, presentation of ideas, or even the unemotional expression of feelings. The Narrative Aria is often sung in four, six, eight, ten, and less often in as many as twenty or more lines. There are also the Erh-liu melody, the Nan-pang-tzu and the Ssu-p'ing melody which are rhythmically similar to the Narrative Aria and are used in a variety of units for relatively quiet moments.

Another type of structural unit consists of a relatively short singing passage--usually only one or two lines--followed by monologue or dialogue related to the subject of the song. This whole pattern is then repeated several times. This is a type of structural unit often used when there is a guessing context; for example, in Ssu Lang T'an Mu (HK 3) when Ssu Lang wants to visit his mother but hesitates to tell his wife, who tries to guess why he looks so unhappy. After each guess (sung), he protests profusely. This sequence continues until she finally guesses the right reason.[24] In this example the singing is done in the Lyric Aria. In Wu-lung Yüan (Black Dragon

Villa) (HK 10. p. 7a-9a) where Sung Chiang visits his unfaithful mistress, Yen Hsi-chiao, and pretends to guess why she is not pleased to meet him, his singing lines are done in the Ssu-p'ing melody.
In Part I of Yü T'ang Ch'un (The Trial of Su San), during her journey the heroine recounts her grievances to her kindly old guard; she sings once in the Lyric Aria, six times in the Narrative Aria, and finally once in the Dramatic Aria. (I shall discuss this below.) Each time, true to the conventions of the performance, the old guard moralizes, indulges in social satire, or pokes fun at his fellow actor on stage. [25] Such a repeated song-and-comment sequence which stretches out a simple question-and-answer episode over a long time usually does not really build up tension. There is no surprise waiting for the audience. [26] What the audience looks for is a playful patterning for its own sake. Like the arias, the spoken portion of each segment is also structurally repeated each time: "Did I guess right?" "No, you didn't." "May I ask why I did not guess right?" "Because of such and such and such," and then the pattern repeats. Although the truth does not come out until the very end (the characters may even have an unexpected change of mood), the audience enjoys in a relaxed manner the virtuosity of the performers.

The third type of structural unit consists of several different kinds of arias sung in succession. The usual sequence begins with one line of tao-pan, the rhapsodic Interjective Aria. The Hsi-p'i female version is especially expressive: it begins on a high note and continues in a tumbling strain with elaborate grace notes, pausing now and then on each step of the pentatonic scale. [27] The Interjective Aria is commonly sung behind the curtain just before the actor appears on stage and serves to announce an impending arrival. If the character is already on stage, he sings with his back turned toward the audience. The Interjective Aria is also used when a person recovers from fainting or state of shock--returning from a journey to another world, as it were. There is normally only one line of text to this kind of aria. However, if necessary an extension called Hui-lung may be used; this is a long melisma which weaves up and down in a narrower range. Literally Hui-lung means "a coiling dragon." With or without the Hui-lung extension, the next aria after the Interjective is the Lyric Aria, usually in two or four lines. The pace then quickens again with the shift to the Animated Aria.

If we call the metre of the Lyric Aria 4/4 time (one heavy beat plus three light beats) and the Narrative Aria 2/4 time (one heavy beat plus one light beat), then the Animated Aria is 1/4 time. Although the metre is constantly split into 2/8 melodically, the tactus that the listener feels, and which is regularly marked by the conductor's clapper, is the single 1/4 note beat. With this kind of steady single beat, the Animated Aria does build up an intensity. Eventually the aria reaches such a high pitch that the only way to bring it to a close is to break down the rhythm in the last line, using more rubato and long, held notes. This process is called ch'ang-san-le, "to shake it loose,"[28] a technique which is also regularly used in concluding other types of arias although the constrast in mood is not always so striking. This kind of slow-to-fast sequence can be further filled out with the addition of the Erh-liu melody between the Narrative and the Animated Arias. It can also be shortened by omitting the Interjective and Lyric Arias. However, it is not always easy to say whether the result is a truncated accelerating pattern or simply a pair of arias. The decision will have to be made partly in terms of dramatic context.

The following is a scene from Yüan-men Chan Tzu (Executing the Son at the Gate).[29] Yang Yen-chao, the father, is having an argument with the grandmother. The text of the arias is as follows: (In excerpted recordings the mother's lines are frequently omitted.)

Interjective Aria (the couplet is labeled a and b)
Yang: a. Suddenly I hear the old matriarch arrive outside my tent;
        [Spoken dialogue]

Lyric Aria
Yang: b. I, Yang Yen-chao, leave my seat, welcome her in.
        [Long melisma; fiddle interlude]
        a. Facing my mother I salute her, I bow prostrate;
        [Melisma; interlude]

Narrative Aria
        b. I ask my mother, "You bother to come here for what reason?"
(Mother: a. I have come, and you, my son, should know the reason;
        b. There is no need to feign ignorance by asking questions.)
Yang: a. The ancient matriarch, full of anger, keeps a stern face;
        b. It is because of the child, Tsung-pao, that unfilial brute?
(Mother: a. The poor boy has violated what regulations
        b. That makes you tie him there and threaten to kill him?)
Yang: a. The mention of him makes me furious, makes my bowels burst;

	b.	How I wish I could seize him and split him in two.
	a.	I gave him strict orders to guard the borders;
	b.	Who could guess, at Mu-k'e Fort he took himself a wife.
	a.	For this reason I arrested him and tied him outside;
	b.	Pray, honorable mother, to execute him, is not this just?
(Mother:	a.	It is true, he misbehaved, he should be punished;
		[Spoken dialogue]
	b.	But please remember that he is still young and ignorant.)
Yang:	a.	If you protest that he is still young, merely a child;
	b.	Let me name you a few young heroes. Just listen to me:
	a.	Ch'in Kan-lo when twelve years old became a minister;
	b.	Shih Ching-t'ang when thirteen was made a general.
	a.	In the Three Kingdoms Chou Kung-chin, a man whom everyone knows,
	b.	At seven years of age mastered the arts of warfare and generalship.
	a.	At twelve years old he led the State of Wu and commanded the navy;
	b.	In his eyes, that man Ts'ao Ts'ao was merely a baby.
	a.	At the Red Cliff, he fought with fire that defied gods and spirits;
	b.	He slaughtered Ts'ao Ts'ao's eight hundred thousand men, there was no place to bury the corpses.
	a.	In all these cases, their parents were human, they were no gods descending to earth;
	b.	Now tell me, is my son (ritardando-rubato) born of a beast?

In the above example the accelerating pattern of arias matches the mounting emotional intensity in Yang Yen-chao. In the quarrel scene in San Chi Chang[30] (Three Parting Blows) in which the father threatens to disown his daughter who insists on marrying a poor beggar, we see a clearer example that involves two singers both fiercely arguing back and forth. Less contentious is the duet in P'ing-kuei Pieh Yao (P'ing-kuei Bids Farewell at the Kiln) (HK 10), where the hero and his wife sing in the Narrative Aria as they instruct each other to take care, alternating line by line. Then as they express their sorrows more directly, they sing alternately in the Animated Aria, which builds until finally the rhythm breaks down as they simply call each other's names in the form of k'u-t'ou, the one-line Lament Melody. In Wu Chia P'o (Wu Chia Hill) (HK 10, p. 4b), an episode from Lady Precious Stream, P'ing-kuei returns after eighteen years and teases his wife. The liveliness of their conversation is further intensified by splitting single lines of the Animated Aria between the two.

It is not surprising to see the events of a narrative fitted to this accelerating pattern. The courtroom scene in "The Trial of Su San (Part II)" is a well-structured example. The pattern not only fits the story related by Su San but also the dramatic happenings in the court. As the heroine presents herself before the judges, she sings one line of the Interjective Aria. Immediately there arises a misunderstanding about her legal name and she is threatened with punishment. She pleads for a chance to explain. Her appeal to the judge is done in the Hui-lung melody. She goes on to explain in the Lyric Aria, and this leads to the entire story of her life in the brothel and how she met her lover, Master Wang. When she has to give an account of all the gifts and money he spent on her, how he became poor and she in turn helped him to make his way home, she tells all in the Narrative Aria. Here the recurrent pattern of a few lines of aria followed by comment begins and is repeated eight times. By this time it is clear to the two assistant judges that the chief judge is Su San's former lover, and the speech dialogue makes him the butt.

Next is a short passage of the medium tempo aria, the Erh-liu melody, in which Su San tells of their parting promises. Following this, her singing changes to the Animated Aria in which she tells how she became involved with the Shen family, how the jealous wife accidentally poisoned her husband and put the blame on Su San. The musical flow is continuous in this section. The questions in shorter phrases of the assistant judges are inserted during the instrumental interlude which bridges the stanzas. The excitement mounts when the judges scold Su San for confessing to a crime that she did not commit, and she argues back that she could not stand the torture. The whole dialogue is in short single sentences, one singing, one speaking. Finally the tempo breaks down as the assistant judges teasingly ask her whether she would ever like to meet her former lover again. Her tearful reply is sung in a rubato, highly declamatory style. The opera ends with a small coda of additional excitement: with the assurance that she will be acquitted, Su San leaves the court while singing another Erh-liu melody. However, at this point she begins to recognize the chief judge. She tries to catch his

attention in several lines of the Fast Animated Aria. Of course, it
is impossible for him to respond, and she leaves dejectedly singing
in the rhythmically irregular Declamatory Aria. Except for the short
introduction, this framework of the accelerating pattern covers the
entire act or, for that matter, the whole opera as it is normally performed. [31]

The pattern of slow-to-fast arias is not always used so skillfully; in fact, sometimes the device seems dramatically pointless.
In Ch'ing-wen Pu Ch'iu (Ch'ing-wen Mends a Coat) (HK 8), an adaptation of an episode from the novel Dream of the Red Chamber, a
loyal young maidservant who is ill sacrifices her health to stay up
all night to mend a coat for the young master, Pao-yü. She first
sings in the Lyric Aria about the cold and her feeble condition.
After offering to mend the coat, she sings in the Narrative Aria to
describe the procedure. As she grows more exhausted and sick
from the strain, she sings in the Animated Aria and finally faints
when she finishes the last stitch. She recovers in a line of the Interjective Aria, and the short opera ends with her wailing in self-
pity in the Declamatory Aria. [32] This opera must have been put
together hastily. Portions of the text are lifted directly from the
novel, including details that do not make sense here. For example,
without knowing the context of the novel, no one could understand why
another maid, Yüan-yang, is so rude to Pao-yü in the opera. Musically, the formulas and the ready-made framework are applied quite
mechanically.

There is a device that keeps the arias moving which is not really
a musical one. It is the periodic sounding of the night watchman's
beat between arias. Typically, the scene is that of a man or woman
waiting or pondering over a difficult problem. Take for example
"Wen Chao Pass" (HK 3), in which the fugitive Wu Tzu-hsü waits
anxiously in a friend's house for a chance to escape across the border. The night progresses slowly from watch to watch as he sings.
The whole passage is very effectively balanced by the startling dis-
covery at dawn that his beard has turned completely white. In "The
Capture and Release of Ts'ao Ts'ao" Ch'en Kung sits in the inn at
night regretting having joined forces whether or not to kill him. By
the fifth watch he grows wary and escapes. In "Black Dragon Villa,"
which I have cited before (p. 71), the melody used throughout is the
moderate tempo Ssu-p'ing melody. (It is a melody that is generally
used in such light-hearted plays as "The Drunken Yang Kuei-fei,"
or "Mei Lung Town" (HK 10). However, in the present context the

mood seems ominous.) Sung Chiang and his mistress both pretend to be asleep. They in turn get up and sing of their mixed feelings toward each other. At the third watch he pulls out his sword but decides not to kill her. At the fourth watch she reaches for her scissors with the same muderous intent but changes her mind, unwisely, as we see shortly after the fifth watch.[33]

For the first two types of structural units discussed, the aria-centered type and the recurring aria-comment type--as well as the type with incremental repetition that uses the device of the five watches --we can easily find analogous structures in Chinese folk ballads and narrative entertainments.[34] On the other hand, the sequence of blocks of arias with contrasting speed, in an accelerating direction, especially when complete with introduction and coda, probably finds its best analogy in the more organized instrumental music, such as the ch'in melodies,[35] although there is a Shantung rhythmic speech style of storytelling (see below) that often accelerates conspicuously during performance. Joseph Kerman notes in his Opera as Drama[36] the analogy between the dramatic progression in classical music and that in the operas of Mozart. While the sonata form is essentially a drama of melodic contrasts and tonal contrasts, the ch'in melodies illustrate best the drama of melodic contrasts and rhythmic contrasts. This is not to suggest a direct relationship between ch'in music and the Peking Opera. We also find this pattern of sequence in some pieces of p'i-pa music,[37] and above all, regularly in the jo-ha-kyū movements of the highly sophisticated gagaku.[38] The rhythmic scheme is simply a very old and well-developed artistic concept. It should be noted that the analogy between Western classical music and Western opera is much freer than in their Chinese counterparts. For example, while the close resemblance of the Trio in Act II of Don Giovanni to the sonata form is an exception, the adherence of Peking Opera to the slow-to-fast rhythmic scheme is the general rule.

Some of the arias seem to function at times simply as elevated speech, although it is by no means always easy to draw the line between arias and elevated speech. The short rhapsodic melodies of the Interjective Aria and the Declamatory Aria are perfect vehicles for emotional outbursts or dialogue during dramatically tense moments, as in Ch'en Kung's attempt to stop Ts'ao Ts'ao from killing Lü Po-she's family (HK 3, p. 9). In these two aria types the rhythmic irregularity of the melody is reinforced by the fiddle accompaniment, which repeats the more prominent singing notes here and there, as if drawing them out further.

The Dramatic Aria is probably the one most often used for elevated speech. It has a steady fiddle accompaniment and regular beats on the clapper in the background, while the singer seems to be constantly avoiding the beat. This creates two levels of contrasting rhythm: a pseudo-speech rhythm and a constant forward-driving succession of beats.[40] A good example of its use is the arguing scene in Chao Shih Ku-erh (The Chao Family Orphan) (HK 3, p. 5b)[41] in which Ch'eng Ying, a loyal minister, wants his wife to give up their son to save the heir to the throne. Another example from the play Cha Mei An (The Execution of Ch'en Shih-mei) (HK 9, p. 5-9) is the big quarreling scene among four people (Judge Pao; Ch'en Shih-mei, the convicted man; Ch'in Hsiang-lien, the deserted wife; and the princess who is Ch'en's new wife).

It is interesting that the Animated Aria differs from the Dramatic Aria essentially in that it also has regular rhythm in the voice melody (see p. 72); the two even have the same instrumental prelude and interlude in the fiddle. In fact there are operas with places where the Animated and Dramatic Arias are interchangeable.[42] I have described above the use of the Animated Aria as the latter portion of a larger structure of an accelerating pattern (p. 73). In dramatic content, especially when sung in dialogue (either both roles singing or one singing and one speaking), the function of the Animated Aria is often clearly that of elevated speech.[43]

The singing of a Dramatic Aria can also be used merely for formal purposes, that is, serving as entrance and exit songs, markers of transition from one scene to another, and even markers of short episodes within a scene when a new subject of discussion is introduced. The singing is usually fairly short: two or three lines, which can be shared among two or more people. As the initial marker, it provides the setting for the conversation which follows. After the speech another two or four lines are sung to summarize the content or mood. Quite often only one of the two markers is used. Arias sung as formal markers are frequent in operas that emphasize plot development, such as the ones adapted by Lu Sheng-k'uei in the latter part of the nineteenth century from episodes in The Romance of the Three Kingdoms.[44] The other aria types, such as the Narrative and Animated Arias and the Erh-liu melody, seem also to function at times as formal markers. This is especially true in some of the operas featuring Kuan Yü, e.g. Tseng P'ao Tz'u Ma (The Gift of the Robe and the Horse), Pai Ma P'o (White Horse Hill), and Kuo Wu Kuan (Through the Five Passes) (HK 5).

It is perhaps relevant here to mention a kind of rhythmic speech which is often used in Peking Opera. Technically, it is called shu-pan or nien kan-pan (recitation of an unaccompanied aria?) a kind of delivery of spoken words fitted to continuous steady beats marked by the clappers. The syllables are grouped mostly into units of three and seven (separated by measured pauses) which resembles the style of recitation in the popular entertainment form known as shu-lai-pao[45] (The Beggar's Jingles) or that of Shantung story-telling.[46] Both genres use the accompaniment of steady clapper beats without melody. In "Wu Chia Hill" (HK 10, p. 7), the singing dialogue in the Animated Aria has several additional short, three-syllable phrases interpolated in the text. (The musical expansion here is technically known as to-pan.)[47] If one were to omit the melodic element in this dialogue, the resemblance to the popular styles of recitation is quite striking.

Rhythmic speech is extensively used in Cantonese Operas today[48] by both serious and comic roles. In Peking Opera it is most often used by the comic characters. In the hilarious play Wu P'en Chi (The Tale of the Black Bowl) (HK 3, p. 6a-7a), an old cobbler of straw sandals receives as payment a black bowl which has an invisible ghost attached to it. He goes to a temple to ask the deities to help him get rid of the ghost but then tries to cheat the deities out of the reward that he promised them. Naturally, he is stuck with the ghost. All this is presented in a series of repeated patterns similar to the ones I have described earlier but with rhythmic speech taking the place of arias.

On rarer occasions rhythmic speech is also used for more serious moods. However, the phrasing is organized into a definite pattern of beat-groups called P'u Teng Erh (The Fluttering Moth on the Lamp). For example, the general Chao Yün recites in this pattern in the opera "Ch'ang Pan Hill" (HK 6, p. 9) when he sees that Mi Shih, the wife of Liu Pei, has thrown herself into a well in order to make it easier for him to escape through enemy lines with her son, who is the infant heir to the throne. There is an example of the use of P'u Teng Erh in dialogue form between Sung Chiang and his mistress, Yen Hsi-chiao, in "Black Dragon Villa" during their struggle just before he stabs her.[49] Here, in addition to the clappers in the accompaniment, the muted cymbals are also used to add to the tense atmosphere.

Thus it appears that from the point of view of dramatic function, while some of the arias seem to be employed as speech, the speech-like recitation is also employed as aria. There are, of course, actual spoken portions which are equally important to the over-all structure of a Peking Opera. Speech in Peking Opera does more than move the story forward and provide excuses for the arias; it exists in its own right. Even in the more natural style of speech there is subtle manipulation of rhythm, which should also be regarded as a kind of musical performance.[50] However, it is beyond the scope of the present paper to discuss this subject in detail. I shall merely summarize by saying that one finds expressive resources comparable to the arias in the reading of long documents,[51] in the declamatory speech by the serious dramatic roles which is rhythmically pliable and periodically balanced in parallel phrases, in the snappy repartee by the comic figures, and in the recitation of entrance and exit poems.[52]

Some operas are predominantly sung; in others spoken dialogue plays a major role.[53] In various proportions, the two media are integrated and held together by subtle rhythmic currents, which are reinforced by the use of the percussion patterns. Just as the fiddle accompaniment helps the singer shift from one aria to another, the percussion patterns are the binding medium for the arias and speeches.[54]

I may have given the impression that Peking Opera is a stereotyped form limited by pre-existing melodies and mechanical arrangements of its components. Actually it is enormously varied, as any opera-goer can testify. The form can accommodate the most diverse materials, from the acrobatics of military plays to the lyric pathos of love stories, with ample room for humor and satire as well as high tragedy and lugubrious sentiment. It draws on many literary sources and other art forms for its plots, which are usually familiar to the audience;[55] as a result, the plot of a given opera may be incomplete in the acted version, but it remains an artistically satisfying performance because of the structural symmetry of the smaller patterns.

FOOTNOTES

1. Due to ill health I was not able to finish my article in time for the celebration of the sixtieth birthday of my friend Professor Lee Hye-ku of Seoul University in 1969.

2. See notes 7, 12, 40 and 54.

3. Hereafter HK. Edited by Liang Shan-ch'ing and Hsü Chih-hao. Shanghai: Ta-tung Book Co., 1934, 4th ed., 10 vols. Note that each work is paginated separately.

4. On most of these artists see A. C. Scott, The Classical Theatre of China. N. Y.: Macmillan, 1957, pp. 78-91.

5. Chou Chih-fu in his Ching-hsi Chin Pai-nien Suo Chi [Miscellaneous accounts of Peking Opera during the last 100 years] 1932, 2nd ed. Hongkong, 1951, p. 4, cites an 1825 list of plays of the Imperial Theatre Troupe, in which the total is 272 titles. Ch'i Ju-shan had compiled a list of 1747 titles that were performed between 1860 and 1910 (see Ch'i Ju-shan Ch'üan-chi [The complete works of Ch'i Ju-shan], Taiwan, 1964, Vol. IV). However, many are alternate names of the same piece.

   T'ao Chün-ch'i in his Ching-chü Chü-mu Ch'u T'an [A preliminary investigation of the Peking Opera repertory], Shanghai, 1957, has given a list of 1230 titles, all with a brief summary of the plot. Many are alternate versions of the same story or episodes from a longer story.

   In Hsi-k'ao [Sources of Peking Opera], published c. 1915, 2nd printing, Shanghai, 1920, by the editors of the Chung-hua Library (a complete set of which is not available to me), the total is about 500 titles. Many of these are not in the common repertory today.

6. Some are preserved in the Academia Sinica, Nankang, Taiwan (See my forthcoming report "Primary Sources of Materials from the Oral Tradition" in CHINOPERL (Chinese Oral and Performing Literature) NEWS, no. 3, 1971, Cornell University, Ithaca); some are found in the Nagasawa Kikuya Collection in the Tōyō Bunka Kenkyūsho, Tokyo, Japan.

7. In Yü T'ang Ch'un [The trial of Su San], for example, the most common grouping of the Animated Aria (see below) is four couplets. For more details on the verse form, see my article, "Text Setting with the Shipyi Animated Aria," in Words and Music: The Scholars' View; a Medley of Problems and Solution, Compiled in Honor of A. T. Merritt by Sundry Hands. Ed. by Lawrence Berman. Dept. of Music, Harvard University, January 1972, pp. 237-270.

8. For example, if Line a ends on d', Line b would end on c'; if Line a ends on g, Line b ends on f. The two pairs of cadential notes can also be used in a criss-crossed arrangement (ibid.).

9. See Jaroslav Prusek, "Chui-tzu-shu Folk Songs from Honan" (in German and Czech, 1954) in English: in Chinese History and Literature, a Collection of Studies, Prague, 1970, pp. 170-198; also Zdenek Hrdlicka, "Old Chinese Ballads to the Accompaniment of the Big Drum," Archiv Orientální, 25, 1957, pp. 83-145.

10. Formally, there is a device to counterbalance this asymmetry when it is felt necessary, that is, for the orchestra to play a particular kind of percussion pattern called Sao-t'ou. See Chang Yü-tz'u, etc., Ching-chü Ta-chi-yüeh Hui-pien [A compendium of Peking Opera percussion patterns] Peking, 1958, p. 358.

11. Ssu Lang T'an Mu [Ssu Lang visits his mother] (HK 3) p. 11b. In A. C. Scott's translation in his Traditional Chinese Plays, Wisconsin, 1967, p. 55, he has omitted this portion of the dialogue.

12. See R. C. Pian, "Rewriting of an Act of the Yuan Drama, Lii Kwei Fuh Jing, in the Style of the Peking Opera: A Field Worker's Experiment," (presented at the CHINOPERL Conference, April 1970, Berkeley, Cal.), in CHINOPERL NEWS, no. 2, December 1970, p. 21.

13. There is a good sampling of Peking Opera arias on record (Lyrichord #LLST 7212, The Chinese Opera; Arias from 8 Peking Operas). However, see my review in Ethnomusicology, XV (May 1971) 2, p. 313-15, on corrections of several labels of aria types.

14. See transcriptions into staff notation of many examples in Liu T'ien-hua, Selections from the Repertoire of Operatic Songs and Terpsichorean Melodies of Mei Lan-fang, Peiping, 1929. 106 pp. plus 84 pp. of the same pieces in the kung-ch'e notation. Explanations are both in English and Chinese. It is to be noted that all melodies in this collection are female melodies. (See discussion below.)

15. See Pian, "Text Setting . . . ", esp. conclusion.

16. For example, the tune "Chi San Ch'iang" [The triple thrust] for drinking scenes, "Yeh Shen Ch'en" [Deep in the night] for accompanying dancing, and the numerous songs generically called p'ai-tzu, e.g., as used by the hero in Lin Ch'ung Yeh Pen [The flight of Lin Ch'ung at night].

17. See analysis of the Hsi-p'i female melody by Liu Chi-tien in Ching-chü Yin-yüeh Chieh-shao [Introducing the music of Peking Opera], Peking, 1960, p. 183.

18. For example, T'ien Tan Chiu Chu [T'ien Tan saves the prince], Erh Chin Kung [Twice entering the palace], and Wu P'en Chi [The tale of the black bowl] are not tragedies but are all set to Erh-huang melodies. Furthermore, several light comedies are set to the Ssu-p'ing melody, which traditionally belongs to the Erh-huang category.

19. For a detailed discussion of the fan-melodies with illustrations, see Ho Wei, "Hsi-ch'ü Ch'ang-ch'iang Ch'uang-tso Yen-chiu" [A study of the process of creating Peking Opera arias] in Hsi-ch'ü Yin-yüeh Lun-wen Hsüan [Selected essays on operatic music], Shanghai, 1958, p. 103-107.

20. The instrumental interlude played on the fiddle is identical for both.

21. A good example can be found in the Lyrichord Recording LLST 7212, The Chinese Opera, Side 1, Band 4.

22. See edition by Ting Ping-sui, etc. Taipei: Far East Book Co., 1957, p. 24.

23. See <u>Ching-chü Ch'ang-ch'iang</u> [Peking Opera arias] compiled by the Chinese Institute for the Study of the Musical Drama, Peking, 1959, Series I, Part 1, pp. 35 and 40.

24. See Scott, 1967, pp. 39-42.

25. The Taiwan performance of 1964 by the Ta-p'eng Troupe. Recorded by R. C. Pian (transcription in manuscript form). For a slightly different version, see for example <u>Yü T'ang Ch'un</u>, ed. by Ting Ping-sui, Taipei, 1956. The more recent version, called <u>Nü Ch'i Chieh</u> [She goes to court] as transcribed by Lin Lu, Peking, 1962, which is based on the performance by Mei Lan-fang and Hsiao Ch'ang-hua, is much more serious in tone.

26. Perhaps this is analogous to certain types of Ming dynasty short stories described by Patrick Hanan ("The Early Chinese Short Story," <u>HJAS</u>, 27 (1967), pp. 192-195) in which the revelation aspect of the plot is not the most important factor.

27. The Interjective Aria: (from "The Trial of Su San")

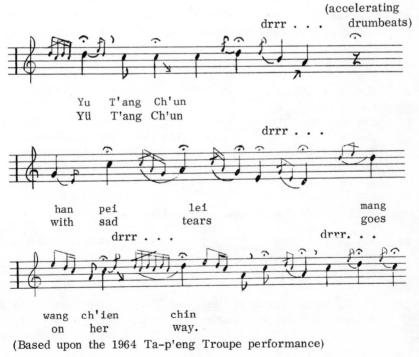

(Based upon the 1964 Ta-p'eng Troupe performance)

28. Pian, "Rewriting . . . in the Style of the Peking Opera . . . ,"
    p. 23.

29. See transcription into staff notation in Ching-chü Hsüan Ch'ü
    [Selected arias from Peking Opera]. Ed. by the Chinese Insti-
    tute for the Study of the Musical Drama. Peking, 1956, pp.
    6-10. The mother's singing is omitted in this transcription.

30. This opera and the two following mentioned pieces, P'ing-kuei
    Pieh Yao and Wu Chia P'o, are three episodes from the same
    story, collectively known as Hung Tsung Lieh Ma [The red
    maned horse], which has been translated into English by S. I.
    Hsiung as Lady Precious Stream, Liveright Publishing Co., N.
    Y. 1935.

31. This story has a happy ending in the original. See Ching Shih
    T'ung Yen compiled by Feng Meng-lung (1624), No. 24. "Yü
    T'ang-ch'un lo-nan feng-fu" The Jen-min Wen-hsüeh Ch'u-pan-
    she edition, Peking, 1956. However, in the present day opera
    form the tale has an ambiguous conclusion.

32. Apparently this work was not frequently performed. It is not
    listed in most common collections.

33. Later, he kills her in a quarrel.

34. See Z. Hrdlička, op. cit.

35. For example, P'u An Chou [A Buddhist chant]. See transcrip-
    tion in Ku Ch'in Ch'ü Chi [A collection of Ch'in melodies].
    Peking: The Music Press, 1962, pp. 203-210. (There is a
    recording of this peice in Chinese Classical Masterpieces, as
    played by Liu Tsun-yuen, Lyrichord LL-82.)

36. N. Y.: Alfred A. Knopf, 1956, Chap. 3.

37. For example, Ch'un Chiang Hua Yüeh Yeh [Moonlight over Spring
    River]. Lyrichord LL-82. However, this could have been influ-
    enced by ch'in music.

38. W. P. Malm, Japanese Music and Musical Instruments. Rutland,
    Vermont and Tokyo: Charles E. Tuttle, 1959, p. 102.

39. Kerman, op. cit., p. 86.

40. See example in staff notation in R. C. Pian, "The Function of Rhythm in the Peking Opera" in The Musics of Asia, (Papers read at an International Music Symposium, Manila, April, 1966. Pub. by the National Music Council of the Philippines. Ed. by José Maceda, Manila, 1971), p. 123.

41. Sometimes under the title of Pa I T'u [Portrait of eight virtues], p. 5b.

42. For example, the aria "People Say that the Loyang Blossoms are Beautiful," in Act II, scene 2 of "The Trial of Su San," is sung in the Animated Aria by Mei Lan-fang but in the Dramatic Aria by Yen Lan-ching (see note 25).

43. Good examples can be found in Pai Ling Chi [The white silk strategy] (HK 9); and Erh Chin Kung [Twice entering the palace], the Ching-chü Ts'ung K'an edition, Shanghai, 1955, pp. 490-491.

44. There is an account of Lu's work in the Introduction to Hsiao Ch'ang-hua Yen-ch'u Chü-pen Hsüan Chi [Selections from Hsiao Ch'ang-hua's repertory], Peking, 1958.

45. There is a recording of an imitation of this in Hsiang Sheng Chi Chin [The best of comedian's dialogues], Vol. IV. Recorded by Wu Chao-nan and Wei Lung-hao. Taipei: National Language Daily Inc., 1969.

46. Examples can be found in C. Stevens, Chinese Folk Entertainments: A Collection of Tapes with Matching Texts (see full description in CHINOPERL NEWS, no. 3), Vol. II; and the Ming-feng commercial recording (Taiwan): CO-297-8.

47. For detailed description of this technique, see Hsia Yeh, Hsich'ü Yin-yüeh Yen-chiu [Studies of operatic music]. Shanghai, 1959, p. 88.

48. Frequently performed also in the United States in the Boston and San Francisco areas by professional troupes from Hongkong.

49. HK 10, p. 17; there is a commercial recording of this, M-299 (Peking).

50. Pian, "Function of Rhythm in the Peking Opera," pp. 118-120.

51. A good example is the reciting of the plaint by Chia Kuei in
     Fa Men Ssu [Buddhist temple]. A detailed analysis of the
     speech patterns in it is given by the artist Hsiao Ch'ang-hua
     in his article "T'an Chia Kuei Nien Chuang" [On the reading
     of the plaint by Chia Kuei], in Hsi Chü Pao [Journal of music
     drama], Peking, 1963, 2, pp. 42-46.

52. See for examples K'ung Ch'eng Chi [The ruse of the empty city]
     (HK 3); also Folkways recording, FW 8882.

53. The play Wu Chia P'o [Wu Chia Hill] is a good example of a
     predominantly singing piece, and Ta Yü Sha Chia [The fisher-
     man's revenge] (HK 4) represents a predominantly spoken play.

54. R. C. Pian, "Contribution of the Percussion Orchestra to Dra-
     matic Structure in Peking Opera." (Unpublished paper read at
     the 27th International Congress of Orientalists, Ann Arbor,
     Mich., 1967.)

55. Most Peking Opera stories seem to be from the major novels,
     classical short stories, the Yüan and Ming dramas, currently
     popular historical novels, many kinds of regional dramas, and
     occasionally from certain forms of popular narrative genres.
     See T'ao Chün-ch'i, op. cit.

BIBLIOGRAPHY

Chang, Yü-tz'u, et al. Ching-chü Ta-chi-yüeh Hui-pien [A compendium of Peking Opera percussion patterns]. Peking, 1958.

Ch'i, Ju-shan. Ch'i Ju-shan Ch'üan-chi [The complete works of Ch'i Ju-shan]. Taiwan, 1964.

Ching-chü Ch'ang-ch'iang [Peking Opera arias], compiled by the Chinese Institute for the Study of the Musical Drama. Peking, Series I, 1959, part 1.

Ching-chü Hsüan Ch'ü [Selected arias from Peking Opera], edited by the Chinese Institute for the Study of the Musical Drama. Peking, 1956.

Ching Shih T'ung Yen, compiled by Feng Meng-lung (1624). Peking: Jen-min Wen-hsüeh Ch'u-pan-she, 1956.

Chou, Chih-fu. Ching-hsi Chin Pai-nien Suo Chi [Miscellaneous accounts of Peking Opera during the last 100 years]. Hong Kong, 1951.

Hanan, Patrick. "The Early Chinese Short Story." HJAS. 1967, p. 27.

Ho, Wei. "Hsi-ch'ü Ch'ang-ch'iang Ch'uang-tso Yen-chiu" [A study of the process of creating Peking Opera arias]. Hsi-ch'ü Yin-yüeh Lun-wen Hsüan [Selected essays on operatic music]. Shanghai, 1958.

Hrdlička, Zdeněk. "Old Chinese Ballads to the Accompaniment of the Big Drum." Archiv Orientální. 1957, p. 25.

Hsi-hsüeh Hui-k'ao [A compendium on Peking Opera dramaturgy] (HK), ed. by Ling Shan-ch'ing and Hsü Chih-hao. Shanghai: Ta-tung Book Company, 1934.

Hsi-k'ao [Sources of Peking Opera]. Shanghai, by the editors of the Chung Hua Library, 1920.

Hsia, Yeh. Hsi-ch'ü Yin-yüeh Yen-chiu [Studies of operatic music].
Shanghai, 1959.

Hsiao, Ch'uang-hua. "T'an Chia Kuei Nien Chuang" [On the reading
of the plaint by Chia Kuei], Hsi Chü Pao [Journal of music dra-
ma]. Peking, 1963, p. 2.

Hsiao Ch'ang-hua Yen-ch'u Chü-pen Hsüan Chi [Selections from Hsiao
Ch'ang-hua's repertory]. Peking, 1958.

Hsiung, S. I. Lady Precious Stream. New York: Liveright Publish-
ing Company, 1935.

Kerman, Joseph. Opera as Drama. New York: Alfred A. Knopf,
1956.

Ku Ch'in Ch'ü Chi [A collection of Ch'in melodies]. Peking: The
Music Press, 1962.

Liu, Chi-tien. Ching-chü Yin-yüeh Chieh-shao [Introducing the music
of Peking Opera]. Peking, 1960.

Liu, T'ien-hua. Selections from the Repertoire of Operatic Songs and
Terpsichorean Melodies of Mei Lan-fang. Peiping, 1929.

Malm, W. P. Japanese Music and Musical Instruments. Rutland,
Vermont and Tokyo: Charles E. Tuttle, 1959.

Pian, R. C. "Contribution of the Percussion Orchestra to Dramatic
Structure in Peking Opera" (unpublished paper read at The 27th
International Congress of Orientalists, Ann Arbor, Michigan).
1967.

_____. "Rewriting of an Act of the Yüan Drama Lii Kwei Fuh
Jing, in the Style of the Peking Opera: A Field Worker's Experiment." CHINOPERL NEWS. No. 2, Dec. 1970.

_____. "The Function of Rhythm in the Peking Opera," ed. by
José Maceda. The Musics of Asia. Manila, 1971.

_____. "Primary Sources of Materials from the Oral Tradition."
CHINOPERL NEWS. Cornell University, Ithaca, no. 3, 1971.

Pian, R. C. "Text Setting with the Shipyi Animated Aria." Words and Music: The Scholars' View; a Medley of Problems and Solutions, Compiled in Honor of A. T. Merritt by Sundry Hands, ed. by Lawrence Berman. Dept. of Music, Harvard University, January 1972.

Prušek, Jaroslav. "Chui-tzu-shu Folk Songs from Honan" (in German and Czech, 1954) in English. Chinese History and Literature, A Collection of Studies. Prague, 1970.

Scott, A. C. The Classical Theatre of China. New York: Macmillan, 1957.

_____. Traditional Chinese Plays. Wisconsin, 1967.

Stevens, C. Chinese Folk Entertainments: A Collection of Tapes with Matching Texts (see full description in CHINOPERL NEWS, no. 3), vol. II.

T'ao, Chün-ch'i. Ching-chü Chü-mu Ch'u T'an [A preliminary investigation of the Peking Opera repertory]. Shanghai, 1957.

Ting, Ping-sui. Feng Huan Ch'ao. Taipei: Far East Book Company, 1957.

DISCUSSION SECTION ON RULAN CHAO PIAN'S PAPER

Pian: In former studies I have dealt with rhythm in Peking Opera, the problems of text setting in Peking Opera, and the use of percussion patterns in Peking Opera--all small technical problems. In this study I am attempting something larger than vocabulary. I do not treat whole operas but large structural units which can be equated with the larger problems of syntax, and meaning as a result of syntax. I have not dealt with the structure of a whole piece or the division of a Peking Opera into acts for the simple reason that I have not yet examined all of the Peking Opera repertory. This is different from my friends who are dealing with Yüan drama and the Noh plays, which are closed systems. Thus far, in the pieces I have studied (about seventy) I do not find a consistent form, nor do I see a definite form emerging. It is also difficult to decide as I encounter some very interesting pieces whether or not they are influenced by their literary origins. Some come out of novels, Yüan dramas, the k'un-ch'ü tradition, and even some story-telling mediums (t'an-tz'u,[1] for example), which are all literary sources of Peking Opera.

As far back as the late eighteenth century, according to Chou Chih-fu's book entitled Ching-hsi Chin Pai-nien Suo Chi (An Account of Peking Opera in the Last Two Centuries), there were among the court entertainments the k'un-pu (k'un-ch'ü division) and the hua-pu, whatever hua means. In the hua-pu, there were nineteen titles, some of which are still seen in regional opera today: the Hsiao-kua-fu Shang-fen, for instance, which Lu Hsün mentions in his Shao-hsing Hsi, and Chü Ta Kang which we find in Chekiang opera and other types of regional operas. From the titles we can tell that they were vaudeville types of entertainment.

Malm: You said that a Peking Opera is basically a series of rhyming couplets seven or ten syllables long. You also say that the musical scheme indicates which is the first and which the second line of the couplet. This is fascinating to me and I yearn for an example.

90

Pian: O.K. Suppose there is a scale from f to f'. This is the normal range for the female voice in Peking Opera. The first line will usually end on d' or g, and the second line usually ends on the notes a major second below, that is c' or f.

Malm: "Each aria melody can vary in detail without losing its identity." (p. 68)

Crump: That's the kind of thing I'd like to understand.

Pian: I wouldn't want to answer that in a footnote. The whole issue of tune identification is a very large one. What about Bayard's study on the tune family? There has been a good deal of work done on ballad music and on American folksongs. These apply very well to this kind of music.

Sesar: The question of architectural form or texture interests me. Speaking of form, I find, sometimes hits a dead end. You discover that the form was fixed after the play was written. Whatever we mean by form must undergo further exploration. Again, we need more concrete examples. What we need to do is produce cheap plastic records with examples recorded on them.

Malm: This is the latest thing.

Pian: Of course, with Yüan drama and the Noh there is a form and a theory and the repertoire is limited. With Peking Opera I sometimes think of people who ask about form in a fugue. You can talk about the process, but because each piece is different you can only talk about texture.

Teele: I don't think it is quite as fixed in the Noh. You speak of dialogue and lyrics and aria moving to the Narrative Aria. I immediately though of kotoba where you have sage-uta and age-uta. This may sound terribly well defined, but in fact it is not. Line number or line length is unlimited. I'd like to see examples of Peking Opera text here where you are defining your couplets. In Japanese you have 7 5, 7 5, 7 5, going on and on ad nauseum.

Pian: Do you have rhyme schemes?

Teele: No.

Pian: In Peking Opera that is very clear.

Teele: I thought how similar many of these things appeared to be, and I wondered if in fact they are so similar after all.

Sesar: I have never really liked opera.   One reason I can't tolerate it is because I could never understand what they were saying, even in English.   People do attend the Noh drama, but no one understands what is being sung.   How much of Peking Opera is truly understood?

Pian: People attend Peking Opera for many things.   Why do they attend?   Do they go to see a plot unfold?   Is the plot development important?   Is it part of the excitement they are waiting for?   It isn't important in Peking Opera.   They go to hear beautiful arias, to hear humorous dialogue.   They go to hear interesting patterning, and I tried to stress the patterning aspect in my paper.

Sesar: There is always the big moment too.

Pian: Yes, the big moment, not the surprise of the big moment, but the technique of building up to it.

Johnson: You go to hear famous performers too.

Pian: There is some of that too.

Johnson: In Taipei people urge you not to miss the performance of so-and-so.   What he is performing is less important; ask them the name of the opera and a common reply is, "Oh, I don't know, but it doesn't matter."

Pian: That's universal.

Crump: In contemporary opera what are people interested in seeing? What about the pageants of the life of Christ?   What do they go to see there?

Pian: Well, we can summarize modern Peking Opera plays simply by pointing out that the followers of Mao Tse-tung want
to use it as a message carrier. Here the playwrights are
more self-conscious. They are no longer treating a basically traditional art; it becomes personal.

Crump: But in the past there must have been things newly written
that did not use traditional themes. They became traditions in time, but why did people go to see them in the
first place? You say yourself, Iris, that there are so
many twists on the conventions that it was contingent on
the audience's knowledge of the convention for them to
appreciate it.

Pian: There were successful ones and unsuccessful ones.

Teele: On page 72 you speak of a third type of structural unit.
I was thinking of a series of arias which are grouped together as arias and not as part of a structure involving
prose/aria/prose/aria types. This sounded to me much
like the kuri/sashi/kusemai[2] series which occurs over and
over again in the third part of the ha section of the Noh
drama. Is your example similar in that it is part of a
fixed group that goes together and leads someplace? Is
it a structural unit that belongs in a particular place and
serves a particular function?

Pian: Thus far I have merely pulled out these patterns and I
have not yet discovered a consistent locational pattern.
Sometimes in Peking Opera a pattern appears throughout
the entire play; sometimes it is found in one act only.

Malm: You quote that "Joseph Kerman notes in his Opera As
Drama the analogy between the dramatic progression in
classical music and that in the operas of Mozart. While
the sonata form is essentially a drama of melodic contrasts
and tonal contrasts, the ch'in[3] melodies illustrate best the
drama of melodic and rhythmic contrasts." (p. 76) I need
that translated into more intelligible terms.

Pian: Yes, what do we mean by dramatic elements? Dramatic
means sudden changes. Perhaps a long, boring, unchang-

ing passage is another way of showing drama too, but change and the lack of change can both illustrate dramatic elements. In a sonata you have statement, contrasting statement, restatement with variations, and change of tonality from tonic to dominant; you might return, or perhaps you expect to return to the tonic but the music surprises you and goes to the subdominant. These are what I mean by dramatic elements. This is how I interpreted Kerman.

Malm: Perhaps drama is an unfortunate choice of wording. Contrast is perhaps what you really mean.

Pian: No. I think Kerman means the support of the human drama on the stage with this musical drama. If you accept a sonata as a drama then the music that supports the action on stage functions in similar ways. You can listen to music that has no program and feel that it is dramatic. I tried to use this analogy employing a different set of materials. As for Chinese music, I find in ch'in music that rhythmic contrast from movement to movement can be achieved in very interesting ways, in very dramatic ways.

Johnson: Do you mean it would be very easy to imagine a program behind a ch'in melody? You can take a Haydn piano sonata (and I have a specific one in mind) and find a heroine and a villain; she is pursued by the villain and screams at the moment when she is attacked.

Pian: I suppose so. But I hope the point is clear.

Malm: Here you continue in your paper: "In a Mozart opera the close resemblance [of ensemble singing] to the sonata form is an exception, while the adherence to the slow-to-fast rhythmic scheme in Peking Opera is the general rule." (p. 76)

Pian: Kerman points out a specific ensemble and says it is a perfect imitation of the sonata-allegro form. I had better footnote that for the general reader. My point is that, whatever the origin of this sequence from slow to fast, when applied to Peking Opera arias it happens in a more formulaic, automatic way than in Mozart. It is more common to Peking Opera.

Malm: This could be confusing to the general reader who knows nothing about Peking Opera.

Crump: It is unfortunate that we don't have two forms of the adjective as we used to have; dramatic and dramatical. It is archaic now, so we can't use it.

Teele: Is the ch'in melody defined somewhere?

Pian: Ch'in is the seven-stringer zither.

Johnson: I can't quite hear in my mind your Animated Aria because you say in this case it is also simply a form of elevated speech with regulated rhythm.

Pian: My wording is unclear again, probably. This Animated Aria occurs in a place where normally you expect elevated speech. Because of its dramatic position it has the function of elevated speech; it is appearing in a place where you would normally expect elevated speech, but the Animated Aria happens to be used.

Johnson: Does it still have a melody here? The speech I am thinking of is the stylized speech which is not accompanied by musical instruments.

Pian: You could have accompaniment in the background.

Johnson: But it is not an aria then . . .

Pian: That's why I say the text should be altered to read: "The Animated Aria, in such a case, should be considered simply a form of elevated speech." This is what I wanted to express.

Sesar: It is sung then?

Pian: Yes. It goes like this: (sings the melody).

Malm: It would be nice to have that example in our text.

Crump: Iris, in talking of the hui-lung extension, (p. 71) can this
          be used to extend the Interjective Aria, for example?

Pian: Yes.

Crump: Is hui-lung[4] the title of that segment, is it a ch'ü-p'ai?

Pian: It has come to be the proper name.   It is labeled in the
          text.

Crump: So here in modern opera we have the equivalent of the
          musically descriptive labels that we see in tsa-chü and
          Ming ch'uan-ch'i.   The label is describing the music.
          In hui-lung there is a coiling effect, right?

Pian: Yes.   But for that matter then, the man-pan, k'uai-pan
          can also . . .

Crump: Yes, but they are not ch'ü-p'ai in the same way the hui-
          lung is, or are they?

Pian: That's hard to say.   Erh-huang man-pan, for example;
          when erh-huang is combined with man-pan then the slow-
          ness of the man perhaps is not that prominent anymore.

Crump: But the pan-ness of the pan remains, doesn't it?   It is the
          clapper, isn't it?

Pian: No, the word pan means melody here.

FOOTNOTES

1. T'an-tz'u: rhythmic recitations.

2. Kusemai: the chanted-dance, of which the portion of a Noh play called kuse is the survival.

3. Ch'in: the term refers to the seven-stringed chordophone also called ku-ch'in.

4. Hui-lung: a long melismatic melody which weaves up and down in a narrow pitch range, often used to extend the Interjective Aria.

The Musical Characteristics and Practice
of the Japanese Noh Drama in an East Asian Context

William P. Malm

Noh is the best known "ancient" professional Japanese music-
drama parallel in time with the late Yüan and early Ming dynasties
of China. The basis of this knowledge is its performance practice
today plus the lives and writings of its founders, Kanze Kan-ami
Kiyotsugu (1333-1384) and his son Zeami Motokiyo (1363-1443), and
the many excellent historical studies by Japanese and foreign scholars
of its predecessors or of its later developments and influences. The
purpose of this study is to concentrate on technical terms and practices gleaned from these three sources in the hopes that certain Sino-
Japanese music relationships may emerge.

Thanks to the work of scholars like O'Neill (1958) and Araki
(1964), many details of early Chinese theatricals in Japan and their
relations to early Noh are available in English. Therefore, we need
comment here only on some of the musical aspects of this vitally
interesting period. The two most obvious sources of Chinese music
theory and practice are Buddhism and gagaku court music, both of
which were of considerable importance by the sixth century. Nomenclature of Buddhist music (classically known as shōmyō though it has
many forms) and the more theatrical dance forms of the court (bugaku)
will appear and be identified in the technical sections of this essay
that follow. Perhaps of greater interest are the more directly Chinese
and more public theatricals such as gigaku, a masked theatrical found
in Japan in the same sixth century. It arrived, like many other music and drama forms of that period, via Korean versions of T'ang
Chinese traditions which in turn reflected theatricals from all over
Asia.[1] The Chinese traditions of jugglers, acrobats, magicians, and
other side show activities also were brought into Japan under the general title of sangaku (in Chinese san-yüeh, scattered music). By the
tenth century the term sarugaku (monkey music) or sarugō appeared
to be used interchangeably with sangaku.[2] Such activities were inter-
mixed with soothsayers, shamans, and temple or shrine events. They
were more often plebeian entertainments than courtly presentations,
though much of our information about them comes from the diaries of
courtiers out "slumming." They showed an increasing emphasis on
pantomimes and thus on drama. These traditions overlapped with

99

dengaku, a form originating as a folk field work or blessing dance-songs which in turn became yet another professional or semi-professional theatrical of the tenth century (see O'Neill, 1958, 7-9). It is out of the flourishing of sarugaku and dengaku over the next four hundred years plus the continual development of other courtly, temple, or plebeian music and dance forms that Noh eventually emerged. In the context of this very brief historical outline, let us turn then to the musical elements of Noh and concentrate on such terms and techniques as might be germane to our general topic.

Noh music consists of vocal music, known collectively as yōkyoku, plus the use of an instrumental ensemble called the hayashi. The vocal music may be rendered by the primary actor-dancer (shite), the secondary (waki), other performers (tsure), or by the chorus (ji). The instrumental ensemble consists of one flute (nōkan), a shoulder drum (ko tsuzumi) and a hip drum (ō tsuzumi), struck by the right hand and a stick (bachi) beaten drum (taiko) set on a low stand. The taiko is only used during major dance sections, while the other three instruments function as well as accompaniment for certain parts of the singing or as signals for formal units of the play. We will begin with the characteristics of the vocal music.

While the writings of Zeami are filled with formal facts and musical implications to which references will be necessary in this study, the details of more specific music theory and practice of Noh are found in much later works. Our discussion is based on modern practice in the hopes that such existing musical facts may lead us back to more ancient implications and perhaps to some Chinese parallels. The first differentiation to be made in Noh vocal music is between the recitative-like heightened speech style called kotoba (words) or serifu and the melodic sections called fushi. The latter are the source of Noh music theory. The fundamental principle of Noh melody is the use of two or three nuclear tones enhanced by regulated movement between them via other notes in the tone system. Their presence and the distribution of each tone system depends on the dramatic needs of the text or the character or on the placement of a melody in the formal structure of the play. In Zeami's time tones were apparently derived from the old Chinese gagaku scales and their modes (Zeami, Vol. 2, p. 45), Zeami saying that the ryo sound was more cheerful and the ritsu sad (Zeami, Vol. 2, p. 21). Zeami speaks in terms of a lyrical, soft style of melodies (nyūwa) (Vol. 1, p. 547), but by the Edo period there were two basic melodic types, known today as the tsuyogin (strong style) and the yowagin (soft style).

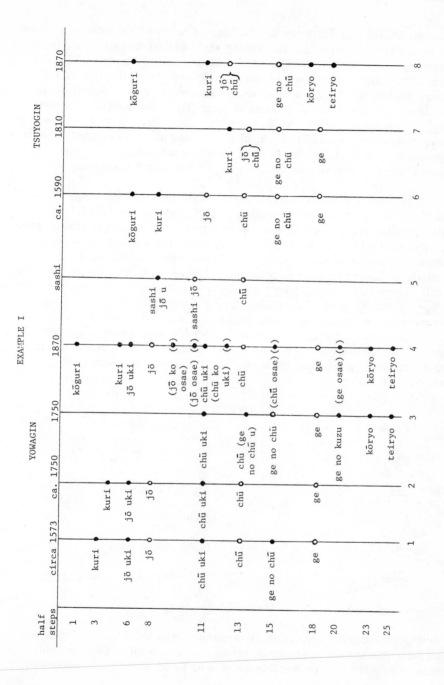

EXAMPLE I

As can be seen in Example 1, the basic pitches of the soft style tend
to be a fourth apart while the strong style places two or three main
tones much closer together. The example, derived from Yokomichi
(1963, p. 12), shows some of the known variants of the two styles
from the late sixteenth century to the present time. The full tonal
repertoire of the various schools of Noh can be carried far beyond
this outline (see Miyake, 1955, 158-59). Note here how the three
essential terms are to be found in all but the most restricted modern
system (no. 5) and, in the context of our study, the use of the Chinese character for ryo as the lowest pitch is significant.

The basic pitches of each system are marked with large circles
in Example 1. Beyond this category each system can be divided
hieratically into pitches of second importance, neighboring tones, and
auxiliary or changing tones which may give that system its special
sound. For instance, the modern yowa shown in Example 1 (no. 4)
has three basic pitches (jō, chū, ge), four of next importance melodically (kuri and kōguri, kōryo and teiryo) and two neighboring tones
(chū uki and jō uki). In addition four pitches marked in parentheses are
temporary substitutes for their neighbors in special melodic situations.
A study of melodies in this particular tone system further reveals that
there are definite rules concerning the movement from one pitch to
another, particularly the basic pitches and their neighboring tones as
shown in Example 2.

EXAMPLE 2

Pitch:	May go to:
ge	chū, or jō, or jō uki
chū	chū uki, jō uki, or down to ge
jō	jō uki
chū uki	jō, jō uki or kuri
jō uki	kuri or down to chū, chū uki, jō, or ge

A Western musician studying this example will think of the rules for
melodic movement in sixteenth century counterpoint. One can only
wonder to what degree similar rules are found in Chinese melodies.

What we do know is that similar rules are found in Japanese Buddhist chant which in turn came from ancient Chinese and Indian musical rules. Of equal importance is the fact that such melodic formulae and rules are found in various secular vocal forms (eikyoku) popular in the Heian period such as rōei and imayō. The latter is of special interest as it was a type of song often used by the shirabyōshi dancing girls of the period. Unfortunately, little is known of the actual musical content of these popular songs, though the study of surviving rōei has begun (Harich-Schneider, 1965). From this study the names and styles of types of ornamentation in rōei, when combined with Buddhist and early Noh nomenclature, provide much helpful information. For example, yuri is one of the most widespread terms for trills in ancient vocal music through Noh and on into shamisen traditions (see Ongaku jiten, Vol. II, p. 37). Example 3 lists such common terminology as it exists in Noh today (see Miyaki, 1955) for various kinds of melodic formulae or ornamentation to give some idea of: 1) how organized the style of Noh music is and 2) how many terms became regular parts of Japanese music theory. The analogy with the historical development of Western music theory is obvious. What we need to know in Asia is the extent to which similar concepts were carried on in parallel Chinese theatrical traditions.

EXAMPLE 3

furi	kuri
hane	mawashi
haru	nomi
iri	sashi
kiri	

At this point it is not as important to explain what the terms listed mean as it is to know that they exist.[3] With that in mind let us cast our net a bit further into the field of the form of Japanese Noh.

The most general formal concept of Noh is the three part jo-ha-kyū. Historically it offers no problems as such divisions were used in bugaku court dances and so probably come from China originally. The terms are found in Zeami's writings as well (Vol. I, p. 79). The manner in which this concept is applied to entire plays, sections of a play, or a single line is discussed in detail in Professor Teele's chapter along with the names and functions of the many other formal terms like age-uta or michiyuki. Among the latter, perhaps the most interesting term historically is kuse, for it is a dance section which derives its name from a dance form of some importance during the founding years of fourteenth century Noh. Zeami's father was quick to learn this style and Zeami himself makes a distinction between the short songs (kouta) of the sarugaku style and the more rhythmically forceful kusemai music (Zeami, Vol. 2, p. 26). He implies that a kuse should consist of a shidai, two sections (dan), and a closing shidai (Vol. 2, p. 400). This opinion is doubly interesting as the form of the lighter weight shirabyōshi dances was similar (O'Neill, 1958, 51) while the kuse dances of today often follow a related pattern. The influence of the more narrative songs of kusemai were important in the founding of Kōwaka mai and Noh (Araki, 1964, 71 ff). However, the dominant reason for the popularity and eventual influence of shirabyōshi and kusemai both seem to be in their rhythmic dynamism. In that context it is time to look at the instrumentation of these two genres and their relation to the hayashi of Noh.

In the best international popular music tradition, the appeal of shirabyōshi seems to have been sex and rhythm. The former is found in the costumed girls who performed the dances and apparently provide extra-theatrical pleasures and the latter was in footstamping and percussion accompaniment. It is the percussion accompaniment which is of particular interest in an Asian context. In the Heian period the percussion instruments of shirabyōshi and some sarugaku sometimes included cymbals (dōbyōshi, in Chinese t'ung-p'ai-tzu, see Ongaku jiten, Vol. 7, p. 232). Such instruments in some form have remained in various forms of Chinese music to the present day. In Japan they are noted in gagaku traditions derived from the Chinese T'ang dynasty court (via Korea?). The most striking examples of the use of cymbals in the early Japanese ensemble are seen in the fifteenth century copy of a twelfth century scroll called the Shinzei Kogakuzu (see Malm, 1959, 80 or Nihon Koten Zenshū, 2nd series, No. 19) in which performances of Rinyūgaku are depicted (Plate I). This particular form of gagaku is said to have been derived from Southeast Asian sources (Togi, 1971, 125). A further study of the scroll reveals yet other percussion instruments that hint of Southeast Asian origin. Two large barrel drums are played with sticks on one head (compared with Thai drums in Yupho, 1960, Plate 2 or page 31), and in both this ensemble and in the accompaniment of a lion dance (Plate II) one sees an instrument that seems to be a knobbed gong. A much larger version of such a gong is seen in a procession in the same scroll and the catalogue of the Shōsōin, an eighth century Japanese store house, includes a gong (shōban) in the accompaniment of sangaku. All these instruments seem to have faded from Japanese theatricals except for the use of cymbals (called chappa) in the off-stage music of the kabuki, but one must remember that their original use in ancient Japan was semi-folkloric and semi-religious. The shirabyōshi, the sangaku, and the sarugaku and dengaku that led to Noh were often part of a Shinto festival or an ennen, a theatrical occurring in a Buddhist temple ground. The double barrel drums do not survive except in the form of two smaller taiko which are always part of Shinto matsuri bayashi (see Malm, 1959, frontispiece). The gong survives in many folk theatricals and festivals today in a small form called by the general term kane (see Ibid., p. 53). The cymbals survive in a few Shinto festival dances (see Ibid., p. 57), but of equal interest is its frequent appearance in pictures of earlier theatrical events. For example, cymbals can be seen in the ensemble accompanying dance drawn as decorations on an eighth century archery bow stored in the Shōsōin (see Hayashi, 1964, pl. 19). They also appear (Plate III) as part of the ensemble for what looks like a shirabyōshi part of seventeenth century ennen (see Konakamura, 1896, Vol. 2, p. 21) in combination with the tsuzumi drum (an instrument discussed later). A study of the various festivals held in the eighteenth century at the Kasuga Shrine in Nara (see Kasuga, Omiya Wakamiya Gosairei Zu, Vol. 3, p. 8) reveals Shinto miko girls and tourists in the Edo period performing an apparently rather lively dance to the accompaniment of a ko tsuzumi drum plus two players of cymbals (Plate IV).

The same collection of festival events at Kasuga Shrine shows (Plate V) an Edo period dengaku ensemble (Vol. 2, p. 21) which used a flute and smaller versions of a previously larger dengaku barrel drum plus the binsasara, an idiophone consisting of rectangular slats of bamboo bound together at one end (see Malm, 1959). They remind one of a folk variant of the type of multiplated idiophone seen in the Rinyūgaku orchestra mentioned earlier. Both these may relate to the various forms of wooden clappers used by directors of East Asian ensembles, such as the Korean court orchestra (aak), and found in some Chinese opera accompaniments. The Japanese dengaku variety seems unique in its size and shape in both ancient pictures and in surviving folk forms. However, of more importance in a comparative study of Noh is the tsuzumi drum seen at the head of this dengaku ensemble.

The earliest use of the term tsuzumi in Japan is found (with different characters) in the Nihon Shoki (Vol. 9) of 213 A. D. The traditional description of the actual arrival of a tsuzumi is credited to Mimashi who in 612 brought four sizes of kure tsuzumi along with other gagaku musical materials from Korea. Of the four sizes the smallest (itsuko) was used in bugaku, the third size (san no tsuzumi) remained in the gagaku of Korean origin (Komagaku), and the other two sizes (ni no tsuzumi and shiko) seem to have been absorbed into more theatrical events such as sangaku. Much of the information we have about the early Japanese uses of tsuzumi drums are found in the records of the eighth century Shōsōin, mentioned earlier, which include materials added to the storehouse from the Tōdaiji in 950.

Twenty-two drum bodies survive in the Shōsōin. One of the later additions from the Tōdaiji is in the shape of the contemporary ō tsuzumi drum but is made of pottery. The rest of the bodies are made of zelkova (keyaki) wood and are lacquered black. The drums vary in size from 39 to 42 centimeters in length and each has a set of three parallel rolls covered at the thinnest point of the hourglass shape (see Hayashi, 1964, 3rd Plate). One of the drums from the Tōdaiji collection is most curious in its gentle sloping contrast between the two ends and the middle of the body. It is particularly unique when compared with the other normal hourglass-shaped bodies and the shapes of drums seen in the sangaku scene pictured on the large archery bow and also present in a picture of entertainers on the back of an elephant shown on the face of a biwa lute (see Hayashi, 1964, Plates 18 and 19).

The type of drum seen in the drawings is more in the style of the san no tsuzumi of Komagaku and of the chango drum popular in Korea today. The larger forms of the kure drums were played with a stick in the left hand while the smaller seemed to be struck on both heads with the hands. In either case, the drum was set before the player or suspended in front of him at waist level by a rope passing behind his neck. Barrel drums in this position can also be seen in old drawings (see Hayashi, 1964, Plate 19) as well as in contemporary folk dengaku ensembles. However, it is the positions and playing methods of the kure tsuzumi that are of special comparative interest. The strap-suspended hourglass drum is seen not only in Korea but also in many folk and theatrical forms of Southeast Asia and India (see Marcel-Dubois, 1941, Plate X). Similar drums set before the performer or on her lap are found in the stone tomb carvings of the T'ang period in Szechwan, China (see Kishibe, 1968).

If we search further into the Buddhist frescos across China into
Central and South Asia, one gets the impression that the Buddhist
angels themselves must have flown such drums in both playing positions throughout the continent and even to the islands of Japan (Togi,
1970, pl. 66-70). Our concern, however, is still with the terrestrial
development of such a drum in the Noh drama.

Two sizes of the kure drum apparently evolved into the ō and
ko tsuzumi of the Noh. The ko tsuzumi is seen first in pictures of
shirabyōshi and kusemai performers (see Araki, 62 and 63). The
manner of its use in ensembles is of special interest. The two ennen
dances mentioned earlier (page 105) show the drum used in combination with cymbals. However, the earlier picture (Konakamura, Vol.
2, p. 21) shows what might be called a transitional playing position
(Plate III). The drum is not suspended in front of the performer
but is held by the lacing ropes in the left hand facing downward and
played by striking the "bottom" skin. This same position is seen in
Plate VI, a picture of sarugaku no Noh (Konakamura, Vol. I, p. 55)
derived from the Yaku Shiji Engi of the fourteenth century. In this
case the drum is combined with a large barrel drum borrowed, perhaps, from dengaku but placed on the ground. The melodic instruments are a flute, a singer, and a shō (mouth organ). Recall that
the shō was seen as the melodic instrument of a sangaku shown on
the archery bow. Such melodic functions have only recently been
implied as a truer picture of the presently harmonically oriented
instrument (Picken, 1969, 401). Yet another picture of ennen (Plate
IIIB) shows two monks singing and the tsuzumi in its present day
shoulder position (Konakamura, Vol. 2, p. 20). This same position
is seen in the Edo pictures of dengaku at the Kasuga Shrine (Plate
V). However, other pictures of Noh (Kasuga, Vol. I, p. 22 and
Vol. 3, p. 34) show the complete hayashi ensemble of flute, ō and
ko tsuzumi plus the taiko. The moment at which such an ensemble
was first formed is not yet known. Zeami's writings mention the
sarugaku tsuzumi (Zeami, Vol. 2, p. 260) and flute (Vol. 2, pp.
262-69). The taiko remains a historical problem as the characters
now used for ō tsuzumi (see glossary) were pronounced either ō
tsuzumi or taiko. By the sixteenth century a separate writing of
the word taiko (see glossary) clearly distinguished it from the ō tsuzumi.
The actual origins of this stick drum are equally hazy and interesting.
The earliest picture (Plate II) of a drum with parts resembling those
of the Noh taiko is found in the Shinzei Kogakuzu (NKZ, Vol. 19, p.
1). The drum is called a kaiko or toro tsuzumi, which literally

means "a wiping taiko." This curious name is matched by the curious playing position. The drum is held against the player's waist with one head facing upward. It would appear that the fingernails of the right hand are flicked or scraped across the head. Though the actual technique and shape of the drum are different, one is reminded slightly of the florid style of the present day India tabla. The important point in relation to the history of Noh is that the small barrel-shaped drum is placed with one of its lashed heads facing upward. It seems a small step from its hand-held position to one on a stand and from the rather exotic sounds of the fingernails on the head to the more forceful tones produced by hitting the drum with two sticks. Such "new" styles of taiko playing are seen in pictures of folk field-planting festivals and of parades from the Kamakura and Muromachi periods and in pictures of Noh from Muromachi such as the dance of Shizuka in the Nara Ehon Yokohon (see Nihon no Bijutsu, no. 52, p. 88). It is difficult to tell precisely when this instrument became part of the Noh ensemble, for in Zeami's times and in his writings, as mentioned earlier, the same characters were used to write either ō tsuzumi or taiko. However, the folk use of such an instrument, the use of the name "Kanze" for the first professional taiko group, and the pictures from periods shortly after Zeami show that the three drums became a standard part of Noh from at least the fifteenth century. One refinement of the taiko drum that seems to have come after its inclusion in the Noh is the placement of a patch of deer skin in the center of the struck head. This addition subtly muffles the tone to give the drum a more "shibui" sound. Early drawings do not show this patch nor can it be seen on any of the pre-Noh drums. It does seem to be on a taiko carried in a procession in the Momoyama period (see the screen on page 137, Nihon Bunkashi, Vol. 3). Edo period pictures show that it was standard by that time.

The melodic instrument of Noh has its own special mysteries and refinements. We have already pointed out that earlier theatricals used a variety of instruments such as the shō, and the flutes seen in such ensembles seem rather thin, in the style of the simple bamboo flute. However, two modal implications in the writings of Zeami concerning the Noh flute (nōkan, see Vol. 2, pp. 262-68) indicate that the instrument was derived from the ryūteki of the gagaku ensemble. Sometime in its early development a major change was made in its construction. One important change was the insertion of a different diameter cylinder in part of the tube of the flute so that much of its overblown system results not in the usual octave but in a seventh (see Berger, 1965). A reason for this novel alteration has not

been given, but a study of the positions of the major pitches of the
Noh tonal system (see Example 1) implies that such a change may
relate to the emphasis on three tones a fourth apart. Though in
contemporary practice the flute and vocal line are only occasionally
related tonally and almost never related melodically, the original
state of the tradition seems to have been quite different. Zeami
(Vol. 2, pp. 262-68) lays great emphasis on the importance of the
flute (p. 262): "Since the flute is the instrument which establishes
the tonality, it is appropriate that it should be regarded as central."
Earlier he says: "After the song and dance have begun, the flautist
must listen to the singing of the actors, help establish the tonality,
and embroider the vocal line." Later he tells a story about a famous flautist, Meishō, which may relate to an early performance by
Zeami and his father (p. 268):

> Once in a performance of Shinji Sarugaku, Tōryō, an
> adult, was singing the rongi in rankei mode with a
> child actor. Since the boy was still a child, his voice
> slipped up to banshiki. As the pair sang the word-
> filled rongi, their voices became more and more dis-
> parate and the sound was not good. At this point
> Meishō, while holding to the original rankei tonality,
> elaborated the boy's singing in banshiki. At the same
> time he decorated the adult vocal part in rankei. It
> sounded as if there was no difference between the two
> tonalities and the performance was a success.

Such an instrumental-vocal relation could be found, perhaps, in parallel Chinese opera practice though, as stated, it does not play an
important role in modern Noh drama.

By the time the hayashi ensemble, the actor-dancers, and the
unison chorus were organized, Noh seemed to be a long way from
Chinese theatricals of the same period. Attempts have been made
to relate Noh to Yüan k'un-ch'u opera (Shichiri, 1927) in terms of
its staging, the nature of its plots, use of masks, and other performance characteristics. The case is not very convincing, but the
musical side of the case has not been studied. With this in mind,
some basic information about the tonal system and vocal forms of
Noh has already been given. We turn finally to one of the most
unique aspects of Noh music, its rhythmic structure in terms of text
and the use of percussion instruments. Only time and further interdisciplinary studies will reveal the degree to which this system may
have East Asian continental sources.

The general laws of rhythmic setting in Noh music are based
on a concept of placing the text in a framework of eight beats.   There
are three basic systems: the ō nori in which there is a syllable for
each beat, chū nori in which there is a syllable for two beats, and
hira nori in which twelve syllables are set in the eight beats.   These
are theoretically set in the tripartite, jo-ha-kyū manner as shown in
Example 4.

EXAMPLE 4

A hira nori setting

| 1 | 2 | 3 | 4 | 5 | 6 | 7 | 8 |

Na -- ni ga na ni   shi   te   na ni   to ya ra

Whenever the hira nori principle is applied, regardless of the number
of syllables, there is a tendency to avoid a syllable on beats 1, 3,
and 5.   The sung sections of Noh drama are not always in the same
poetic forms and there are tempo changes and a certain license in
the lengthening of given words or syllables (mashi bushi, see Yokomichi,
1968, 19-20).   Indeed, the very elastic nature of the beat in much of
Noh music seems to be completely contrary to Chinese practice.   However, in both traditions the functions of named stereotyped rhythmic
patterns in the percussion accompaniment are essential.   In Japan
these are called tegumi and they are our next point of study.   Since
the ō and ko tsuzumi are the major vocal accompaniments we will
turn to their music first.

In approaching Noh drama drum music and its stereotypes one
must be aware that all music exists in a time continuum and that
traditional musics of the world are based on the concept of using
aurally perceivable events which cause the culturally conditioned listener to anticipate what may happen next and thus psychologically progress in time until such moment as a terminating signal is presented.
This important concept is most easily understood by Westerners in
the context of chord progressions in seventeenth and eighteenth century
art music or, for that matter, in the twelve-bar blues.   The patterns
of the Noh drums, like the chords of traditional Western music, can
be classified into families and functions.   For example, the pattern
mitsuji, like Western tonic chords, is one of the most frequently

found patterns and the one most often heard at the beginning of a passage. The specific form of this beginning pattern can be different in each case. In Western music the tune and mood may effect the choice of tonic into, say, major or minor or perhaps a delay or substitute. In Noh drum music the mood and the rhythmic setting of the text by the singers will have an analogous effect.

Example 5 shows a classical version of the "proper" setting of a 7-5 syllable line of text in a hira nori setting accompanied by the drum pattern mitsuji. The triangle △ marks the strong beat on the ō tsuzumi, the circle o the major pon sound on the ko tsuzumi and the dot • the ko tsuzumi lighter chi stroke (for drum strokes see Malm, 1963).

EXAMPLE 5

	8	1	2	3	4	5	6	7	8
Voice:		na	ni ga na-ni shite			na ni to ya ra			
ko tsuzumi				Yo o		Ho	•	Ho o	
ō tsuzumi		yo —————— Ho △							

Note how the drum pattern marks off the tripartite divisions of the text with calls (kakegoe) before and sounds upon beats 3 and 5. The system looks very neat and logical, like the lead sheet for Western popular music or the figured bass in the Western baroque tradition. However, three additional principles should be added for us to understand more of the meaning of the use of such patterns in Noh music: 1) the compliance of drum patterns to the needs of specific vocal passages in terms of the melody and/or the text, 2) the driving force of periodic non-conformity in the rhythmic structure of the vocal and percussion lines, and 3) the sense of "logical" movement in the time continuum through the frequent use of similar pattern progressions. We shall look at these three principles in the order given.

A study of lesson books for drum music (see Ko, 1955) and a listen to recorded performances reveal that accents, such as the beats 3 and 5 shown earlier, are often delayed to coincide with important syllables in the verbal meaning of the text or to follow the deviations in style of a given vocal performer. Zeami implies this procedure in sarugaku (Vol. 2, p. 258):

When the hayashi is playing alone before the actor has
started, they should perform according to the way their
spirit moves them, giving drum calls and playing the drums
to the best of their abilities. When the song, dance, and
acting have begun, they should no longer play with such
independence. Rather, they must be sensitive to the spirit of the actor and the play according to the set standards
of the song and dance.

One could interpret this admonition in the spirit of the setting shown
in Example 5. However, Example 6 shows yet a further meaning as
revealed in a section of the kuse from the play Tamura. The ko
tsuzumi begins with kan mitsuji, one of the mitsuji pattern family,
and is followed by two mitsuji, tsuzuke (the next most common pattern), and another mitsuji. The o̅ tsuzumi patterns are tsukusuma,
two koiai, tsuzuke and a tsukusuma. Note first the relation between
the patterns of the drums themselves. In the ko tsuzumi, the only
difference between mitsuji and kan mitsuji is the use of a lighter
stroke on beat 5 of the latter (compare lines 1 and 2). Examples
5 and 6 show the o̅ tsuzumi matching with the ko tsuzumi mitsuji
pattern in three different ways. In Example 5 it also plays a pattern
called mitsuji, but in Example 6 it starts off with strokes on beats
8 and 1 and a drum call that leads into silence on beat 3. In the
next line the koiai pattern marks beat 8, and uses the drum calls
and stroke theoretically on 3 (marked with parenthesis), nearer the
style of the o̅ tsuzumi mitsuji of Example 5. The fact that the third
beat stroke is delayed, as is the fifth beat stroke of the ko tsuzumi,
relates partially to the text. The line uses a standard count of seven
and five syllables divided into the normal hira nori manner of 4 + 3
+ 5. However, the text reads "hana no Miyako mo, haru no sora"
(the flowers of Miyako also, the spring sky). The first four syllables
do not mark the end of a word, and thus the percussion accent under
the syllable ya of Miyako is a better "rhythmization" of the melody.
The choice is analogous with the kinds of decisions a Western musician might have made in the proper harmonization of a sung melody
in the classical era. In both the Japanese and Western cases artistic
preferences can override the most "logical" settings of a text, but in
general vocal music composers or accompanists are concerned with
communicating the meaning of the text. The word "accompanist" is
included in this discussion as the composer of the vocal line in Noh
does not seem to be the creator of the percussion part as well. Like
kabuki music (see Malm, 1963, 218), the Noh compositions are a
joint effort.

EXAMPLE 6

	8	1	2	3	4	5	6	7	8	
voice				CHI	ZO	NA	NA NI	SHI O	O	3+5
1. kotsuzumi	●	yo △			yo	●		ho	ho ○	
otsuzumi								●	○ ●	
voice	HA	NA	NO	MI	YA	KO NO	HA RU	NO SO	RA	7+5
2. ko	yo		ho (●)	△	yo (●)	○		ho	●	
o									○	
voice	GE	NI	TO	KI	ME	KE RU	YO SO	O	I SE	7+5
3. ko	yo		ho (●)	△	(●)	○		ho	●	
o									○	
voice	I	YO	O	NO	KA	GE	MI DO	RI NI	TE	6+5
4. ko	yo △		ho	●	△ yo	● △	○	ho	○	
o		○							●	
voice				KA	ZE		NO DO	KA NA	RU	7
5. ko	yo △		ho			yo (●) ○		ho	○	
o										

Lines 4 and 5 of Example 6 continue to illustrate the principle under consideration. The 6 + 5 line is "filled out" by an extension of time spent on the syllable no, and this more complicated situation is given firmer rhythmic support with a more active pattern (tsuzuke) played in a more rigid form. Note how the final syllable te is strung out to make up the beginning space of the next eight beats. Line 5 presents yet further compositional demands as only seven syllables are present and they are in the last half of the phrase rather than the first half seen in line 2 and in Example 5. To help out this extension of the former text phrase and the first syllable of the new line, the ō tsuzumi plays a pattern which avoids its usual accent on beat 3. At the same time, the first entrance of the ko tsuzumi is delayed by half a beat in order that the subsequent five syllables get off to a secure start.

The degree to which this give-and-take of rhythmic placements is practiced is not always evident, for professional copies of drum parts merely give the name of the pattern to be used at the spot in the text where it starts. Fortunately, the lesson books in the style of Example 6 give us a fairly clear indication of the degree of flexibility allowed within the tradition. Unlike the lead sheets of Western jazz and popular music, the drum notations of professional Noh are not the basis for improvisation. However, variations in the interpretations of a given passage occur both between performances of different schools of Noh and of different artists in one school. In the preparation for this discussion, a study was made of two different publications of the kuse section of the play Takasago (Kojima, 1900, Vol. 3, pp. 16-25; Senka, 1913, Vol. 4, pp. 1-3) and a recording of the same work (Victor SJ 3005). The degree to which they were the same and to which they were different is a study in itself. An additional fact that it may add to our present research is its implication of the "secret" tradition so common in Japanese music. There is always a "correct" way of performing a piece, but the details of such a rendition are seldom available to the uninitiated. Those of us outside the guilds can only be grateful that so much musical information is available in Noh and that the creation of recordings has frozen given performances for our perusal. One hopes that similar sources may be available in the equally interesting field of Chinese theatrical music.

Examples 5 and 6 give one the impression that Noh music is set in a constant series of eight-beat phrases, but this is not so. The three different overall rhythmic structures (ō, chū, and hira nori), the variety in the number of syllables in a line, and the artistic prolongations of the length of a hold on one syllable create many situations which require longer or shorter phrases. Example 7 illustrates some of the ways in which such situations are handled in an excerpt from the kuse of Funabenkei (Ko, 1955, 58-59). The text translation was done with the kind cooperation of Professor Teele, and the unit divisions of the syllables were authenticated by Professor Yokomichi Mario of the Tokyo National Folk Theatre Research Institute. The first line (I) shows a compromise on the fifth beat of the pattern mitsuji. The reason for this change seems to be a desire to support the first syllable of a four-syllable group beginning at that point. Line II shows a normal tsuzuke pattern support for a line of seven and five syllables, but by line III new factors have arisen. The last syllable of line II is prolonged for two extra beats, perhaps to accommodate the different number of syllables (4 + 4 + 6) in line III. The drum part reaction is the use of a four-beat tori (literally "take out") pattern. The vocal part "on paper" does the same thing, but the aural effect is rather like performing the parts out of synchronization. The tsuzumi patterns clearly begin at the start of line III, but the vocal line starts later. The significance of this change becomes more evident if one compares the beginnings of the first four-syllable units in lines I, II, and III. Each shows the most typical vocal entrance in Noh singing. The first syllable (in these cases "ko") is placed on a pick up beat. In the first two lines this is in its normal position before beat 1, while in line III the charts show it as being before beat 3 of the tori section. However, a culturally conditioned listener might continue to sense this as a typical beat 1 in the manner shown by parenthetical numbers along line III. Japanese music theorists do not accept such a slide rule system of analysis, for they wish things to look neat on paper. Nevertheless, the fundamental point for this analyst is shown by such an unorthodox notation of the rhythmic structure. Aurally, new tension has been created between the vocal and instrumental parts. Such tension helps to drive the music forward through a time continuum, and such a motion is essential to the dynamism of all music. In the context of this principle let us look further at line III. The first four-syllable unit is accompanied by the completion of a drum pattern plus the sound of the first beat of the next one (the first five beats of the line). At this point the ō tsuzumi uses the pattern hikae, with its first beat accent, instead of the other common beginnings for an eight-beat structure which includes the ko tsuzumi mitsuji pattern (as seen in line I). The choice of this pattern may have been made to help emphasize the start of another eight-beat group after the four-beat tori. However, note also that this choice leaves the drums very inactive

EXAMPLE 7

```
         voice              (8)  1   2   3   4   5   6   7   8
  I      6(4+2) + 4              KO - O-MEI    TOMI  TAT-TO- KU
         kotsuzumi (mitsuji)                      yo  O  ho• ho O
         otsuzumi (mitsuji)      • yo ——  ho △
```

```
         voice              (8)  1   2   3   4   5   6   7   8
  II     7(4+3) + 5              KO - KORONO  GOTOKU  NARUBEKI O
         ko (tsuzuke)                 O        • yo•  O ho O ho O
         o (tsuzuke)            yo △ ho  ho •   △ yo△   △
```

```
         voice              (8)  1   2   3   4   1   2   3   4   5   6   7   8
  III    4 + 4 + 6                       KO- O NA- RI    NA TOGETE MISHIRI- ZOKU WA
         ko (tori, mitsuji)              ho • ho O              yo  O   ho • ho O
         o (kake kiri, hikae)   yo △              △     yo ——
                                        (1   2   3   4   5   6   7   8   9   10)
```

```
         voice              (8)  1   2   3   4   5   6   7   8
  IV     6(3+3) + 5              TEN NO MICHITO  KOKOROE-TE
         ko (tsuzuke)                 O        • yo•  O ho O ho O
         o (tsuzuke)            yo △ ho  ho •   △ yo △ho△         • yo
                                (11  1   2   3   4   5   6   7)
```

```
         voice              (8)  1   2   3   4   5   6   7   8
  V      5 + 5                       SHO-O  SEN NI   SAO SA- SHITE
         ko (kizami oroshi→)                      yo •  • •ho O      O
         o (ate kashira)        • ho• ho —— △ ya  a △          •
                                (8   1   2   3   4   5   6   7)
```

```
         voice              (8)  1   2   1   2   3   4   5   6   7   8   1
  VI     3 + 5 + 4               GOKO  NO   E-N- TOO O   TANO-SHIMU
         ko →, kan tsuzuke)      (O) O  O        •      • yo•  O ho O ho O
         o (okuri, kiku, tori)   (•)      • yo     yo- i • yo△ ho△        • yo△
                                     (1   2   3   4   5   6   7   8   9   10)
```

He gained great honors and riches and, in the spirit of Heaven's decree that
a wise man should retire once his great deeds were done and his fame obtained,
he found pleasure in mists and waters while rowing a boat on the Five Lakes.

kōmei tomi tattoku
high name, riches, honored

kokoro no gotoku narubeki o
heart, like, as much as possible, (accusative particle)

kō nari na togete mi shirizoku wa
great deeds, becoming, name attaining, body retiring, (nominative particle)

ten no michi to kokoroete
Heaven's way, (quote particle), understanding

shōsen ni sao sashite
small boat, in, boat pole, extending

go ko no entō o tanoshimu
Five Lakes, smoke and wave, (accusative particle), enjoy

for four beats while the vocal part is busy with the next four syllables. Of equal interest is the fact that the ko tsuzumi delays its first entrance thereafter by half a beat (after beat 5) in order to support more directly the beginning of the longer, fuller six-syllable completion of the line.

The tsuzuke pattern of line IV seems an appropriately active accompaniment for a vocal line filled with six and five syllables (the "n" at the end is a common vocal addition not part of the actual text). Perhaps the most revealing aspect of this line is its continued use of vocal syncopation at the start of each syllabic unit (ten, mi, ko). Such a vital characteristic in Noh singing is not usually mentioned in theoretical studies, but its importance can be understood by comparing the entrances and endings of the four lines discussed so far. They start on the up beat of counts 1, 1, 3, and 2 respectively. Line III ends on the after beat of count 8 and the others on the after beat of count 7. In lines II and IV these endings are extended by three and two beats. In line IV the common practice of a vocal n is added to the actual text syllable (te) in order to accommodate the extension. A musical meditation on all these points shows that such actions are deliberate compositional devices used to enhance the rhythmic vitality of the music. In other words, one can perceive the workings of a musically sensitive mind in the rhythmic settings of Noh music just as clearly as, for example, one can admire the genius of Mozart in the harmonic analysis of a symphony. In each case we are looking at only one aspect of the music, but both limited views helps us to understand the very different logics and beauties of the resultant musical events. With that in mind let us return to the Noh drama passage of Example 7.

Lines V and VI reveal quite different rhythmic styles. Both begin with their first syllables squarely on a beat, 2 and 1. The ō tsuzumi accompaniment, in contrast, begins each first pattern on the last beat, 8, of the previous phrase. It is thus another example of the "slide rule" effect in the motion of Noh music. The ko tsuzumi sound is striking in line V with its first use of two quick strokes on beat 6 and an overlapping quick movement leading into the next vocal phrase. In a textbook this pattern kizami otoshi (see item 43 in Ko) begins after beat 4 and ends on a beat 2 in an okuri, that is, a two-beat unit deleting the normal six additional beats of a drum pattern (see Tazaki, 1925, 17). Thus, the theoretical count for the ten beats of the vocal phrase are 2 plus 8 as shown. All this rhythmic shifting of gears is matched with greater drum activity to create a cadence for the end of the song. Note that the ō tsuzumi uses a new drum call (yoi) to help emphasize the fact that something different (the sectional ending) is about to appear. At the same time note the concurrence of drum calls (yo) before beat 5 has also reinforced the last section of the phrase, as it had done before in lines II, IV, and V. A solid cadence preparation seems in progress, but the last two beats of the line in the ō tsuzumi part reveal the beginning of another pattern (tori). This event seems to defeat the cadential efforts and, in fact, it does. The overlapping pattern marks the beginning of the accompaniment of the vocal entrance of the main actor two beats later (not shown). It provides a smooth rhythmic connection between the chorus and soloist sections and is functionally analogous with similar harmonic transitions such as incomplete or half cadences found in many Western choral works of the romantic period.

The rather mind and eye boggling analysis of Example 7 is done to demonstrate the basic principles listed earlier. It is quite evident that the choice of drum patterns and their actual performance methods are intimately connected with the nature of the vocal part. Secondly, the nonconformity of pattern lengths does indeed create aural tension which forces one to move forward to some moment of rhythmic or phrase resolution. This can sometimes be created in a single pattern such as tsuzuke. Note in that pattern how the two drums rather argue over the first three beats, get together with their one common drum call for beats 4 and 5 and then the ō tsuzumi quits on beat 6 leaving the ko tsuzumi to finish the job. Put such internally dynamic patterns against vocal lines of differing lengths and the forward motion becomes yet more powerful. We have called this phenomenon the slide rule effect. Each line of action has an internally rigid structure, but the lines can be set against each other in different ratios, i.e., their beat 1's are in different places. An additional sense of forward motion is created by an anticipation that one given pattern may be followed by certain other specific patterns. To discuss this principle we will turn finally to the music of the taiko.

Since the taiko is normally used for dance accompaniment its patterns have little significance in relation to text, though the slide rule effect can be found when the taiko is playing in conjunction with the tsuzumi. All we shall look at in this study is a few significant pages from a taiko textbook (Komparu, 1953). Fifty-nine patterns are named and notated as compared with two hundred and four in the ko tsuzumi and one hundred and seventy in the ō tsuzumi books. However, a great deal more information is included in the taiko source.

EXAMPLE 8

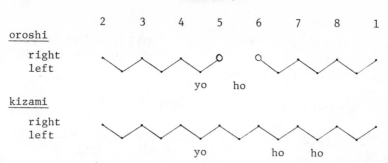

Example 8 shows the patterns oroshi and kizami with the left and right stick strokes, the drum calls, and the size of the stroke, the smaller, more deadened stroke being shown by a dot and the middle and higher strokes being indicated by the size of the circle shown. The implications of a slide rule effect are evident by the very fact that the sound of the pattern and the placement of beat 1 seemed off by a beat. The instruction book makes no point of this, but it does provide other most interesting information. First, it tells the basic use of the pattern. In the case of kizami it says (Komparu, 95), "As the basic pattern for taiko, it is repeated an endless number of times." The next two items of instruction are of even greater interest. One section is called the maete, the patterns that may appear before the given pattern, and the second is the atote, the patterns that may appear after it. Example 9 shows the two lists for both kizami and oroshi.

The uses of oroshi are given as "a connection for types of kashira to types of kizami and types of kashira to types of uchikomi." Such details of use are given for all the standard patterns. This is followed by lead sheets for sections of basic plays in which the taiko performs while singing is going on. The power of progression is so strong that lead sheets of the twelve basic dance pieces of Noh are given in collective sections rather than one piece at a time (Komparu, pp. 254-57). There is yet further information available about the manner in which patterns may move in different nori sections of the vocal music and in special musical situations. However, the point of this study has already been made rather forcefully: rhythmic pattern progression and its anticipation by a listener plays as important and varied role in Noh music as do chord progressions in Western classical music. It remains to be seen what analogies may or may not appear in Chinese opera.

EXAMPLE 9

kizami

PATTERNS THAT MAY OCCUR BEFORE THE GIVEN PATTERN	PATTERNS THAT MAY OCCUR AFTERWARD
oroshi or oroshi makuri	kizami or tori kizami
kizami, tori kizami, or han kizami	takakizami, takakizamikiri, or takakizamisuteru
taka kizami kiri	age or age suteru
nagaji	uke nakakashira or uke nakakashira suritsuke
kashira suritsuke or uke nakakashira suritsuke	nagaji, nagaji kaeshi, or mijikaji

oroshi

kashira	kizami
tori kashira	takakizami
uchikaeshi kashira	takakizamikiri
kasanekashira	takakizamisuteru
	ageyori
	ageyori suteru
	ukenakakashira
	nagaji
	nagaji kaeshi
	mijikaji
	uchikomi
	odorute

We have wandered far through historical, tonal, melodic, and rhythmic principles found in the study of Noh, though the explanations and examples of each actually have been rather preliminary. Each point is worthy of a separate, extended study. This introduction of them all has had but two basic goals: 1) they are meant to enhance one's appreciation of the historical depth, creative imagination, and musical logic of Noh music, and 2) hopefully they invite further explorations along paths that may help us understand what might make East Asian music particularly East Asian and perhaps distinctive from other world musics. The validity of the first goal should be self-evident in the examples. Securing the second goal depends on further intercultural and interdisciplinary research.

FOOTNOTES

1. For a study of gigaku, see Hayashi Kenzō (1951) and for a more thorough study of T'ang music see Kishibe Shigeo (1960) and Edward Schafer (1963).

2. A study of the problems of distinctions between the two terms is found in the appendix of Araki (1964, 199-201).

3. For such explanations see Miyake and Yokomichi.

BIBLIOGRAPHY

Araki, James. The Ballad-Drama of Medieval Japan. Berkeley: University of California Press, 1964, 289 pp.

Berger, Donald. "The Nohkan: Its Construction and Music." Ethnomusicology. Vol. IX, no. 3, 1965, pp. 221-239.

Hama, Kazue. Nihon geino no genryu. Tokyo: Kadokawa shoten, 1968, 442 pp.

Harich-Schneider, Eta. Roei: The Medieval Court Songs of Japan. Monumenta Nipponica Monographs, no. 21, Tokyo: Sophia University Press, 1965, 132 pp.

Hayashi, Kenzo. "Sangaku ni-ko." Toyo ongaku Kenkyu. No. 9, March 1951, pp. 27-46.

_____. Shosoin gakki no kenkyu. Tokyo: Fukan Shobo, 1964, 368 pp.

Iba, Takashi. Nihon ongaku gairon. Tokyo: Koseikaku Shoten, 1928, 999 pp.

Kasuga. Omiya Wakamiya Gosairei zu.

Kishibe, Shigeo. Toji ongaku no rekishiteki kenkyu. Tokyo: Tokyo daigaku, 2 vols., 1960.

_____. " . . . nijuyon gakugi ni tsuite." Toji no gakki. Toyo ongaku sensho, no. 2, 1968, pp. 269-288. English summary.

Ko, Yoshimitsu. Koryu ko tsuzumi shofu. Tokyo: Nogaku shorin, 1955, 162 pp.

Kojima, Isehamaei. Yatsubyoshi. Tokyo: Hinoki, 3 vols., 1900.

Komparu, Soichi. Komparuryu taiko zensho. Tokyo: Hinoki Shoten, 1953, 322 pp.

Konakamura, Kiyonori. Kabu ongaku ryakushi. Tokyo, 2 vols., 1888.

MacKerras, Colin. "The Growth of Chinese Regional Drama." Journal of Oriental Studies. Vol. IX, no. 1, 1971.

Malm, William. "The Rhythmic Orientation of Two Drums in the Japanese No Drama." Ethnomusicology. Vol. II, no. 3, September 1958, pp. 89-95.

_____. Japanese Music and Musical Instruments. Tokyo: Tuttle, 1959, 299 pp.

_____. "An Introduction to Taiko Drum Music in the Japanese No Drama." Ethnomusicology. Vol. IV, no. 2, May 1960, pp. 75-78.

_____. Nagauta: The Heart of Kabuki Music. Tokyo: Tuttle, 1963, 344 pp.

Marcel-Dubois, Claudie. Les Instruments de Musique de L'Inde Ancienne. Paris: Presse Universitaires de France, 1941, 252 pp.

Miyake, Kōichi. Shidai kara kiri made no utaikata. Tokyo: Hinoki Shoten, 1952, 169 pp.

_____. Jibyōshi seikei. Tokyo: Hinoki Shoten, 1954, 222 pp., ex.

_____. Fushi no seikai. Tokyo: Hinoki Shoten, 1955, 155 pp., ex.

Nihon Bunkashi. Kanakura, Tokyo, vol. 3, 1966.

Nihon no Bijutsu. No. 52, 1970.

Noh, Nihon no Koten geinō. Tokyo: Heibonsha, no. 3, 1970, 365 pp.

O'Neill, P. G. Early No Drama. London: Humphries, 1958, 223 pp.

Ongaku jiten. Tokyo: Heibonsha, 12 vols., 1955-57.

Pian, R. C. Sonq Dynasty Musical Sources and Their Interpretation. Cambridge, Mass.: Harvard Press, 1969, 252 pp.

Picken, L. E. R. "Tunes Apt for T'ang Lyrics from the Sho part-books of Togaku." Essays in Ethnomusicology. Seoul: Korean Musicological Society, 1969, pp. 401-20.

_____. "Some Chinese terms for musical repeats, sections, and forms, common to T'ang, Yuan, and Togaku scores." Bulletin of the School of Oriental and African Studies. Vol. XXXIV, part 1, 1971, pp. 115-18.

Schafer, Edward. The Golden Peaches of Samarkand. Berkeley: University of California Press, 1963, 399 pp.

Senka, Haruko. Ko tsuzumi no shiori. Tokyo: Meisho, 4 vols., 1913.

Shichiri, Zukei. Yōkyoku to genkyoku. Tokyo: Sekibun, 1927, 305 pp.

Shida, Engi. Nihon kayō kenshi. Tokyo: Shibundō, 2 vols., 1958.

Shinzei Kogakuzu in Nihon koten zenshū. Tokyo: Funikei, vol. 17, 2nd series, 1928.

Sugawara, Kazunaga. Shichijūichi-ban shokunin uta-awase, reprinted from sixteenth century version in Gunsho ruiji, XVIII. 1904.

Takano, Tatsuyuki. Nihon kayō shi. Tokyo: Shunjusha, 1926, 1090 pp.

Takazaki, Nobujiro. Kadoryū ō tsuzumi keitei. Tokyo: Hinoki, 1925, 81 pp.

Tanabe, Hisao. Nihon no gakki. Tokyo: Soshi sha, 1964, 381 pp.

Togi, Masataro. Gagaku. Performing arts of Japan, V. Tokyo: Weatherhill, 1971, 207 pp.

Yokomichi, Mansatoyuu. Nō, explanation notes for record album Nō (Victor SJ 3005), 1961, 60 pp.

Yupho, Dhant. Thai Musical Instruments, trans. by David Morton. Bangkok: Siva Phorn, 1960, 104 pp.

Zeami jūroku-bu shū hyōshaku, ed. by Asaji Nose. Tokyo: Iwanami shoten, 1960, 2 vols.

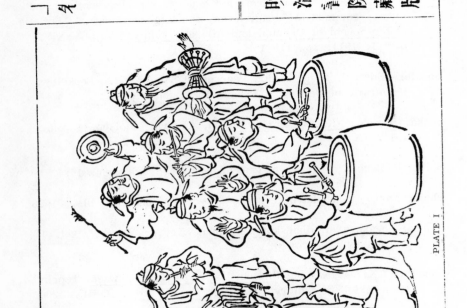

PLATE I

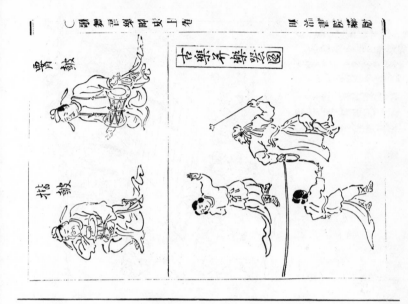

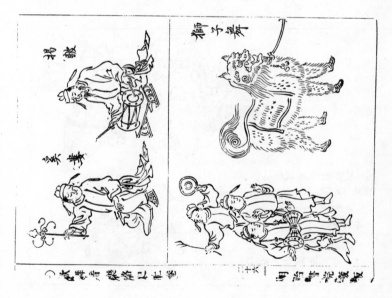

PLATE II

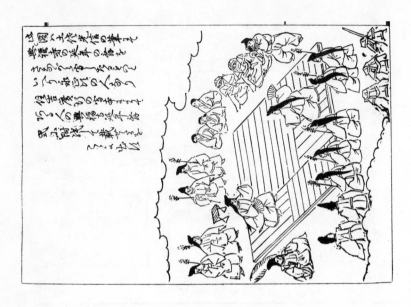

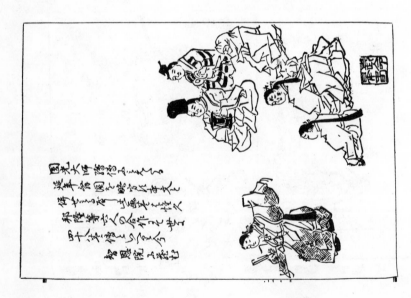

PLATE III

PLATE IV

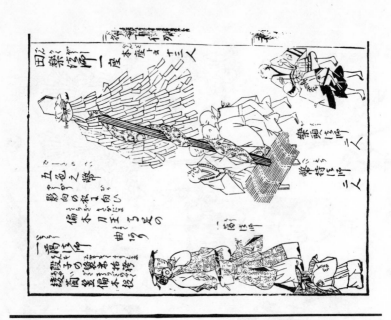

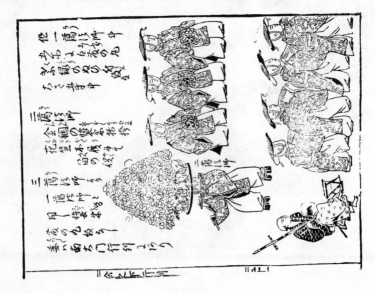

PLATE V

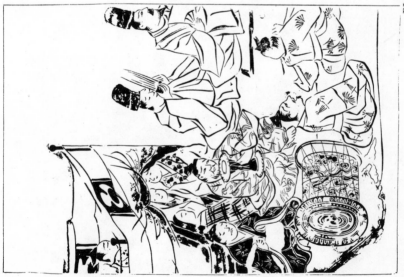

PLATE VI

DISCUSSION ON WILLIAM P. MALM'S PAPER

Malm: First of all, my section on form will be withdrawn in light of Professor Teele's paper.

Sesar: In the uses of the Noh melody, you say that "Their presence and the distribution of each tone system depends on the dramatic needs of the text or the character or on the placement of a melody in the formal structure of the play." (p. 100) Since we don't know exactly how, I think that really requires a formal study. The study I did on the Haku Rakuten,[1] for example, was based on the fact that all the god-plays are fairly uniform in structure. In fact, not only the structure but the nature of the dramatic incidents that occur within each section and the attitudes of the dramatis personae are also uniform. We know that the musical structure is similar as well and follows fairly much the same pattern. I'd like to find out what happens musically in the actual performance of this play Haku Rakuten. One would have to listen to a lot of plays to be sure how these sections (sashi, age-uta, etc.) sound and what effects they have. We also need to ask what variations occur in the music and precisely how they vary in the same sections from play to play.

Malm: Are you asking if the actual tune is related to the emotional situation?

Sesar: That too! I was actually speaking of the ideal situation in which everything was gathered together, after which one could begin to draw important conclusions about these relationships.

Malm: In Sumidagawa the moment when the mother finds the grave of her son is a very important one, and I'm convinced that the quality of the music at that point is influenced by the text.

Pian: You also indicated that narrative songs were a possible source of the Noh. Can you give a specific example in Noh where this occurs? In the dialogue? In certain types of songs? Where in Noh do you find these possible origins?

133

Malm: I was speaking of the use of certain terms like yuri, names of certain stereotype patterns in the melodies. The same tunes do not appear, but the same nomenclature can be found. Yuri,[2] for instance, can be found in the shōmyō and in the Heike Monogatari too. It also occurs in the Noh drama. Obviously, the same words are being used for the same musical techniques.

Pian: So they don't stand for a means of delivery or a certain rhythmic pattern?

Malm: No, the names are the same and some influence must have been felt.

Pian: In another place you noted the use of percussion instruments in earlier forms, and I want to know why there are less and less use of percussion instruments.

Malm: Actually, there is more use!

Pian: What does that prove?

Malm: In the illustrations in my paper we find instruments creeping in and we don't know where they come from. Instruments are used which do not show up in later forms, and I wonder if Chinese music-drama influenced them to some degree.

Pian: What about the cymbals shown in certain illustrations?

Malm: They are pre-Noh.

Pian: Are they ever used in Noh?

Malm: Never. That is what fascinates me. In early forms, sarugaku[3] and dengaku,[4] you found them being used. They got carried over into the Shinto tradition in the Edo period. For instance, in this illustration (Plate IV) all the people are entering the temple. Here are the ladies lighting the magic fires, and here in small print is someone using cymbals. This is Edo, but it isn't Noh. It had connections with religion and some connections with the T'ang dynasty imports into Japan. This is fascinating. My

paper points out many instruments which do not appear
in Noh but are seen in prototypes of Noh.

Pian: Are you sure they are predecessors of Noh? If so, then
my questions still stands: why do they disappear in Noh?

Malm: I wish you could find out for me. I don't have a picture
of that wonderful illustrated hunting bow in the Shōsōin
with me. On it a theatrical is obviously taking place.
Some people are banging cymbals and others play the shō.
None of these instruments were used in Noh, but they
were obviously in existence at the time Noh was being
formulated. Noh picked out instruments that were different, and some of them were defunct in gagaku, [5] for example, the small tsuzumi. Suddenly it begins to be used in
extremely well-organized ways.

Pian: I was hoping that you could provide a dramatic reason for
using these percussion instruments so that dramatic change
might explain the disappearance of some of them.

Malm: One easy answer might be that if you have to bang a
cymbal at an important spot in the text no one can hear
the text. In Chinese opera they don't ring the gong on
an important word. Take the shamisen, for instance.
Why don't singers sing with the shamisen? When the
shamisen plays, the singers sing off the beat. If they
sing on the beat they have to compete with the "chink" of
the shamisen. Why does the drum beat get delayed? It
is because of the text. It is moved over one-half beat to
accommodate the text.

Pian: I disagree, though not completely. I feel that the melodies
in Noh also come on off-beats, but not for reasons of clarity. The answer is rhythmic style. Syncopation can give
the music a drive to continue. It is a rhythmic style.

Malm: It is true, of course, that music exists in a time continuum and that there must be a drive to go forward. You
need to feel assured that it will continue. Western music
uses unresolved chords for this effect. In Noh the same
effect is achieved by delaying a rhythmic pattern, making
one uncomfortable until it is finished.

Pian: It is for rhythmic drive. But that isn't the only reason.

Malm: But it might explain why the cymbals were dropped. They
          were there earlier. Why didn't Zeami use the cymbals
          in the Noh? They were there to use!

Pian: K'un-ch'ü[6] makes far less use of percussion than Peking
          Opera; it is a much more lyrical type of drama. You
          say: "Though in contemporary practice the flute and
          vocal line are only occasionally related tonally and almost
          never related melodically . . . " (p. 109) What do you
          mean by that?

Malm: The flute never plays the tune sung by the singer. Once
          in a while they coincide and collaborate on a single note,
          but that is as close together as they ever get. The singer
          takes his pitch from those notes. I know of no example
          where the flute plays the melody being sung. Melodically
          the two are totally unrelated. In Chinese opera there is
          a heterophonic relationship between the accompaniment
          and the singer. In Zeami's time that apparently was not
          the case.

Sesar: That's true in the Noh dance too. The dances, although
          highly stylized, only rarely reveal a connection between
          the choral parts and the dance. In Yō Ki-hi,[7] for exam-
          ple, there is absolutely no relationship between the choral
          part and the dance. The dance is strictly formal and
          unrelated to the surrounding parts of the drama. Japa-
          nese drama is very demanding on the audience, it seems.
          Many unrelated elements are combined, yet it is precisely
          at that point where the various elements must maintain an
          independence and be aware concurrently of what is happen-
          ing. For instance, I have heard that the drum calls were
          used originally only in rehearsal. It was a conscious
          decision which kept them in the drama. These types of
          phenomena occur over and over again. If we keep them
          in mind it helps to explain many things that are so hard
          to understand. Remember the two plays built around the
          taiko? It is precisely in these plays that the taiko is
          noticeably eliminated.

Malm: This is like asking me why we sing in triads in the west. That is one of the unanswered questions about our own music. There were no triads in the time of Pope Gregory and for a long time after him.

Pian: I think Carl and I are trying to make use of a dramatic crutch to explain some musical phenomena.

Malm: It's a musical crutch.

Pian: It is much harder to explain why people sing in thirds than in some other intervals. You can't adduce dramatic reason . . .

Malm: Nor can you use dramatic reasons here. The reasons have to be musical. I know of no music which does not adhere to some internal logic. No music is totally arbitrary.

Pian: Only in terms of the total musical framework can you explain what function a third serves. If you isolate it, it becomes divorced from . . .

Malm: Now we are becoming a conference on esthetics.

Sesar: But here we have a drummer drumming away on his drum, and a flute player tootling away at his own melody, and a dancer who is dancing a piece that is unrelated to either one of them, yet you have a single play. There must be a unifying factor there, but perhaps it can't be verbalized. There is a sense of harmonizing each extraneous element, but each element has to be harmonized in a way that protects one against giving way to the other. Now and then the drum gives way and retards its beat so that the text of the singer can be heard, but then each returns to its own sphere, each in its own disparate world. The shite, [8] you know, doesn't even rehearse with the waki. [9] They employ an actor who is available without rehearsals. The actors know the music.

Malm: Ah! Enter logic. Each knows the music. It's like a jazz group. The various musicians don't just sit down and each play the tune; one holds back until his turn comes along.

Each adjusts to the other. The performance is in no way set, but there is order in it. They are playing within a tradition.

Teele: I noted a curious thing while singing in recital. We never had a flute player with us, but the beats were absolutely strict. So in a sense I developed the attitude that the flute was not that essential. It was nice to have it fluttering in the background, but we could totally ignore it. It seemed ornamental in function.

Crump: Ha! The "sinew of the music lies in the beat"!

Malm: Rhythm is to the Noh what harmony is to eighteenth century Western opera.

Johnson: Can any comparative statements be made to contrast in terms of melody in Noh and Peking Opera?

Malm: I think if each of us were to present an example in Western notation that some comparative information could be exchanged--not definitive but comparative.

Pian: Let's name something, because I think we can do that. All right, you mention jo-ha-kyū.[10] That theory can be applied to Peking Opera melodies, the introduction, the middle section, and the speeding up to a climax. The jo is pre-rhythm, am I right?

Crump: San-pan.[11]

Pian: Well, maybe san-pan, but more likely man-pan,[12] or better, the interjective aria (tao-pan). In the ha section you would employ man-pan, yüan-pan,[13] erh-liu,[14] and in the kyū section you would find liu-shui-pan.[15] Translated, it would be constructed as the interjective aria, the lyric aria, the narrative aria, the erh-liu aria (which I deliberately leave untranslated). I'm only guessing now from what I know of Peking Opera, but in male roles in Peking Opera (male roles, not male actors), the melody is constantly sung at an interval a fourth or fifth below the female voice. Of course, there are other differences between these two melody types. The ornamentation and melodic turns are dif-

ferent, voice production is different, melodies are different; but in general they do occupy these two different areas
of the same scale. How are they used dramatically? Old
ladies, especially the stoic matriarchs, sing basically a
male melody with female embellishments. Lovesick young
boys sing essentially female melodies with male voice production and male melodic characteristics.

Teele: In the Noh it wouldn't be related in that way; they sing
in the same register all the time.

Sesar: There is something special about child roles, the kokata.[16]

Teele: Where I find the similarity is in the tsuyogin and in the
yowagin, the strong and weak styles. The warrior usually
sings in the strong style, and women's roles tend to be
cast in the weak styles. In old man roles you encounter
a crossing over sometimes. I tried one of those roles
once--the most difficult thing I ever tried. I felt they
were constantly switching over, but my teacher said I was
wrong. Nonetheless, that's what I felt.

Pian: This is very interesting because the fiddle player in Peking
Opera plays the same accompaniment for either male or
female roles. They even share the same titles. If the
aria is the hsi-p'i narrative aria, regardless of the sex
of the singing role, the accompaniment is the same and
uses the same interludes. How much aware of the sex
differential the fiddle player is at the time I can't say.

Sesar: You mentioned before, Bill, that there is little if any improvisation in Japanese music. The shite, for example,
learns his part and the music is handed down from generation to generation as a fixed system. However, looked
at as an entire production, when the performers enter the
stage, they are in some sense winging it.

Malm: That's variation, as in a Mozart opera.

Sesar: In the Noh all the actors are so highly trained from child-
hood that there is literally no possibility of forgetting a
line or missing a cue. Yet it is possible for a group of
actors who have never played together before to assemble
and perform a play.

Pian: Well, there is an expression in Peking Opera: "Tsa-men t'ai-shang chien" (I'll see you on the stage). It means, "We don't need to rehearse before the performance."

Sesar: Yes! That's where the excitement enters. Otherwise everyone is left with a bored attitude toward a series of fixed pieces. This explains why a piece gets boring. But with your "Well, I'll see you on the stage," that is where the spark is touched off and the performance can be an exciting one.

Pian: What about a team in a ball game? There are fixed rules, but the game is improvised.

Sesar: Yes. You are working within a rigid scheme, but no one knows precisely what is going to happen.

Malm: Take the traveling opera troupe. They go on stage cold every night to create a new performance. There are lots of Metropolitan Opera stories about sobering up the tenor who, when pushed onto the stage, sings a brilliant performance. They know the show so well that the performance goes on almost by itself. In Japan, you know, there are books that tell you exactly where to place your feet on the stage, just like an Arthur Murray handbook. (laughter) Now there is absolutely no improvisation there, yet nothing happens in the same way twice. That's why the chant syllables yo and ho were retained in the Noh drama. They were drum signals which kept everyone together. With one actor on stage wearing a heavy mask, through which he can't see, the signal provided by yo-o-o-o-o-o-o-o-o-o-o-o is the vital key for keeping everybody together.

Teele: My teacher was full of stories about actors, their masks acting as blinkers, falling off the stage during performance.

Malm: That's true. Sometimes if you don't move exactly one step at a forty-five degree angle at the proper moment, you'll fall off the stage.

Crump: There's where improvisation would become truly dangerous!

FOOTNOTES

1   Haku Rakuten: a Noh drama by Zeami Motokiyo (1363-1444) about a fictional visit to Japan by the Chinese poet Po Chü-yi --Haku Rakuten in Japanese. See C. Sesar's article, pp. 143-167.

2.   Yuri: one of the most widespread terms for trills in ancient vocal music in the Noh and in the shamisen tradition.

3.   Sarugaku: a mixture of masquerade, song, and dance entertainments; one of many early spectacles from which the Noh emerged.

4.   Dengaku: folk or field entertainments. One of many early forms which contributed to the eventual formulation of Noh.

5.   Gagaku: classical court music imported into Japan from T'ang dynasty China.

6.   K'un-ch'ü: the classical Chinese theatre of the Ming dynasty which combined features of the local style of music in the K'un-shan region with the refinements of Wei Liang-fu and Liang Po-chün.

7.   Yō Ki-hi: a Noh drama about the renowned courtesan of the T'ang Emperor Hsüan-tsung; adapted from Chinese dramas of Yüan and Ming times on the same subject.

8.   Shite: the main actor in a Noh drama.

9.   Waki: the secondary actor in a Noh drama, whose role is in opposition but subordinate to the shite.

10.   Jo-ha-kyū: the structural divisions of Noh drama. The function of the jo section is introductory, ha is the major section composed of an unprescribed number of subdivisions (dan), and kyū is a closing section.

11.   San-pan: music without a regular rhythmic pulse; unmeasured music.

12.   Man-pan: the lyric aria; a slow, ornate melody in regular triple meter comparable to 4/4 time (one heavy and three light beats).

13.　Yüan-pan:　the narrative aria; the same melody as the lyric aria but without so much ornamentation, in triple meter comparable to 2/4 time (one heavy and one light beat).

14.　Erh-liu:　a lyrical aria with sparse ornamentation; near the close, it accelerates and concludes with a free and unmeasured section.

15.　Liu-shui-pan:　the animated aria; a fast, sparsely ornamented aria with a steady driving beat.

16.　Kokata:　the parts of emperors and kings are always played by boy actors.

China vs. Japan: the Noh Play Haku Rakuten

Carl Sesar

The attempt by Japanese to define Japan's national and cultural
identity in relationship to China and her influence constitutes a major
theme running throughout Japanese religion, thought, literature and
the arts.   Just as this theme found different areas for expression, so
it also resulted in widespread differences of opinion and attitudes
ranging all the way from total adulation of China to complete disavowal
of her cultural presence in Japan.   The extremity of such views pointed
up a deep-seated ambivalence in Japanese attitudes toward China that on
the one hand could not help but acknowledge the weight and prestige of
Chinese culture and its influence upon Japan, but at the same time stub-
bornly refused either to subordinate native Japanese culture to it or to
forfeit claims to Japanese inventiveness and originality in assimilating
it.   As a dramatic form that dealt with major religious, intellectual
and artistic concerns of a sophisticated court audience, Noh drama was
not exempt from this theme or from its ambivalences, and so it is not
surprising to find the question of Japan's cultural relationship to China
treated as the central theme in certain of the plays themselves.

Some of these plays, Ryōko and Shakkyō, for example, are in
the balance respectful and even somewhat deferential toward China.
In each case Japanese Buddhist monks land in China as part of a
pilgrimage to famed religious sites there and in India, and are treated
to wonderful and miraculous spectacles; one senses that Japan is regarded in these plays to be on the fringe of the Buddhist world rather
than at its center.   Nevertheless, the Japanese pilgrims are accorded
by the Chinese the civility given to equals and there is no apparent
hint of cultural conflict.

The play Tōsen is an extremely moving presentation of Chinese
and Japanese cultural conflict depicted in terms of the competing demands of filial piety, national origin and acculturation.   Filial piety
emerges the victor over national origin and clearly this moral ideal
in Tōsen is viewed as the common property of both countries.   The
conflict is resolved by an equitable decision: the Japanese lord grants
the Japanese-born children permission to go with their Chinese father
back to China in the name of sympathy, kindness and respect for the

143

children's natural affection for their parent. While this is an unusual play in many respects, it does not really concern itself with questions of Chinese cultural influence in Japan except in an indirect way.

Aside from the plays mentioned above in Noh drama the issues are for the most part one-sided and heavily weighted in Japan's favor. Zegai, Fuji-san and Haku Rakuten all deal with the arrival of a Chinese visitor to Japan. In Zegai and Haku Rakuten the visitors who represent potential threats to Japan's cultural integrity are soundly defeated and sent packing back to China, while in Fuji-san the Chinese traveller is an imperial envoy on whom the native Japanese gods condescend to confer blessings and rewards.

Two other plays, Genjō[1] and Kasuga Ryūjin,[2] treat situations in which someone intending to travel to China is persuaded to remain in Japan. In Genjō the famous lute player Fujiwara no Moronaga, desiring further training in the instrument, is about to sail for China. On the way he stops for one night at Suma Bay and plays a piece on the lute for an old couple in whose house he has taken lodging. They admire his playing so much that when a rainstorm drumming down upon the roof threatens to drown out his playing they spread straw mats there to deaden the noise. Moronaga then asks them to play and their performance on the lute and zithern proves to be so highly accomplished that he abandons his plan to study in China. The old couple then reveal themselves to be Emperor Murakami and his consort, Lady Nashitsubo. They explain that the Emperor had performed on the famous lute called Genjō in the hope that after hearing it Moronaga would decide to remain in Japan. The old couple then vanishes, but soon afterwards the Emperor reappears, summons a dragon-god from the sea and obtains from him another famous lute which he presents to Moronaga. Similarly, in Kasuga Ryūjin a priest planning to journey to China and India is told by an old man that he need not go abroad because followers of Buddha can now find all that their faith requires in Japan. Revealing that he is a messenger of the god Kasuga Myōjin, the old man then disappears. Later a dragon-god appears, tells of the many Buddhist gods that are to be found at Kasuga and makes the priest swear to abandon all thought of traveling abroad.

By far the best known and most telling play on this theme of cultural conflict is Haku Rakuten. Concerned with the relationship between the poetic arts of China and Japan, the work is an encapsulation in dramatic form of the major issues involved and as a

Noh play itself, <u>Haku Rakuten</u> also exemplifies these issues in an immediate way as they pertain specifically to Noh drama. The object of the play, of course, is to show the superiority of Japanese poetry over Chinese poetry. Several kinds of arguments are voiced in the course of the play to substantiate this view, some of which are quite familiar and rest on traditionally established views about poetry held by the Japanese for centuries prior to the play's composition. But because we are given a Noh play and not a critical treatise, the total argument is inseparable from the dramatic context. To appreciate the argument fully, therefore, requires a close examination into the play's construction, plot and manner of performance.

To begin with, <u>Haku Rakuten</u> belongs to the first group of Noh plays, variously known as <u>kami-mono</u>, <u>waki-nō</u> and <u>shobamme-mono</u>. As the variety of nomenclature for this and for all the five groups of plays shows, such classifications are not just simple, general groupings of plays, but rather a complex system of classifications that indicate in part formal characteristics, in part thematic content and in part the musical mood and over-all poetic effect of each play in the group. All of these features are closely interrelated. Firstly, plays generally follow the established formal requirements for their class. These requirements govern such matters as a play's structure and sequence of parts, the music and dance, costumes, masks and, of course, the types of roles and characters in the play. Secondly, though fixed, such requirements are not in force purely as matters of convention, but serve more importantly to provide a detailed framework within which raw material can be molded in the interests of the special thematic concerns and aesthetic aims of the class of play they govern.

If we examine plays in a class one by one, some variations in form and exceptions to specific requirements will almost always be found. Such variations are of greater or lesser significance in a single play depending upon the degree of uniformity shared by all the plays of its class. The considerable disparities in form that exist among plays of the fourth group or fifth group, for example, would make these differences hardly worth examining closely in any given play in these two groups.

The plays in <u>waki-nō</u>, however, are on the whole consistent in their themes and regular in form. There is a certain range of variation among <u>waki-nō</u> according to the different kinds of dances that

are performed, but these have been recognized as established sub-
classes of waki-nō, each having special but uniform characteristics.
Thus, while plays with a chū dance conform rather closely to other
waki-nō in both their form and their auspicious themes, all feature
the shite in a female role, so that the effect of their performance is
actually closer to the elegance and emotional qualities of kazura-mono,
or woman-plays.   Similarly, gaku-mono all tend toward exoticism because of the gaku dance, and their themes are to some degree com-
mensurate with this effect.   Hataraki-mono are one more sub-class
of waki-nō having special features.   Hataraki dances are most often
performed in the fifth group or demon-plays; thus in waki-nō the deities who dance hataraki are usually dragon gods or the like, and the
total effect of these plays is swift and abbreviated, again much like
kiri-nō.

   The most typical and represtative of waki-nō, however, are the
kami-mai-mono and the shin-jo-no-mai-mono.   In each of these kinds
of waki-nō, the shite appears in the first act in the guise of an old
man of humble station and in the second act reappears in his true
identity as a god and performs a dance.   The basic difference between
these two kinds of waki-nō is that in kami-mai-mono the dance performed by the nochi-jite is rather vigorous and direct so as to characterize a youthful god, while in shin-jo-no-mai-mono, the nochi-jite
is always an aged god and so the dance is extremely slow, solemn
and dignified.   In each case the actor is costumed and masked accordingly; thus the mask for Sumiyoshi in the kami-mai-mono Takasago is
the Kantan-otoko mask worn by the young traveler Rosei in Kantan,
while in Haku Rakuten, which is a shin-jo-no-mai-mono, the same god
Sumiyoshi wears the mask of an old man.   In other respects, theme,
structure and development, most waki-nō of these types are quite regular.   But within the standard formal scheme of waki-nō, Haku Rakuten
displays a number of subtle shifts and variations.   If we examine these
special features of Haku Rakuten against the standard for waki-nō, it
becomes apparent that, far from being accidental or arbitrary, they
represent a careful and ingenious working of material within the con-
fines of a fixed form in such a way as to give added meaning and impact to both the dramatic situation and the play's theme.

   The theme of Haku Rakuten, the superiority of Japan's poetic
art over that of China, is itself an interesting example of variation
within waki-nō.   The basic thematic ingredient in plays of the first
group is that of shūgen, "congratulatory words."   Central to the play
and voiced by the god himself, these "congratulatory words" take the
form of religious hymns of praise dealing with such themes as peace

and long life, benedictions for the Imperial Way and the splendor
and glory of the age, assurances for the continued protection and
safety of the country and so forth. The occasions for such encomiums
by the god may vary somewhat according to circumstance or setting,
but in almost every case they take place as a direct consequence of
a pilgrimage made by the waki to some famous shrine or devotional
site associated with the deity in question. By casting the play Haku
Rakuten into the form of waki-nō, the author at once links the question of supremacy in the poetic arts to larger religious themes and
by making the occasion of the play the arrival of a Chinese visitor
on the shores of Japan herself, he succeeds in altering the shūgen
content from an expression of simple praise or congratulation into
a proclamation of victory won in a holy war waged to protect the
land from foreign invasion.

The play opens with the waki, Haku Rakuten (Chinese: Po
Chü-yi), taking the stage accompanied by two attendants (waki-zure).
As a rule, the role of the waki in plays of the first group is designated by the term daijin-waki, literally "grand minister waki," to
indicate that he is a person of high rank. In waki-nō, this is almost
always either a Shinto priest or an imperial envoy. Haku Rakuten is
given somewhat similar status when he identifies himself as an official
of the Chinese court, but his identity as a poet is a marked exception
to the rule. For special costume touches he carries a tō-uchiwa, or
round Chinese fan, and instead of the usual daijin-eboshi, or "grand
minister cap" worn by daijin-waki, he wears a tō-kammuri, or
"Chinese crown." His entrance is as follows:

WAKI: (sashi)

    Know that I am Haku Rakuten,
    An official in the service of the Prince of China.
    East of here lies a country whose name is Nippon;
    I have orders to hurry forth to that land
    To take reckoning of Nippon's accomplishments.
    I am now bound that way across the track of sea.

WAKI and WAKI-ZURE: (shidai, michiyuki)

    Rowing our ship out to the sun's beginning,
    Rowing our ship out to the sun's beginning,
    We seek the country lying there.
    Across the Eastern Sea,

148

>
> Our ship rides the distant track of waves,
> Our ship rides the distant track of waves.
> Behind us, in the last light of the setting sun,
> Cloud pennants soar above the empty sky;
> Out where the moon once more is rising,
> Hills come into view; in but a moment
> We have reached the land of Nippon,
> We have reached the land of Nippon.

WAKI: (tsuki-serifu)

> So swiftly have I crossed the track of sea, that
> I have already reached the lands of Nippon.   I would drop
> anchor here for a time and view the sight of Nippon.

This concludes the jo section.

Instead of the usual sequence of shidai, nanori, michiyuki and tsuki-serifu found in most waki-nō, here the first two parts are reversed, and, rather than being spoken, the nanori is chanted as a sashi.   This sort of entrance is known as a han-kaikō, or "semi-formal entrance," which sometimes results in the shidai being omitted altogether.   The kaikō, or "formal entrance," upon which this is based was a special variant reserved for performances given on important occasions.   The han-kaikō is very rare, occurring in only two other plays in the current repertory, Mekari and Tama-no-i.

The effect of this kind of entrance is to draw particular attention to the waki, who delivers his lines in a more solemn manner than is common, thus lending a greater measure of dignity and rank to his role than held by the usual daijin-waki.   In this respect, as the single most influential Chinese literary figure in Japan, Haku Rakuten takes the stage with overpowering credentials.   Moreover, because of the lack of a shidai verse and musical accompaniment at the start of the play, the opening in Haku Rakuten resembles that used for the great majority of karagoto-mono or "Chinese pieces."   Among waki-nō, for example, both Seiōbo and Tōbōsaku open with a kyōgen kuchi-ake, followed by the waki who initiates a sashi.   In Tsuru-kame, the waki and shite enter together and so the shite initiates the sashi after the kyōgen kuchi-ake.   Thirteen other karagoto-mono open without a shidai: Kantan, Kanyōkyū, Kōtei and Sanshō all begin with a kyōgen speech; Kappo, Shōjō, Taihei Shōjō, Shōki, Shōkun, Tōsen, Chōryō,

Tenko and Bashō open with a nanori by the waki. Thus the han-kaikō entrance in Haku Rakuten not only emphasizes the Chinese poet's stature but, by structural analogy with other karagoto-mono both in waki-nō and in other classes of Noh plays, gives the entire jo section of Haku Rakuten a certain "Chinese" flavor as well.

The content of this jo section sets forth the situation in much the same way as other waki-nō, but again with significant differences. First, echoes of an old rift between China and Japan can be heard as Haku Rakuten sets sail eastward to "the sun's beginning" while behind his ship in China the sun is sinking. This alludes to an official message sent to the Sui court in China by Empress Suiko which reads, "The Son of Heaven in the land where the sun rises addresses a letter to the Son of Heaven in the land where the sun sets. We hope you are in good health."[3] The Sui history records that when the Emperor saw this letter he was displeased, thought it discourteous and ordered that such a letter not again be brought to his attention. More important, however, is the fact that instead of the usual religious journey made by the waki in god-plays, the purpose of Haku Rakuten's sea voyage is to take measure of Japan's cultural accomplishments. His journey is thus undertaken in a spirit totally at odds with the reverence and respect that characterizes the waki's travels in other waki-nō. Haku Rakuten's lack of these attitudes in a god-play already hints at blasphemy and immediately transforms his arrival in Japan into an ominous event.

The ha-no-ichidan follows the standard form. It begins with the entrance of the shite (and tsure) to issei musical accompaniment, in this case a so-called shin-no-issei-no-hayashi, or "formal issei accompaniment," which, since the play is a waki-nō, serves to impart a solemn, grave mood to their entrance. They sing an issei verse together, which is followed by a sashi, sage-uta and age-uta, as follows:

SHITE and TSURE: (issei)

> Dawn breaks over the sea
> At Tsukushi of the Unknown Fire.
> Look, the sight of the moon alone is left!

SHITE: (sashi)

> The giant waters heave and swell,
> The blue waves inundate the heavens.

SHITE and TSURE:

> So we think it must have been
> When Han Rei left the country of Etsu,
> Pulling the oars of his small boat
> Across the misty waves of the Five Lakes.
> How fine the sea looks!

(sage-uta)

> West of the beach of Matsura,
> In the hilless dawn,

(age-uta)

> The moon sets;
> The hovering clouds, the boats offshore,
> The hovering clouds, the boats offshore
> Are anchored together in the early dawn;
> And there across the sea, from China,
> A ship's journey is not far,
> A single night's voyage, it is said . . .
> Look, the moon has already gone away!
> Look, the moon has already gone away!

The scene is set at dawn, in sharp contrast to the sunset in the jo section. This not only establishes the time sequence of the waki's journey but also vividly reinforces the point made earlier about the two countries. These passages are filled with broad hints about a ship and a man from China, though presumably, as Arthur Waley suggests,[4] the two fishermen are not yet consciously aware of Haku Rakuten's arrival.

Sumiyoshi fits the humble station prescribed for the mae-jite in waki-no by entering in the guise of an old fisherman. But in most god-plays there is also a certain touch of elegance and nobility in the mae-jite's mask and costume which, despite his lowly station, serves to suggest his true identity. The mask most often worn is the kouji-jo. This is the most dignified of all masks for old men and in god-plays is actually meant to represent the features of a Shinto god in disguise. In waki-no this mask is usually worn along with the jo-gami, or old man's wig, the mizugoromo, a long-sleeved gown made of un-glossed silk and the shiro-okuchi, a broad, white divided skirt whose use in society was restricted to persons of samurai status or court rank. Sumiyoshi, however, enters wearing the warai-jō, or "smiling old man," the least dignified mask for old men, since a smile or laugh in Noh is felt to be an indication of low breeding. Further, instead of the standard mizugoromo, Sumiyoshi wears a rougher shike-mizugoromo, or raw-silk gown and the courtly shiro-ōkuchi is omitted altogether. In this play then, Sumiyoshi's position is made to appear even more lowly than usual. Taken together with the added stature accorded the waki by means of the han-kaikō entrance, this device is deliberately aimed at creating as much contrast as possible between the two characters. This contrast has far-reaching implications that first become clear in the mondō, or dialogue between waki and shite, which follows.

As in most waki-nō, this dialogue constitutes the second part of the ha section. It starts with spoken lines and builds up into song, culminating in the shodō.

WAKI:

> Having endured ten thousand miles of waves,
> I have come at last to the land of Nippon. Here is
> a small boat floating by. I see an old fisherman.
> Can he be an inhabitant of Nippon?

SHITE:

> That is correct.
> I am an old fisherman of Nihon.
> Are you not, sir, Haku Rakuten of China?

WAKI:

> How very strange!
> This is the first time I have come to this land,
> Yet you see that I am Haku Rakuten!
> How can this be?

TSURE:

> Though you are a gentleman of Kan,
> Your name has come to Nihon before you
> And is widely heard and spoken of.

152

WAKI:

> Even supposing you have heard my name,
> How could you recognize me?
> I cannot believe that is possible!

SHITE and TSURE:

> All through the land where the sun begins,
> It has been told that Rakuten would come
> To take reckoning of Nihon's accomplishments.
> We looked out toward the west,
> And when we saw a ship had come off shore,
> Each in our hearts thought, "It is he!"

CHORUS:　(shodō)

> Will he come now?
> Will he come now?
> Thus we waited,
> And when to Matsura's shore
> A ship came openly into view,
> A Chinese ship, and a man from China,
> How could we fail to see that it was Rakuten?
> But how tiresome, your noisy talk!
> You are Chinese,
> And your speech is a meaningless gabble;
> Listen as I might,
> I can make no sense of it!
> Enough, then!
> Our time is too precious,
> Let us cast our hooks!
> Our time is too precious,
> Let us cast our hooks!

In waki-nō, the established pattern for the ha-no-nidan is that the waki acts as the questioner and the shite responds accordingly. This generally begins with a simple request for directions or information about the place the waki is visiting. The replies given by the god in disguise are always more provocative than the waki might expect from a person of low rank and prompt him to further questioning, which finally results in a gradual revelation of intimate, detailed knowledge of the history and lore of the shrine or god under discussion. In this fashion the way is paved for the all-important ha-no-sandan to follow, in which the _kuse_ is delivered and the _shite_ eventually reveals his true identity.

The passages above, however, differ markedly from the usual pattern in several respects. First, since this is a god-play, the _waki's_ destination is understood to be a sacred spot, in this case Japan herself. But Haku Rakuten, traveling there for other than devotional reasons, is ignorant of this fact and is thus unwittingly a trespasser upon sacred grounds. The force of this is even further emphasized by his demeanor; Chinese, he is convinced of his supe-riority and so does not display the proper reserve and quiet respect characteristic of the usual _daijin-waki_. He is not only blunt with the fisherman but also acts rudely toward Japan herself by continually referring to the country as "Nippon" while Sumiyoshi uses the name "Nihon." In all this, Haku Rakuten becomes the perfect foil for the _shite_ who, in the guise of a humble fisherman, can pretend to be deferential, modest and even crude when it suits his purpose.

As a result, the focus of the content of this section is centered upon the arrival of the _waki_, Haku Rakuten, rather than upon matters pertinent to his destination or to the deity concerned, and so consti-tutes a complete reversal of the standard pattern. His reception is seemingly cordial and even respectful at first, but the sense of the entire _mondo_ here accentuates the inappropriateness of his visit. Haku Rakuten's identity and reasons behind his arrival are exposed, his cre-dentials are challenged and the fisherman (actually the chorus in the _shodo_ speaking for him) abruptly announces that he will have no further dealings with him. Thus, in effect, the play has nowhere else to go, unless another _mondo_ takes place.

The _ha-no-sandan_ is made up of this second _mondo_, which con-tains the poetry contest, followed by a _kuse_ and _rongi_. By itself, the _mondo_ here resembles the usual dialogue found in _waki-no_ and concludes with an _age-uta_ very much like the _shodo_. This ending acts as a sub-stitute for the usual _kuri_ and _sashi_ which generally precede the _kuse_ but which are missing here. Thus the entire _ha-no-sandan_ is really two sections combined into one and so is conspicuously longer than is normal. Coming after the fisherman's refusal to talk further with Haku Rakuten, the dialogue opens as follows:

WAKI:

> Just a moment, I wish to ask you something.
> Bring your boat closer! Now, old fisherman, tell me,
> what does one do for amusement in Nippon these days?

SHITE:

And in China, pray, how do you gentlemen divert yourselves?

WAKI:

In China we play at making poems.

SHITE:

In Nihon we take pleasure in composing uta.

WAKI:

But what are uta?

SHITE:

Out of the sacred texts of India, Chinese poems and fu have been fashioned, and from Chinese poems and fu our country fashions uta. Having in this way blended in Three Countries, we in writing term it "The Great Blend," from whence comes the reading "Yamato-uta." But this you know, and wish only to make trial of an old man's heart.

WAKI:

No, no! I meant nothing of the sort. But come, I will make a poem about the scene before us:

"A cloak of green moss hangs upon the shoulders
     of the cliff;
A sash of white clouds encircles the waist of
     the mountain."

Do you understand it, old fisherman?

SHITE:

"Green moss . . ." means, does it not, that the green moss hanging from the shoulders of the cliff resembles a cloak? Then, "A sash of white clouds encircles the waist

of the mountain." Very good, very good. Now an <u>uta</u>
of Nihon would go something like this:

> "The cliff wears
> a cloak of moss
> but has no sash,
> and the cloakless mountain
> wears a sash it would seem."

WAKI:

> How strange!
> He is but a lowly fisherman,
> Yet he caps my verse so aptly!
> What sort of person can he be?

SHITE:

> I am scarcely human, a creature of no account.
> Nevertheless, the singing of <u>uta</u> is not confined to men
> alone; among all living creatures there are none who do
> not sing <u>uta</u>.

WAKI:

> Yes, of creatures that live,
> Even the birds and beasts

SHITE:

> Compose Yamato-<u>uta</u>.
> Of such instances,

WAKI:

> In the land of Yamato,

SHITE:

> Songs abound.

CHORUS: (age-uta)

    The warbler who sings among the flowers
    The frog who dwells within the streams . . .
    I know not what may be in China,
    But in Nihon we compose uta;
    Even an old man will fashion
    Yamato-uta in this form.

(kuse)

    Yes, and among these uta
    The warbler has sung, it is told that
    During the reign of Emperor Kōken,
    In the Temple of High Heaven,
    A man of Yamato once dwelt;
    Each year in spring,
    When the warbler came to the plum tree
        by his window,
    He would hear her sing this verse:

        Shō yō mei chō rai
        Fu sō gen ben sei.

    He wrote it down in words,
    And when he looked at them,
    There were thirty-one letters
    In the words of an uta:

SHITE:

    "Though I come
    Each dawn
    At spring's beginning,

CHORUS:

    I return unmet
    To my old nest."

    Thus first was heard the warbler's voice,
    And thereafter all birds and other creatures
    Singing uta after the fashion of men.

The instances are many,
Many as the countless pebbles
Strewn along the shores of the sea at Ariso.
Of things that live,
Each and every one sings uta.

(rongi)

Truly then, the ways of Yamato,
Truly then, the ways of Yamato
Lie in the heart of this man of the sea!
Most excellently does he practice them!

SHITE:

Among the many pastimes of Yamato,
There is the fashioning of uta
As well as the arts of dance and song;
Many such have we to show you.

CHORUS:

Truly so!
You speak of the pastime of Bugaku,
But who shall be the dancer?

SHITE:

Though none are here,
Behold! Even one such as I . . .
And in the Bugaku,

CHORUS:

For drums, the sound of waves,
For flutes, the call of dragons,
For the dancer, this old, wrinkled man
Upon the wrinkled waves shall stand,
And hovering over the green-colored sea,
Shall dance the Sea Green Dance!

SHITE:

Land of the Reed Plains,

CHORUS:

For myriad ages inviolate!

This rather long ha-no-sandan, as the "ear-opener" of the Noh play, voices the major arguments brought forth to show the supremacy of Japanese poetry over Chinese poetry. First, the fisherman makes a clear distinction between the verse forms used in the two countries, the shih and fu in China as opposed to the uta in Nihon. The fisherman admits quite freely that the uta has developed out of these Chinese forms, but his strategy here is to show that far from being an imitation of Chinese poetry, the uta represents instead a higher stage of poetic development. Rather than deny the influence of Chinese poetry in Japan, the playwright turns the fact to advantage by implying that inherent in the process of transmission between the Three Countries from India to China to Japan there exist varying levels of cultural achievement and perfectibility whose summit is to be found only in Japan. This argument is given special weight through the use of a clever play on the word Yamato, which means "Japan," but whose Chinese characters also may mean "The Great Blend," in which all foreign influences, Indian and Chinese, have been molded into a unified cultural whole hitherto nonexistent. Having established this point, the scene is set for a concrete demonstration of its truth in the form of a poetry competition. It is not the humble fisherman who suggests it, but Haku Rakuten himself who confidently offers the couplet describing the scene about them. In turn the fisherman, seizing on the fact that sash and cloak should be worn in combination and not separately as in Haku Rakuten's lines, responds with the uta version that cleverly caps the Chinese couplet.

One scholar has shown that the passages in the play that put forth this argument are an abbreviated version of opinions on Japanese poetry set down by the poet-priest Jien (1155-1225) in his poetry collection, the Shūgyoku-shū. Furthermore, the fourth chapter of this collection contains 100 waka written after lines in Po Chü-yi's (Haku Rakuten's) poems taken from the Hakushi monjū. He concludes after careful analysis that the germ of the idea for the play Haku Rakuten and precedence for the poetry contest both have their source in Jien's collection, and that Zeami drew heavily upon it.[5] This being so, one might expect that one of these matched Chinese couplets and waka from Jien's collection would have been quoted for the poetry contest. But the couplet offered by Haku Rakuten in the exchange of poems is not part of Po Chü-yi's works at all, but rather a slightly altered version of lines taken from the Kōdanshō, and the uta in reply is verse written after this couplet in the same work, by an anonymous woman.[6] Since a misquotation of this kind was not likely to go unnoticed by the audience, one must assume that it was deliberate.

There are several possible reasons for this misquotation. One may be that Zeami refrained from using actual lines from Po Chü-yi's works out of a measure of respect for the poet's work. It is true that the play on the whole treats him rather harshly, but the representation of Po Chü-yi on the stage as a symbol of Chinese cultural influence in obviously fictional circumstances and the use of actual lines from his poetry are two different matters. An actual quote might have been inappropriate on artistic grounds as an unwarranted touch of literal accuracy and realism.

More importantly, since the contest needed a clear victory to make its point effectively, the uta used to cap an actual couplet from Po Chü-yi ran the risk of being somewhat less than convincing in the minds of a critical audience and so might have detracted from the play's impact and larger purposes. It was probably no easy task to find a suitable matched pair of verses for use in this poetry contest.

This moment in the play is important because it serves as a prelude to the fisherman's second major argument for Japanese poetry. Briefly, the argument asserts that the making of uta is not confined to human beings, but that all living creatures, the birds and the beasts, the warbler and the frog and even an old, lowly fisherman such as the speaker himself, compose Japanese uta. The argument is a condensed version of passages contained in Ki no Tsurayuki's famous and often quoted preface to the Kokinshū:

The poetry of Japan has its roots in the human heart
and flourishes in the countless leaves of words. Because human beings possess interests of so many kinds,
it is in poetry that they give expression to the meditations
of their hearts in terms of the sights appearing before
their eyes and the sounds coming to their ears. Hearing
the warbler sing among the blossoms and the frog in his
fresh waters--is there any living being not given to song?
It is poetry which, without exertion, moves heaven and

earth, stirs the feelings of gods and spirits invisible
to the eye, softens the relations between men and
women, calms the hearts of fierce warriors. [7]

In its entirety, Tsurayuki's preface represents the classic expression
of traditional Japanese views on poetry and for this reason alone
such an authoritative source could hardly fail to be cited in the play.

The preface in the Kokinshū is also used as the basis for theme
in the plays Takasago and Shiga. The former deals with the twin pine
of Takasago and Sumiyoshi, which are cited in the preface as symbol-
izing longevity and conjugal fidelity and further associated in the play
with the two early poetry collections, the Manyōshū and the Kokinshū.
The latter play, Shiga, deals with the poet Otomo no Kuronushi (fl.
860), one of the "Six Poetic Geniuses" (Rokkasen), so-called because
they were singled out for mention by name in Tsurayuki's preface.
Kuronushi, later deified and worshipped as the god Shiga, wrote poetry
which is described in the Kokinshū preface as being "light in spirit but
poor in form, like a mountain rustic bearing twigs on his back resting
beneath a cherry tree, "[8] and in the play he appears in the first act as
a woodcutter fitting this description. Both plays are in the first group
and so treat poetry accordingly as an instrument whereby the prosperi
and stability of Japan under imperial rule is maintained, a view impli
in the entire preface. For the play Haku Rakuten, Tsurayuki's prefac
also has special relevance because it represents the first complete
statement of Japanese poetic theory and practice as an art on a par
with, but distinct from, Chinese literature and its influences. Writter
at a time when the prestige of Chinese poetry in Japan had reached
such heights that the writing of Japanese verse with serious intent wa
all but in danger of extinction, Tsurayuki's preface provided, in effect
a response to the same threat of cultural invasion from China that thi
Noh play treats, a fact of which audiences were well aware.

More immediately serving the play's purposes, however, are the
particular passages from the preface that have been chosen for the
mondō. The main characteristic of a mondō is that during the exchange of dialogue between waki and shite, the shite's responses constitute a gradual accumulation of subtle hints as to his divinity. Here
the first hint of the fisherman's divinity occurs after Haku Rakuten's
surprise and discomfiture over his defeat in the poetry contest when,
in response to his puzzled question about the fisherman's identity, the
fisherman declares himself to be "scarcely human, a creature of no
account" (hito ga mashi ya na na mo naki mono nari). The expressio

hito ga mashi means "like a human being" and is roughly equivalent to ningen rashii. Negated, the phrase becomes ambiguous and can be taken to mean either one so low in status that he can scarcely be considered human or as a hint of divinity in the sense of someone other than a human being. Actually, both meanings apply here as each in its special sense is integral to the argument. So, following upon the ambiguous hint concerning the fisherman's identity, quotations from Tsurayuki's preface declare that Japanese poetry is a national calling, a practice shared by high and low alike and by all living things as well and finds its fullest expression only in Japan, the land of the gods. In Japan, then, even the lowliest of creatures partakes of the divine through poetry, as vividly exemplified here in the play by a crude fisherman who is in reality a god.

Japanese poetry also possesses magical powers and in this way the recital of all its other virtues by the fisherman in the mondō acts as a kind of spell or incantation that immediately sets these powers in motion against Haku Rakuten. Caught up at once by its eloquence, Haku Rakuten is drawn almost against his will into participating in this recital. He gradually becomes entranced until, by the time the age-uta that signals the end of the mondō is completed, he is totally still and unmoving, remaining so to the close of the play.

The kuse then adds to the argument with a fable telling how in antiquity a warbler's chirping in the form of a Chinese couplet was set down in writing in the form of a Japanese uta. This story, adapted from an anecdote in the Soga Monogatari, [9] is not the original source of the play, but since it is told in the kuse, it carries considerable weight there as a quasi-historical account of the origins of the uta and its intimate connection with the voices of nature. Thus the kuse serves as a further demonstration of how Chinese verse was transformed and made intelligible in native Japanese form.

By the end of the kuse, the arguments made for Japanese poetry are complete. The rongi that follows now shifts both the arguments and the focus of the play away from literary questions toward matters that bear directly upon the Noh art itself, dance and song. In effect this marks the conclusion of the "ear-opening" section and the rongi serves as an introduction for the "eye-opening" section to follow in the second act. The rongi does this by concentrating once more upon the old fisherman, no longer just as a maker of Japanese poems, but now also as a practitioner of two other great cultural accomplishments of

Japan, the arts of dance and song. The case made for Japanese supremacy in these arts takes essentially the same form as the case made for poetry. No true dancer is present and yet none is really necessary; even an old Japanese fisherman is capable of performing with sufficient excellence to show how Japan has nurtured these arts to perfection. The dance to be performed, we are told, is a bugaku piece entitled the "Sea Green Dance." Thus a dance originally imported from China is now transformed into a Japanese version which, as we eventually witness in the second act, proves to be far superior to the Chinese original, since it drives the Chinese invader from Japan's shores. In this way both the "ear-opening" section on poetry and the "eye-opening" section on dance and song demonstrate the point of the play according to their respective modes.

In all of the above, the rongi adheres fairly closely to the established pattern; the chorus acts first as an objective spokesman and then participates in an exchange of dialogue with the shite. One radical departure from the usual form, however, is that unlike most other plays, the declaration of the shite's true identity as a god in Haku Rakuten is not given toward the close of the first act but takes place in the second act instead. This is probably because such a declaration of divinity in the first act would lessen the force of the act's main argument on behalf of the "folk" superiority of the Japanese arts as exemplified by the lowly fisherman.

The second act opens with one more striking departure from the standard form, the omission of the machi-utai, or "waiting song," which is commonly recited by the waki in the form of a prayer heralding the appearance of the shite in his godly form. It must be remembered that because Haku Rakuten has been entranced ever since his defeat in the poetry contest, he is thoroughly incapable of delivering such passages. Their absence is thus dramatically effective because Haku Rakuten's trance is thereby carried over smoothly into the second act. Furthermore, by its nature the machi-utai can only be delivered by someone who already has knowledge of the shite's true identity, a fact withheld from the waki in the first act. Indeed, the fisherman's divinity has for all intents and purposes been withheld from the audience as well. This makes Sumiyoshi's appearance in divine form at the very start of the second act come as an unexpected relevation. The sudden contrast between his identities in the two acts thus further underlines the message that the divine spirit pervading the Japanese arts may be found everywhere in Japan, even in the least likely circumstances.

Sumiyoshi enters wearing the usual mask and costuming for an aged god in shin-jo-no-mai-mono. The mask is the shiwa-jō, or "wrinkled old man"; this is worn along with the shiro-tare, a white, long, hair wig (a black wig is worn by young gods, white by aged gods) and the ui-kammuri, or "manhood ceremonial crown." His garments include the awase kariginu, or "lined hunting robe," the atsuita, which is a heavy silk kimono and the iro-ōkuchi, a dyed broad divided skirt; he enters carrying an ordinary fan.

After the opening lines delivered by the shite and chorus, the shite begins the dance. When this is over he chants the waka, which is then taken up by the chorus. The dance is then resumed to the accompaniment of the remaining passages.

SHITE:

> Upon the sea,
> Its waters green in the mountain shadows,

CHORUS:

> The Sea Green Dance,
> To the drum of waves!

(Sumiyoshi dances)

SHITE: (waka)

> From the Western Sea,
> Out of the waves of the Green Plains,

CHORUS:

> He has risen,
> The God, Sumiyoshi!
> The God, Sumiyoshi!

SHITE:

> He has risen, Sumiyoshi!

CHORUS:

> The God, Sumiyoshi!
> Whose powers are such
> That he will not let you conquer Nihon.
> Go in all speed back, O Rakuten,
> Across the waves of these shores!
> Sumiyoshi has risen!
> Sumiyoshi has risen!
> Now come the gods of Ise and Iwashimizu,
> Of Kamo and Kasuga,
> Of Kashima and Mishima,
> Of Suwa and of Atsuta,
> And the God of Itsukushima in Aki,
> Third Princess of Shakatsura, the Dragon King.
> Hovering above the waters,
> They dance the Sea Green Dance.
> The King of the Eight Great Dragons
> Performs the Music of the Eight Voices,
> And as they all flutter above the sea-void,
> From the sleeves of their dancing robes
> A wind arises, a sacred wind that blows
> The Chinese ship back to the land of Kan.
> We are truly thankful!
> We thank you for this land, O Gods,
> And you, our Sovereign,
> For this land eternal and inviolate!

Little else remains to be said about the conclusion of the play. The gods that arrive to join with Sumiyoshi in his dance do not actually appear on stage. Generally, however, the god or gods who perform a dance are from one particular locale. The reason for including such a host of divinities from diverse parts of Japan is after all to indicate that although those events are taking place at Matsura in Kyūshū, they are of great moment and concern for the country as a whole. The sacred wind (kamikaze) raised by the dancing sleeves of the gods assembled is a close relative of the storm winds which destroyed the invading Mongol fleet centuries earlier, a clear and intentional parallel. It is worth noting that all the action has taken place at sea and that at no time does Haku Rakuten actually set foot upon the shores of Japan.

To recapitulate the arguments briefly, we first have the claim that Japan represents the culmination of literary achievement in the Three Countries, followed by a demonstration of this assertion in the

form of a poetry contest; a further argument telling of the divine
powers at work in the gift of song that in Japan allows all living
creatures to compose poetry and a demonstration of the same in
the kuse by means of an old fable; and thirdly an enlargement of the
scope of the argument to include all other Japanese arts as well, but
particularly dance and song, closing with an enactment of this claim
in which an originally Chinese musical entertainment is performed by
a Japanese god and drives the Chinese invader away from the shores
of Japan.   Finally, in each step along the way all these arguments
are given full weight and impact through a careful working of their
elements into a meaningful formal structure prescribed for Noh plays
in the first group, the waki-nō.

The question remains, do the arguments presented in this play
and the attitudes toward China they reflect have any visible effect upon
the art of Noh drama, particularly upon the fashioning of Noh plays
utilizing materials originally derived from Chinese sources?

A partial answer may be found in the Kadensho, where Zeami
discusses the origins of the Noh art itself.   Zeami begins by ascrib-
ing the primal beginnings of Noh drama to the Age of the Gods when
the Sun Goddess, Amaterasu, shut herself up inside a cave, whereupon the realm was covered in darkness.   According to the legend, a
number of gods and goddesses then assembled outside, performed sacred songs and dances and thus eventually lured Amaterasu out of the
cave so that the realm was once again illuminated.   There is a for-
malized ring to Zeami's assertion of these native mythic beginnings,
but his intention is clear.   By establishing this archaic precedent for
all of the Japanese performing arts, later influences and importations
from elsewhere immediately acquire secondary status.   Once having
established this, Zeami states further that the art does have certain
origins in India as well, where he claims entertainments were used
during Buddha's lifetime as an aid to his sermons.   This in part
speaks to the presence of Buddhist themes in Noh, just as his former
assertion speaks to the native religious content in Noh plays.   Finally,
Zeami allows that the Indian practice of praising Buddhist scriptures
and popularizing Buddhism through song and dance was transmitted to
Japan by way of China.   Here then, China is only the intermediary
between India and Japan through which Buddhist religious entertainments were passed along and there is no independent mention of Chinese forms of music and dance in their own right having been brought
to Japan.

Thus whatever the actual historical origins and development of Noh drama and its antecedents, it is clear that in Zeami's account of them China plays only a minor part. But nowhere in Zeami's writings does one find any outright disavowal of the contribution Chinese elements made towards the eventual formation of Noh drama, nor is there any hint of a tendency to exclude Chinese materials on doctrinal or ideological grounds in order to keep the Noh art "pure." Indeed, the very existence of so much Chinese material in Noh, both in karagoto-mono and in plays dealing with Japanese subjects, is a tacit acknowledgement of traditional Chinese influences. Still, widely used as Chinese elements are in Noh drama, they should not be considered influences except in the vaguest, broadest sense. Chinese literature, music and dance were so carefully worked into the Noh and underwent such extensive modification in the process that they became all but indistinguishable from other elements in a play, remaining conspicuous only when their "Chinese-ness" was a quality playwrights wished to emphasize for dramatic effect, as in the use of gaku dances, for example.

In any case, the pattern of Zeami's account of the origins of Noh drama is in many respects very much like the argument advanced in the play Haku Rakuten concerning Japanese poetry. Whether or not this was Zeami's intention, the link between the two is evident and in this sense at least Zeami's Haku Rakuten is an argument that bears directly upon the Noh art. Furthermore, Noh plays after all are themselves a blend of Chinese and Japanese elements and Zeami's use of the Noh play Haku Rakuten to deal with themes concerned with this cultural blending process, togehter with his working of the material so skillfully into the formal requirements of that class of Noh play, combine to make Haku Rakuten an exemplification of the argument, not merely a vehicle for it.

But the extent to which the attitudes revealed in Haku Rakuten operated as a key factor in the actual choice of material to be fashioned into a Noh play is difficult to determine. Other than general considerations of the familiarity and widespread appeal of certain Chinese stories or poems, there is no way of knowing, for example, why certain sources were adapted into Noh plays and why others were not. Many Chinese tales and poems that met these requirements were, of course, never turned into plays at all. Since the criteria for the suitability of Chinese material for dramatic adaptation rested on the same grounds that applied to native Japanese sources, it is probable that Chinese stories had somewhat less appeal for playwrights or audiences or both than Japanese ones did. Furthermore, while Zeami considered the Noh art in general to be a consummate blend of foreign and native elements, there is no evidence to suggest that when he or other playwrights actually chose to write a Chinese piece they were in any way in conscious competition with the original source, or that they were attempting to fashion a final and perfect version of a tale, poem, or idea which they considered was transmitted from China to Japan in an imperfect state. A good deal of polishing and modification was of course necessary in order to meet the conventional requirements of the Noh stage; but even in the best of those karagoto-mono the author's intention did not go beyond the making of a good Noh play, so there was little if any ideological resistance to Chinese material or struggle to surpass it in Japanese form.

On artistic grounds, however, there was a tendency to regard the aesthetic and thematic possibilities of Chinese materials as somewhat limited. This is clearly shown by the relative paucity of karagoto-mono among the all-important first three groups of Noh plays and by the special status accorded karagoto roles among the categories of mime. Native Japanese sources were naturally closer than Chinese sources to fundamental concerns reflected by these groups and role categories, despite the fact that such concerns and the native literature expressing them were themselves influenced and even molded to some extent by China. Thus the limited artistic possibilities of Chinese materials in Noh drama were in largest measure due to their exoticism, though even this quality often enhanced the total effect of a play rather than impeding it.

FOOTNOTES

1. Sanari Kentarō, Yōkyoku Taikan [A complete collection of Nō plays]. Tokyo: Meiji Shoin, 1954, Vol. II, pp. 1043-1060. (Hereafter YT.)

2. Ibid., Vol. I, pp. 667-680.

3. See de Bary, et al., Sources of Japanese Tradition. New York: Columbia, 1958, p. 12.

4. Arthur Waley, The Nō Plays of Japan. New York: Grove Press 1957, p. 250.

5. Minemura Fumito, "Yōkyoku 'Haku Rakuten' tenkyō-kō" [Study of the source of the Nō play 'Haku Rakuten'], Kanze (October 1943).

6. See note, YT, Vol. VI, p. 2475.

7. Trans. by Robert H. Brower and Earl Miner, Japanese Court Poetry, (Stanford, 1961), p. 3.

8. Nihon koten bungaku taikei (hereafter NKBT), Vol. VIII, p. 101.

9. See note, YT, Vol. IV, p. 2477.

BIBLIOGRAPHY

Brower, Robert and Miner, Earl. Japanese Court Poetry. Stanford:
   Stanford University Press, 1961.

Minemura, Fumito. "Yōkyoku 'Haku Rakuten' tenkyō-kō" [Study of
   the source of the Noh play "Haku Rakuten"]. Kanze. October
   1943.

Nihon koten bungaku taikei (NKBT).

Sanari, Kentarō. Yōkyoku taikan [A complete collection of Noh plays]
   (YT). Tokyo: Meiji Shoin, 7 vols., 1954.

Sources of Japanese Tradition, ed. by Wm. Theodore de Bary et al.
   New York: Columbia University Press, 1958.

Waley, Arthur. The Nō Plays of Japan. New York: Grove Press,
   1957.

DISCUSSION ON CARL SESAR'S PAPER

Crump: It would seem that Zeami and his father came upon a theatrical form that was already mostly formulated. Zeami analyzed what he had received as a heritage and then wrote prescriptions for his own concepts of what the drama should be?

Sesar: It was Zeami who wrote the prescriptions, but of course his father was really the genius behind the scenes. Actually what Kanami did was to take the form which was already called Noh and incorporate another kind of entertainment into it. He sculptured it and . . .

Crump: He made quite a different thing of it?

Sesar: Not a very different thing. He just took the kusemai, a form of entertainment actually stemming from dances called shirabyōshi[1] dances, but based on quite a different kind of music than had been used prior to this. Since it was good, moving entertainment and was useful for narrative recital, he stuck it into the third section of the ha and a form was created out of it which we call Noh. Zeami admitted this, and later when he wrote his prescriptions, he was merely intellectualizing on his own art.

Crump: It seems to me that in thinking comparatively about Japanese and Chinese drama, the prominent feature is that the Noh geist seems to cast its material in terms of the transcendental, where the plot always, or very nearly always, is in a "this world" and "other world" context. This is something that is totally un-Chinese and almost organic to the Noh. Did this exist prior to Zeami and his followers?

Sesar: I can't say for certain. I know that even the Heike Monogatari[2] itself speaks about people already dead, and Japanese literature in general deals very often with people who are dead and return as ghosts. By the time the Noh plays came into being, events were being presented as they actually happened, genzai-mono.[3] Most plays deal with

171

departed spirits. The most powerful theme in Noh por-
trays a soul which must atone for former deeds because
it is bound by attachments to its former life. Many people consider the Noh play to be a mass said for the salvation of someone's soul. The waki, for example, is a
priest. The ghost appears with the burden of its woes
and the ghosts are all very famous people. Warriors
repent of their deeds of violence or boast of their prow-
ess and women speak of their loves.

Crump: Is the milieu Shinto or Buddhist here?

Sesar: More Buddhist, I think. Where there are historical figures the tone is more Buddhist, but the god-plays are
closer to the native religion; most of the god-plays, of
course, deal with the Shinto religion and some plays in
that category deal with a Shinto-Buddhist merger. This
is significant from my standpoint because the plays in
the first group (the god-plays) which use gaku[4] dances
in them actually deal with the Shinto-Buddhist merger;
the gaku dance is one way of having a native god performing a dance which exemplifies this merger.

Crump: Therefore classification of the plays is based on these
things?

Sesar: That whole problem of classification is very tedious.
Classically speaking, there are five types. Plays are
also classified according to the dances, which tells you
only about the kind of dances in them.

Malm: Now I'm intrigued. I think of the play Hagoromo, the
angel who has her clothes stolen while she is bathing.
That is a Chinese story. I don't remember the dance
in the second half, when they finally return her clothes
to her.

Sesar: I can't tell you what the dance is now in terms of Noh.
But the most interesting thing is that the dance is sup-
posed to be the same kind as that performed by the Moon
Maiden.

Crump: Let me clarify something. When you say <u>bugaku</u>, that means it was connected in the past with . . .

Teele: Just to call them <u>bugaku</u> meant that they were Chinese in origin.

Malm: Whenever <u>gagaku</u> is performed as a dance it is called <u>bugaku</u>. The curious thing is that no instruments used in <u>gagaku</u> were incorporated into the Noh. The <u>hichiriki</u>[5] was not used nor was the <u>shō</u>.[6] They show up in the illustrations I produced for you, but by Zeami's time they had lost much ground.

Pian: The exoticism is really quite different from the spiritual aspect associated with Buddhism, isn't it?

Sesar: As it happens, each serves not to separate but to reinforce. If a play is set in China, it is, of course, exotic. That aspect can simply represent something very far away; on the other hand it lends the play a great deal of prestige. It deals with the remote past and it is Chinese, and therefore it carries considerable impact. It is like anything else in Japan that has a Chinese reference: it is always treated with two conflicting and deeply felt attitudes. On the one hand, it is accorded great reverence and on the other, it is sensed as a threat to native culture. The strangeness is there, but that aspect is only a jumping off point . . .

Pian: I was wondering how the Chinese treat the same subject in relation to the way the Japanese treat it. Buddhism is foreign to both, you see . . .

Sesar: I discussed that in the final chapter of my dissertation; that chapter was <u>Yō Ki-hi</u> (Ch.: Yang Kuei-fei). One of the reasons why <u>Yō Ki-hi</u> is such a great play is because in one sense the theme of the original work is very close (although not identical) to the general kinds of themes referring to women in Noh which depict the soul in torment. In the original work the spirit journey is a perfect constituent for the other world. The Noh play has that spirit journey. The <u>waki</u> is the priest. He meets Yang Kuei-fei in the original poem; she weeps, and the Song of Everlasting Sorrow is performed. This is especially interesting. Most plays conclude with a hint of the eventual salvation of the soul. Yō Ki-hi is a really tragic work in the sense that woe is eternal. She ends up in the tower weeping eternally, knowing she will never be reunited with the Emperor. In another play the hero is Hsiang Yü. Ssu-ma Ch'ien harshly criticizes Hsiang Yü as a tyrant. The source of the Hsiang Yü play in Noh is the Heike Monogatari. There the theme is the evanescence of fame, power and glory. In the opening lines of the Heike Monogatari four Chinese historical heroes are mentioned. Their fates were the same as the heroes of the Heike wars. There is a definite relationship, of course: the Heike Monogatari is more Buddhist and Ssu-ma Ch'ien's attitude is more Confucian, but in each case we are faced with men who sought power and had it turn to dust. There is common ground there.

Pian: I am more interested in how they take on different forms, if they can be said to do so.

Sesar: Well, there is no Buddhist element in the biography of Hsiang Yü. But by analogy to military plays in the Noh repertory, this element is introduced while telling the story of Hsiang Yü. In the play Hsiang Yü is a humble boatman. The scene is Wu-chiang, the scene of his defeat. Two Chinese woodcutters ask to be ferried across the river and they begin talking about the place; the ferryman finally admits he is the ghost of Hsiang Yü and tells them about his battles with Han Wu-ti. He also talks about his horse and his love for the Lady Yü. In other sources about Lady Yü she is connected with a flower that grew out of her grave. The woodcutters gather a wreath of that particular kind of flower and that is the way the stories are blended.

Crump: Of course, Buddhism was a foreign religion . . .

Sesar: Everyone knows that and the Japanese developed a way of using those things to their own advantage if there was an issue at stake. They could consider themselves the final receivers of Buddhism which had come across from China to Japan and the ones who made a "Great Blend" of it. The other extreme is, of course, the view that things Japanese can never really equal things Chinese, affording China a great deference. I think Zeami was prejudiced and in his view Japanese art was actually superior.

Pian: My view has always been that no matter what the content an art always takes the shape of its container and that when themes or art forms are lifted from one source and given new containers they adapt themselves to these new containers according to the time or the region.

Sesar: I agree. Most Noh plays that can be traced back to Chinese sources are, in fact, based on Japanese retellings, so the stories are altered according to the nature of the retelling. The Kara Monogatari, for example, contains tales from China in the late Heian period. The anecdotes from China are retold there and one can observe how they have been refashioned in Heian court style. The Kara Monogatari belongs to the genre of poem tales, so a poem is crafted at the peak of the particular anecdote, but it is a Chinese story.

Malm: Well, with one exception, there are no attempts to recreate a Chinese play. The one attempt is a very short piece, the Tsuru-kame, and it is an attempt only in the simplest way. The Tsuru-kame attempts to represent the performance of dances at the court of Hsüan-tsung. It does not pretend to say that this is the way the dances were executed but is a re-creation of that type of event. These were the dances in the Moon Palace and in Hsüan-tsung's palace.

Pian: What caught my interest was when you spoke of the masks, the formal standardized masks, like the ones with the sad face. This is a symbol and it emphasizes the visual aspect. I'm uncertain about my contrast here, but in Peking Opera, although there is a certain amount of visual symbolism, the aural aspect is strong too. The gongs are a case in point. The small gong represents important personages. You also mentioned the character's real station in life, which may be outside the drama at the moment. A role portraying a high official would automatically signal high official clothing.

Sesar: Yes, but in the Noh drama even great characters appear, just as Hsiang Yü did, first in humble guise . . .

Pian: But there is always something to indicate who he really is; there is an absolute value imposed which is outside the drama.

Sesar: Of course. Everyone knows the play beforehand and the very manner of performance lends a tremendous amount of dignity. Humbleness in the Noh drama does not involve a loss of dignity.

Pian: I can think of an excellent example in "The Ruse of the Empty City" (K'ung Ch'eng Chi), where the main character is K'ung-ming, the shrewd strategist. He appears on stage accompanied by the small gong, and Ssu-ma Yi, the great general and antagonist, is accompanied on stage by the large gong.

Johnson: Is it because of K'ung-ming's self-demeaning nature? Humbleness is what I was thinking of: he never brags about his feats.

Pian: Well, I'm merely thinking of the attitude of the audience, the general public and the playwright toward K'ung-ming. He rates only the small gong. There is a debate among Chinese artistic critics about whether or not Ssu-ma Yi deserves that big gong.

Malm: I'm trying to decide now whether or not there is a musical difference in the section for entrances (the nanori). I don't really think there is. In the first act everyone enters in the same way. In the second act, of course, they enter differently.

Sesar: In Noh plays with Chinese subject matter, there is a characteristic opening which contrasts with the classical openings in Noh, but that is because of their exotic nature. The fact that the play is about a foreign subject is the prime factor. The play Yō Ki-hi, however, opens in a manner which is consistent with all other woman-plays, so when I was speaking of the "Great Blend" referring to those few plays of Chinese origin which did reach the great heights of achievement in Noh (and there are only a handful; no other plays with this characteristic opening are equal to them in quality), there was an attempt not simply to perform Chinese plays but to make them come up to the standards of the native plays.

Teele: I find that I am in disagreement here with some of your points. When you say that Tsuru-kame is a reproduction of a Chinese play, you have to clarify that it is not a Chinese play but a Chinese dance.

Sesar: Yes, that is what I meant.

Crump: I need enlightening on Tsuru-kame.

Teele: The Tsuru-kame is "The Tortoise and the Crane," primarily a ceremonial dance performed by two spirits. After they dance, the Emperor (a shite this time) performs a gaku dance.

Sesar: My point was that this was an attempt to re-create that setting. There was no real play as such; there were actually dances only performed by the Crane and the Tortoise. The Japanese must have been captivated by the idea and decided to perform it in this play. Hsüan-tsung must have been very much admired by players of this period. It was precisely because he was known as a patron of the arts that he seemed to be a favorite in Noh. One reason Yō Ki-hi was so famous as a play is because of Po Chü-yi, the most famous Chinese poet in Japan. His Ch'ang-hen Ko was the most famous work. Some quotations from the Tale of Genji referring to that work are incorporated into the play too and in the Yō Ki-hi there is an attempt not only to achieve that medieval flavor of the Noh play but also to use quotes from the Tale of Genji. They were intended to suggest a Heian flavor.

Malm: They wanted to obtain a kind of balance, too, because Haku Rakuten is a very special kind of play. Many of the other Chinese plays are very different: Kantan, for example, or Shōjō. In these plays one gets an entirely different view, which should be brought up. Of course, Shōjō and <u>Kantan</u> are basically folk tales. <u>Kantan</u> is the man who sleeps on a magic pillow and dreams of being an emperor; <u>Shōjō</u> is the spirit of wine. On stage these are magnificent plays, and I think the audience senses no feeling of antagonism toward them. My basic feeling about the Chinese plays was that they are rather a happy adoption of a basic heritage which the Japanese have accepted as part of their own.

Sesar: Yes, many of them are plays which the Japanese find an enjoyable and artistic blend of the two cultures and the audience reacts accordingly, but still there are a few which reveal this deep sense of cultural conflict. The conclusions I came to were that for the most part Chinese materials were treated as expertly and artistically as the playwright found possible. There are real attempts at full incorporation into the Noh setting; others were less successful.

Crump: If one were to come into the theatre in the middle of one of these <u>Karagoto-mono</u> and notice the costuming, would he know he was watching a story originally placed in China?

Sesar: I think the connoisseur would, but the common spectator wouldn't.

Crump: There are no attempts to make Chinese plays look Chinese?

Sesar: No. There are costume touches that appear, but they are small. If you see a Chinese fan, it is a dead giveaway. If you're not up on Chinese fans, however, then you would not notice it. Other costume features are hats and one or two kinds of jackets.

Malm: Were there no masks created for Chinese roles?

Sesar: Yes, there were. The best one was for <u>Kantan</u>, the <u>Kantan</u> mask, but that play depicts a man in the throes of a religious identity conflict. It carried such ennobling qualities that it was later used to portray Japanese noblemen.

Teele: I'd like to introduce another subject. In your very fine paper you assume a well-established norm from which Zeami is deviating. I wonder how you justify that?

Sesar: I looked at almost all the plays in the first group (the god-plays), and it's very clear that despite some standard variations that stem from the dances used in these plays all of them follow basically the same pattern. It was for those reasons that I began to feel that the deviations in this play were really significant. Since this play is so unusual in theme and treatment and the role of the waki is so unusual, it dawned on me that anyone familiar with the standard form of the god-play would be keenly aware that Haku Rakuten's attitude as a waki was a unique and dramatic portrayal. Audiences must have been thoroughly familiar with the standard god-play because there were so many of them. In every one the waki is a priest on a religious pilgrimage to a sacred spot; here the waki does not follow that pattern at all. Furthermore, he is unaware that his destination is a sacred spot. This places an entirely different dimension on the play.

Teele: Zeami wrote a good many of those plays. Have you ever calculated how many of the god-plays are Zeami's?

Sesar: I realized that authorship was significant and to be able to pin Haku Rakuten down to Zeami would be important, but no one has been able to do that. People were loose with their attributions and Zeami got credit for many plays that we know he didn't write. The authorship is doubtful. I tend to think he wrote Haku Rakuten because his approach in theme and content is so close to the form of the Noh play in the Kadensho, his history of the Noh drama. There is a clear difference in feeling about the Noh art of Zeami and that of Zenchiku, who wrote the Yō Ki-hi. Zenchiku, Zeami's son-in-law, was very much interested in Chinese, far more interested than any other Noh playwright known. Kanami was already a mature man traveling about giving performances when the Noh drama suddenly came under imperial sponsorship; therefore neither Kanami nor Zeami was very well versed in Chinese. At that time there was a high premium placed on Chinese learning; naturally, Zeami could never hope to catch up, so his attitude was clearly "to take his stand with the talents he had." And those who did not partake of Chinese learning felt the pressure. It's fair to say that Shōnagon paraded Chinese verses and Lady Murasaki

writes in her diary that she doesn't like it. Shōnagon
is called a showoff. Lady Murasaki also says that she
was better at Chinese verse than her brother, who was
forced to take lessons in it, because she listened outside
the door. For these and other reasons I think Zeami was
intimidated by Chinese learning. Zenchiku, on the other
hand, was younger than Zeami and was brought up in the
atmosphere of learning and respectability. He tried to
elevate the Noh to a status more in line with the latest
in intellectual trends, which were Chinese.

Teele: It seems to me that a different interpretation is possible.
For instance in the sashi nanori of this play Haku Rakuten
says not "Nippon" but "Dai Nippon." Does that make a
difference in your stand? Then in the shidai[7] that follows
they are going to the "hi no moto." Couldn't this be interpreted as going to the "root of the sun?" I know it is
not safe to look simply at opening lines, but I have the
feeling that perhaps he felt he was en route to a sacred
spot.

Sesar: Well, this can be put into Haku Rakuten's mouth, but it's
also clear that he doesn't really understand the significance
of his utterance. Although he is en route to hi no moto,
why should he be aware of the feelings of the Japanese who
feel that this is really profound? I prefer to think that
these are not just accidents.

Teele: You make quite a strong point about the shite coming on
stage in the second act without the machi-utai, which is
rather surprising. The machi-utai is missing; there is
no doubt about that, but I'd like to check more thoroughly
into the functions of the machi-utai. However, it isn't at
all surprising that the shite comes on in glory, because
this is always the case. I thought perhaps you overstated
your case on that point.

Sesar: Yes, but hint or indication of this, which is always given
before the second act commences, is missing in this example; as far as we are concerned, we think we are still
dealing with a fisherman. Since the declaration does not
take place, the illusion is maintained. It's very subtle!

Pian: I wonder if your points about whether or not there are subtleties in these areas might not be proven by the musical background in the play? Can music provide these subtle dramatic characterizations? Again I am reminded of some examples from Peking Opera that are borrowed directly from very sophisticated literary sources. There are details that I am fairly sure are usually missed in performance, because they depend on a knowledge of the entire book on the one hand and on the other I just don't see how that particular point can be brought out clearly in the opera.

Malm: Well, look at it this way: if it were a special passage where the text contained a word with a particular word-tone, isn't it possible that the singer would compromise in that direction? In my passage from the Noh, the singer added two extra beats in order to avoid splitting a word.

Pian: Yes, a word-tone can be made prominent at the sacrifice of changing the melody. But here I am not doubting, even in the absence of musical support, that the author of <u>Haku Rakuten</u> is trying some very subtle interpretation, because from the literary point of view it could be as subtle as you indicated . . .

Sesar: But from the musical point of view . . .

Pian: There could be strong support there or it could be totally unrelated. How about the possibility of very subtle support in the percussion section reinforcing the drama?

Malm: Symbolism can be involved. In the <u>naga-uta</u> piece <u>Gorō Tokimune</u> there is an interesting example. The actor has just received a Dear-John letter from his girl friend and gets drunk. This is the only place in the entire text where you find dotted rhythm. Suddenly two bars of drunken music appear. The scale of the music changes too, so it isn't an accident. If you look at the text it reads, "and he sent her back a rough reply." The effect is an instant of rough tonality which disappears again. That is terribly subtle. In another example, <u>Sumidagawa</u>, there is a scene where a woman is looking for her kidnapped son only to discover a grave; in the scene where she realizes that this is the grave of her own son, the actual note sung by the singer is not accidental. Once for a Western audience, I took two settings of the text of <u>Curlew River</u> by Benjamin Britten and the Japanese Noh drama version and placed them side by side. When the woman recognizes the grave of her own son and weeps, it is thoroughly identifiable by a Western audience ignorant of Japanese. It is very deliberately done in the lamentation style.

Sesar: One interesting point on the use of the instrumentation in Noh is the use of the <u>taiko</u>. In all but three of the plays that contain <u>gaku-mono</u> in the Noh repertory, the <u>taiko</u> is used. Of the three, two of them deal specifically with drums: one is <u>Tenko</u> (Heavenly Drum) and the other is about the musician who is an expert <u>taiko</u> player. He is murdered. His wife is overcome by grief and puts on her husband's robe and begins to beat the <u>taiko</u>. In this play the <u>taiko</u> is not on stage. The playwright does not want to be too representational; he feels it is more forceful to suggest it rather than actually to use it.

Malm: Of course, the <u>taiko</u> used in <u>gagaku</u> and the <u>taiko</u> used in Noh are two different drums.

Pian: Does Zeami say anything about the use of certain melodies for certain types of dramatic situations?

Sesar: I don't recall seeing anything about that. However, I felt incompetent to handle the parts that dealt in great detail with music.

Pian: Well, does Zeami associate particular notes like <u>ryo</u> and <u>ritsu</u>[8] with certain emotional connotations? That might also be a way of supporting your thesis.

Sesar: Even if it was in the text, I'm afraid I couldn't understand it. Music described in intricate detail, I'm afraid, goes beyond me.

Malm: With the help of an assistant, we did in fact search around in Zeami's writings to locate specific information about music.

Pian: I'm just trying to retaliate, you know, by asking you now if there are distinctions between ryo and ritsu melodies. (laughter)

Malm: Oh, they are there in his text.

Pian: How are they applied?

Malm: It hasn't been researched.

Pian: There are no descriptive writings about them?

Sesar: Yes, there are some. I remember that he deals specifically with Kanami's suggestions for the use of the kusemai. Just what the nature of the music was I'm not able to say, but apparently it was much livelier, more agitated and had an irregular beat. That kind of music was incorporated into the main kernel of the music in the third section of the ha. He claims that this music is particularly effective for telling stories. Of course, this is not simply a recital of actions in the past for the spectator's information; they are recitations of events troubling the soul. They are more than just an outpouring of a narrative, they are an outpouring of events which the actor has hitherto kept secret. Many times it is preceded with an expression of shame.

Pian: Perhaps this is like the Yüan writer who can specify melodies and fit them to texts but still not be able to hear a note.

Malm: I want to refer to that section in my own paper where the flute is described:

> Once in a performance of Shinji Sarugaku, Toryo, an adult, was singing the rongi in rankei mode with a child actor. Since the boy was still a child, his voice slipped up to banshiki. As the pair sang the word-filled rongi, their voices became more and more disparate and the sound was not good. At this point Meisho, while holding to the original rankei tonality, elaborated the boy's singing in banshiki. At the same time he

> decorated the adult vocal part in <u>rankei</u>.
> It sounded as if there was no difference
> between the two tonalities and the perfor-
> mance was a success. (p. 109)

Pian: That's an interesting case as far as music is concerned, and it shows how far you can go in discussing music without understanding it yourself. This is true in the Noh, in Yüan drama and perhaps in Peking Opera as well.

Crump: What do you mean by that, Iris?

Pian: I mean being able to juggle modes or melody types for dramatic purposes without being a musician, without being able to play a musical instrument.

Crump: Let me intrude here. You were speaking about the fact that different skewed versions of the same story appear depending on the age of the version in question. This preoccupation with the real and the unreal, the transcendental and the worldly and the juxtaposition of the two . . . does it signify that this type of preoccupation was characteristic of the world of Zeami and his followers?

Sesar: Any discussion of the Noh has to deal with this question. I interpret it this way: they fight all the time. Their lives were an endless bloody battle. This was the life of the military and the artistocracy; both had their hands dipped in blood. Military plays deal especially with this problem and it must have been a difficult psychological burden to bear. In military plays the characters are tormented by their deeds of violence because they are destined to go to <u>shura-mono</u>, the warrior's hell. There is a view of history here similar to that in China. People of the past lived in the present in a more palpable way than is the case with our own society. When ghosts appear on the stage it is their historical presence and they appear with an emotional dimension which is very important to the audience. Because their hands are steeped in blood, they wonder how to escape their fate. The notion of Buddhist salvation dominant in these plays is bound to the notion of attachment. These souls are tied to their former existence through emotional bonds. In order to enter Nirvana one

must shed these emotional bonds. One way of achieving
this is to spill everything out and I don't regard this as
especially transcendental because it's too common. It is
like group therapy today. After you relate your problems
you feel better. This is what operates in the ghost scenes.
Audiences identified very strongly with these scenes. Ono
no Komachi was admired for centuries because she was so
full of emotion. No less than five Noh plays deal with
themes connected with her because of her passionate nature.
Naturally, all the figures in the Heike wars appealed to such
audiences because they were living under the same stresses.
The woman-plays present the softer and more human side.
If achieving Nirvana meant a severing of emotional bonds,
then a real contradiction emerges. One can't help being
emotional and yet the only plan for salvation was to keep
from it. This conflict which appears again and again is
closely linked with a term so difficult to define: yūgen.
Yūgen in early poetry can be narrowed down to certain very
definite directions. In the Shin Kokinshū it approaches the
mysterious, dark, stark, black and white. This becomes
prominent right after the Heike wars and is among the most
profound experiences in Japan. It is total blood. Afterwards bleakness entered, as did talk of the apocalypse.
Before Yūgen there was mono no aware, basically an emotional attachment which is used as a theme. If emotional
ties are the very things that stand in the way of salvation,
then one must look elsewhere. Yūgen is a search for a
higher beauty which is emotionless in one sense and yet
capable of moving one in another sense. It aims at a kind
of mysterious beauty, which, if appreciated, is enlightening
rather than binding to this world. In the Noh the prime
attribute was yūgen. In a sense one might, through watching a Noh play like Yō Ki-hi, feel a sense of relief as the
heroine seeks a release from her torments. It is a very
powerful theme.

Crump: How is the Noh viewed by young people today? When
Johnson was in Taiwan and interested in any surviving performance of opera, he tried to interest younger Chinese in
going with him, but they were not enthusiastic at all. Do
young Japanese view the Noh as a sort of Musica Antiqua
these days?

Sesar: My impression was that there are a few young people who go to the Noh out of a genuine interest in it. What the basis of their interest is, I can't say. It might be that modern Japanese are caught in the same pressures of technology that plague us. I am under the impression that many Japanese youths take Noh lessons today, be it dance or singing.

Crump: There are a fair number of amateur Noh troops out in the boondocks.

Sesar: Yes, there is a type of regional Noh throughout the country

Crump: Were the kyōgen always built into the Noh structure, or were they simply interludes that could be cut out and used as fillers?

Sesar: They are not really part of the play proper, but they are used to link the first and second acts. Was this a habit predating Zeami?

Teele: There is a danger in mixing up the kyōgen interlude with the farce. The small interlude can be left out. It originally was used while the artists were changing costumes between scenes.

Crump: My understanding was that these came out of the farce skits themselves.

Teele: The actors were the same and there are only one or two plays with the farcical elements actually built into the play itself. But it is so very rare.

Pian: What do young people look for in Noh today? Is it really the same thing that was found in them at earlier times?

Sesar: When I attend a Noh play, I either fall asleep or I'm enthralled. Time changes for me in the theater. The play proceeds very slowly. It may be the same thing as the tea ceremony performed amid all the bustle . . . just to achieve a moment's quiet and peacefulness. And then, not many people in Japan, even if they go to see the Noh dram know very much about it. Yet they go.

Teele: I'd like to add a footnote. We speak of Noh as being all of one kind and yet in the Komachi plays there are five that deal with her; one is a <u>genzai-mono</u>. That one has to do with a poetry contest. It is very lively. The same is true of Noh plays in general: about one-fourth of them are <u>genzai-mono</u>. The picture is not monolithic.

Crump: Is there a tradition for Noh outside the performing tradition, the writing of a Noh drama for its own sake?

Teele: There are plays that were written which the author never expected to have performed.

Crump: Just like the Ming drama.

Sesar: Well, a Noh text can be considered simply as an example of long poetry.

FOOTNOTES

1. <u>Shirabyōshi</u>: female temple and palace dancers.

2. <u>Heike Monogatari</u>: "The Heike Tales"; tales of the wars between the Heike and Genji clans.

3. <u>Genzai-mono</u>: a "contemporary product."

4. <u>Gaku</u>: <u>hayashi</u> interludes in the Noh.

5. <u>Hichiriki</u>: a double-reed <u>gagaku</u> instrument.

6. <u>Shō</u>: an organ-like wind instrument.

7. <u>Shidai</u>: a short introductory song in the Noh drama.

8. <u>Ryo</u> and <u>Ritsu</u>: the two traditional Japanese musical scales.

The Structure of the Japanese Noh Play

Roy E. Teele

Any attempt to study the structure of the Japanese Noh play
must perforce start with Zeami Motokiyo, its greatest practitioner
and critic. Therefore, at the risk of repeating what is known to
most students of the Noh, let us begin by discussing Zeami's Nōsakushō, "Treatise on Writing Noh Plays." He begins:

> Involved in writing a Noh play are three elements (sandō,
> "three ways"): materials, construction, and writing. The
> first is knowing the materials to use; the second is the act
> of putting them together; the third is writing. Choosing
> materials carefully, dividing the five sections (dan) into
> introduction, intensification, and rapid close (jo, ha, and
> kyū) sections, writing down the words, and then putting
> music to them, that's the process.[1]

The second part of the Nōsakushō stresses the importance of
music and dance and suggests that characters in the plays should
always be chosen to whom song and dance would be natural: courtiers and court ladies, supernatural creatures, priests. He lists specific names such as Ariwara no Narihira, Ono no Komachi, and Prince
Genji. The choice of places with special associations is also important.[2]

It is in the third section that Zeami makes his most specific
statements about the construction of a play:

> First, the five sections must be arranged so there is one
> in the introductory part, three in the intensification, and
> one in the rapid close. When the actor comes on stage
> he sings a shidai and a song; this constitutes the first dan.
> After this is the intensification: the shite comes out, sings
> the issei and a song; this constitutes a dan. After this the
> shite and waki meet and converse, then sing together, mak-
> ing another dan. After this there may be a kusemai, or
> simply the unison singing of songs, making another dan.
> After this the rapid close, a dance or hataraki set to
> hayabushi or kiribyōshi (fast music), another dan.[3]

189

Depending on the material of the play there may be four _dan_ or six _dan_ (instead of five).   In any case, the author must be careful that suitable music is set, and that the different parts of the intensification section are different in character.

We shall skip over a section on the kinds of Noh Plays, such as ceremonial Noh, congratulatory Noh, or those dealing with love or the recollections of the dead, and all incorporating the names of famous people and places as well as great passages from past literature into the text. [4]   We find more detailed descriptions of the song forms in the next section.   Making use of still another kind of classification, Zeami says that of the old man, woman, and warrior plays the first (called _waki_ plays, usually somewhat ceremonial or congratulatory) should start with a _shidai_ and go on to a song made up of seven or eight 7-5 syllable lines following an opening 5-7-5 syllable sequence.   These 7-5 syllable lines, Zeami explains, are a form taken from the _waka_ (the thirty-one syllable poem which dominated Japanese poetry from the _Manyo Anthology_ on).

When the _shite_ enters he sings the _issei_, a song form made up of 5-7-5-7 syllables: this is followed by a two line form, and then a longer song now called the _sashi_, running to about ten lines in the same 7-5 syllable form.   From singing in a low range the actor moves to a high range, ending with a song about ten lines long.

In the next _dan_ the actors exchange prose speeches, about five each, followed by two or three verses each, sung in the high range, ending with a unison song of about ten lines.

The third _dan_, when there is a _kusemai_, opens with a song of about five lines in the high range, then a _sashi_ of five lines, followed by five or six lines in the low range.   The _kusemai_ consists of twelve or thirteen lines in the low range followed by twelve or thirteen lines in the high range.   After this comes the _rongi_ or discussion, consisting of two or three sung speeches each, closing the _dan_ lightly and rapidly.

The _kyu_ or rapid close reveals the _shite_ in his divine or "true" shape, singing an _issei_ from the _hashigakari_ or passageway, followed by a song in unison in high range, long and rich, ending in the low range.   Then comes a _rongi_ or exchange of two or three verses each, sung lightly and flowingly.   The _shite_'s dance is performed to a fast beat (but more or less so depending on the role), followed by a short song, not defined but relatively short. [5]

With this basis from the Nōsakushō's opening sections, and adding definitions from later in this work and from other works by Zeami (as well as the analysis of various Noh texts), later Japanese writers and scholars, and scholars writing in Western languages, like Noël Péri, Hermann Bohner, Minagawa Tatsuo, and Donald Keene, have set up an idealized or "normal" structure of a Noh play.[6]

In his No, Einführung, Professor Bohner gives an abbreviated form which I translate with slight modifications:

1. Jo, Introduction: The waki or secondary actor (a messenger of the emperor, a pilgrim, a wandering priest) comes on stage. Shidai, a kind of opening song; nanori, he tells his name; michiyuki, travel song: he briefly describes his journey and names the place, the scene of the play, where he has just arrived.

2. Ha$_1$, Development: The shite or chief actor (god in disguise, deceased hero or heroine) comes on stage along the passageway; issei, first song, followed by other songs describing his appearance.

3. Ha$_2$, Meeting of the shite and waki: Mondō, dialogue, closing with an alternating song, and the first song of the chorus.

4. Ha$_3$, Rising to the high point of the play, the calling up of the "true form" of the shite, whereupon the first shite disappears. (Kusemai)
   Ai-kyōgen, interlude by kyōgen actors.

5. Kyū, Fast: After a waiting song and a song in high range, the shite appears as a god or hero or heroine in his (her) true form. Dance. Final high range song. Conclusion.[7]

This abstraction may be illustrated by the songs from Takasago, as translated by the Japanese Classics Translation Committee. The waki is Tomonari, a priest, accompanied by two attendants; the shite is an old man of Takasago who appears in his true form as the god of the Sumiyoshi shrine.

1. Shidai: To-day we don our travelling dress,
                  To-day we don our travelling dress,
                  Long is the journey before us.
   Nanori: I am Tomonari, priest of the Aso shrine. . . .
   Michiyuki: Clad in traveling attire
                  To-day we take boat
                  And set out for distant Miyako,
                  And set out for distant Miyako.

Soft spring breezes belly our sails;
Gazing ahead and behind,
For days past count
Naught can we see save clouds and sea,
Till what once seemed remote
Now drifts into view
And Takasago Bay is reached at last,
And Takasago Bay is reached at last.

2. <u>Issei</u>:   The spring breezes
Murmur in the Takasago Pine.
The day is closing in,
And the bell on the hill
Tolls the curfew.
The shore mists veil the waves
That with their voices tell
The sea's ebb and flow.
"Who is now left that knew me well?
This Takasago Pine,
Though venerable indeed,
Is not my old-time friend."
. . . .
How we have aged,
Sweeping away the fallen needles under the pine!
Shall we live on for many a year to come
Like the ancient sturdy pines
Of long-famed Iki,
Of long-famed Iki.

3. <u>Mondō</u>   'Tis passing strangely.
(<u>Waki</u>)   This aged pair should dwell apart,
He in Suminoye and she in Takasago!
Tell me, I pray, how this can be.
(<u>Shite</u>)   You speak stangely.
Though miles of land and sea may part them,
The hearts of man and wife are joined by love;
Naught do they reck of distance.

4. <u>Kuse</u>:   In this auspicious reign
Jewelled words, like glistening dew-drops,
Light up our people's minds,
Awaking in all living beings
The love of poetry.

> For as Chōnō writes,
> All nature's voices
> Are instinct with poetry.
> Herb or tree,
> Earth or sand,
> Sough of wind and roar of waters,
> Each encloses in itself the Universe;
> Spring forests stirring in the eastern wind,
> Autumn insects chirping in the dewy grass,
> Are they not each a poem?
> Yet of all trees the pine is lord
> Endued with princely dignity.
> Changeless from age to age,
> Its fadeless green endures a thousand years. . . .

Machi-utai:
> From Takasago Bay,
> Hoisting our sails,
> Hoisting our sails,
> Under the climbing moon
> We put out on the flowing tide.
> Leaving behind the isle of Awaji
> And passing distant Naruo
> To Suminoye we have come,
> To Suminoye we have come.
>
>   . . . .

(Shite in
"true form")
> From the waves of the western sea
> That beat on Aoki-ga-hara,
> I first arose--the God himself. . . . (Dance)

Final song:
> Dread spirits quelling, arms are stretched out,
> Life and treasure gathering, arms are inwards
>   drawn,
> "A Thousand Autumns"
> Rejoices the people's hearts:
> And "Ten Thousand Years"
> Endows them with new life.
> The soughing of wind in the Twin Pines
> With gladness fills each heart,
> With gladness fills each heart![8]

This quotation is extensive, but it will serve, I hope, not only to put some flesh on an abstract skeleton, but also to reinforce this simple pattern on the one hand, and on the other show that the songs themselves do carry the structural weight and are in fact a part of the structure. It is only one pattern, but it is the most frequently used structural pattern. It may be seen in what is possibly the most popular of all Noh plays, Hagoromo, from the opening waki-issei,

> Loud the rowers' cry
> Who through the storm-swept path of Mio Bay
> Ride to the rising sea,[9]

through the magnificent kuse (perhaps even more magnificent in Waley's translation),

> Now upon earth trail the long mists of spring;
> Who knows but in the valleys of the moon
> The heavenly moon-tree puts her blossom on?
> The blossoms of her crown win back their glory:
> It is the sign of spring.
> Not heaven is here, but beauty of the wind and sky.
> Blow, blow, you wind, and build
> Cloud-walls across the sky, lest the vision leave us
> Of a maid divine! . . .[10]

on to the closing lines of the kyū,

> Over the mountain of Ashitaka, the high peak of Fuji,
> Very faint her form,
> Mingled with the mists of heaven;
> Now lost to sight.[11]

It is used in Kantan, Yuya, and in dozens of other plays, and is a step toward the elaborate chart of the "normal" play which I have made by combining the table in Minagawa's "Japanese Noh Music,"[12] and Bohner's analysis of song forms in his No, Einführung:

I. First Part
    A. Entrance of the second actor (waki) and his attendants
        1. Entrance music (shidai, issei, or nanori-bue) by instrumentalists
        2. Entrance song (shidai or issei) of the second actor and his attendants (omitted if nanori-bue is played as item 1)
        Shidai in fixed-rhythm, higher melodic style; poem of two twelve-syllable lines followed by a line of eleven syllables, each with a caesura after the seventh syllable; simple, without rich ornamentation; repeated by

       chorus in low voice
          or
       Issei in free-rhythm, rich melodic style; poem consisting of seventeen-syllable line, with caesuras after syllables 5 and 7, and a twelve-syllable line, with a caesura after syllable 7

  3.   Self-introduction (nanori) by the second actor; in speech style
  4.   Travel song (michiyuki) of the second actor and his attendants; in fixed-rhythm, higher melodic style; opening line of five syllables, followed by seven or eight lines of twelve syllables, with a caesura after syllable 7
  5.   Arrival of the second actor at a certain place (tsuki-zerifu); in speech style

B.   Entrance of the first actor (shite) and his attendants
  1.   Entrance music (issei or shidai) and his attendants
  2.   Entrance song (issei or shidai or yobi-kake) of the first actor and his attendants
      Issei in free-rhythm, rich melodic style (cf. IA 2)
      Shidai in fixed-rhythm, higher melodic style (cf. IA 2)
         or
      Yobi-kake, a call from the distance in speech style
  3.   Tri-sectional descriptive or lyrical passage for the first actor and his attendants
      Recitative (sashi), about ten lines of twelve syllables with caesura after syllable 7
      Song in low pitch (sage-uta) in fixed-rhythm, lower melodic style; usually two to four lines
      Song in high pitch (age-uta) in fixed-rhythm, higher melodic style, usually in five to ten lines

C.   Dialogue between the first and second actors
    Dialogue (mondō) in speech style
    Narrative (katari) in speech style
    Preliminary Recitative (kakari)
    Recitative (sashi) (cf. IB 3)
    Reading of a letter (fumi) in recitative style; usually in yowa
    Lament (kudoki) in recitative style; in yowa; begins on chū (middle)
    Kakeai, two 12-syllable lines, caesura after syllable 7
    Shodō, up to ten 12-syllable lines, caesura after 7

D. Explanation and development of the subject of the first actor and chorus

Sage-uta (cf. IB 3)

Age-uta (cf. IB 3)

Shidai (cf. IA 2)

Kuri in free-rhythm, rich melodic style; frequent use of of the pattern named kuri; ends in ge (low) through hon-yuri cadence; number of lines not fixed

Sashi (cf. IB 3)

Kuse (name borrowed from a pre-Noh dance); consists of three sections, the first and second being in fixed-rhythm, lower melodic style, twelve or thirteen lines, and the third being in fixed-rhythm, higher melodic style, twelve or thirteen lines; except for the first line of the third section, sung by chorus

E. The close of the first section: dialogue between the first actor and chorus

Discussion (rongi) in fixed-rhythm, higher melodic style, in response form (three or four exchanges, then ten 12-syllable lines, caesura after syllable 7)

F. Instrumental exit music (rai-jo or haya-tsuzumi, etc.)

II. Interlude (ai-kyōgen)

Dialogue between the second actor and the kyōgen actor; new explanation of the same subject by the kyōgen actor, speech style

III. Second part

A. Waiting song (machi-utai) of the second actor and his attendants in expectation of the reappearance of the first actor; in fixed-rhythm, higher melodic style; 5;7.5;7.5--to 7 or 8 lines.

B. Reappearance of the first actor
1. Entrance music by the instrumentalists (issei, deha, sagariha, haya-fue, or obeshi, etc.)
2. Entrance song (issei) of the first actor in free-rhythm, rich melodic style (cf. IA 2)

C. Dialogue of the first actor, second actor, and chorus

D. Dance by the first actor to instrumental music (mai, gaku, or hataraki-goto, etc.)

E. Conclusion (nori-ji, kiri, or chū-nori-ji)
Nori-ji in ō-nori rhythm; usually employed if the play deals
with the supernatural, but not with warriors; colorful melodic contours
        or
Kiri in hira-nori rhythm, usually employed if the play deals
neither with the supernatural nor with warriors
        or
Chū-nori-ji in chū-nori rhythm; usually employed if the play
deals with warriors
(After the conclusion of the Noh proper:
    Exit of the first actor
    Exit of the second actor, chorus, and instrumentalists)

This may be considered an abstract construct of an ideal or
normal Noh play, but we must be careful of words like "ideal" and
"normal" until the model has been tested. First, let us examine two
plays which are a standard part of the repertory, but very different.

Tsuru-kame, "The Crane and the Tortoise," is what Ezra Pound
aptly called an eclogue[13] or ceremonial congratulatory play, which
always charms when produced. It is short and easy, one of the first
pieces taught to students of Noh-singing. [14] Omote and Yokomichi's
text in the Iwanami edition, like the utai-bon or singing text from
which I learned to sing the play, begins with the shite and chorus
alternating in a sashi which is descriptive of the courtiers assembled
in the great hall. There follows a song describing the palace and
garden, which announces the appearance of the crane and the tortoise,
whereat the waki, a courtier, asks the shite, the emperor, to have
them dance. Afterwards the shite himself dances to the accompaniment of a kiri, or fast closing song, which describes a dance of
moon maidens.

There is no shidai or issei, no nanori, no michiyuki, and, to
go on to the second part, no machi-utai and no kuse (to mention only
major forms). As for dances, the shite performs a gaku or Chinese
court dance. Since such exalted figures as emperors are more often
played by kokata, or child actors, this is somewhat unusual. Moreover, child actors do appear, in the roles of crane and tortoise,
which here require neither speaking nor singing, only dancing. Dancing being most often reserved for the shite, it is also somewhat un-

usual to have the two tsure or companions dance. It scarcely matters
however, in one sense, for the roles are little differentiated. There
is no semblance of dramatic action, and one feels that when Nogami
divides the play into jo, ha, and kyū sections, it is only a perfunctory
gesture, without reference to changes in mood or form. There is
a single exchange of prose speeches between the waki and shite, but
this is not enough to constitute a mondō. It is only fair to add, however, although I do not remember it from the performance and it is
not in the Kwanze utai-bon or the Iwanami text, that Nogami[15] prints
a brief opening speech by a kyōgen actor (unusual in itself, since
only eleven plays in the whole repertory of nearly 240 plays have
such an opening), in which he identifies himself as a minister of the
T'ang Emperor Hsüan-tsung and tells that seasonal dances are about
to be performed.

No author or date is suggested for the play, sometimes called
by a variant title Gekkyūden, but neither this fact nor any of those
cited above should suggest that this is an "odd" or orphaned sort of
piece, for it is in the repertories and texts of all five schools of
Noh-acting. In contrast with this play, let us now consider Funa
Benkei, "Benkei in the Boat," a very different sort of theatrical
experience.

It is a long, complex, dramatic piece by Kwanze Kojiro Nobumitsu (1435-1516), which Nogami divides into two cycles of jo, ha,
and kyū sections, and Yokomichi and Omote divide into thirteen sections (since they do not use the jo, ha, kyū analysis).[16] The waki,
Benkei, is as active and important in the drama as the shite, who
plays Yoshitsune's mistress, Shizuka Gozen, in the first part of the
play and the ghost of the Taira warrior Tomomori in the second part.
A kokata plays the role of Yoshitsune, the usual treatment of the role,
but the ai-kyōgen is anything but usual, for the interlude is not a
mere retelling of the basic plot but a part of the developing plot.
Moreover, the kyōgen actor takes an active and largely comic role
as he rows the boat into the rising storm which precedes the appearance of the ghost, the shite of the second part. It is extraordinarily
effective theatre from the Western point of view.

As to lyric and prose forms, the author has seemingly gone down
the list of possible items and put in virtually everything: shidai,
nanori, sashi (which takes the place of the michiyuki here), sage-uta,
age-uta, mondō, right up to the kuse in the first ha section and the
waka and chu-no-mai in the kyū section. The second half of the play

is not quite so "complete" but it does have an _issei_ and _mondō_ in the second _jo_, _mondō_ and _uta_ in the _ha_, and the _hataraki_ dance and grand closing song to _ō-nori_ rhythm in the _kyū_ section.

Looking at the piece as a whole, having twice seen how completely it fills out the framework, we may note on the one hand the unusual amount of prose and on the other the vividness of the clash between Benkei and Shizuka in the first part, and between Benkei and Tomomori's ghost in the second. It is as if the play were splitting the Noh form at the seams, the dramatic action committing violence on the lyric form. On stage the dance and mime are brilliant, providing unusual contrast between the slow and elegant _chū-no-mai_ of Shizuka in the first part and the mimed combat of Benkei and Tomomori's ghost in the second.

There is a double problem here, of course. First, there is the problem of subsuming the extreme simplicity of _Tsuru-kame_ and the extreme complexity of _Funa Benkei_ under the same structural framework. Are they not in fact too different to be included in the same genre? The second problem is to understand what happens in a play with a double _jo-ha-kyū_ structure. Since a whole Noh program might include five plays in the order of "god," "warrior," "woman," "mad," and "demon" plays (to use the traditional abbreviated forms), it is clear that the spectator was expected to be able to follow such changes, such cycles of _jo-ha-kyū_ structure, in succeeding plays. However, the program ideally had _kyōgen_, or comic plays, interspersed among those five, inserted, it is sometimes said, to allow the spectator to relax between the "serious plays." Thus, a double cycle in a single play prevents following this theory, there being no opportunity for this use of a comic play and consequent relaxation.

Among possible solutions or approaches are two we may consider. First, perhaps _Funa Benkei_ would be better if divided into two plays, the first a woman-play, the second a warrior-play or _shunen-mono_ of the fourth class, or even a _kiri-mono_ of the fifth class. As a theatre-goer, I would not want such a division, but it would be rather tidier to consider from a theoretical viewpoint.

The second approach is to examine Nogami's divisions more closely. Is he justified in such a schema which other editors do not follow? There is no reference to this double structure in the _Nōsaku-shō_. Moreover, it is not simply _Funa Benkei_ which Nogami divides in this way. There are sixty-four so analyzed in Nogami's six-volume edition. There are none in the first group, the forty god-plays; twelve among the sixteen warrior-plays; twenty-seven among the forty-three woman-plays; thirteen among the eighty-five fourth class plays, and two among the fifty-one fifth class plays. Proportionately, there are more such plays among the warrior- and woman-plays, a matter worth investigation, though not here. It is not simply a matter of an analysis of so-called "two-act" plays, although these are all two-act plays in Nogami's analysis. The fact is that he analyzes over one hundred and eighty plays as two-act plays, basically plays in which the shite of the second part appears in a changed form from that of the first part.

Two plays by Zeami, Sanemori and Kiyotsune,[17] will serve to illustrate this analysis from the vantage point of the warrior-play. In the first, the spirit of the aged warrior Sanemori, who received a red brocade robe to wear and dyed his hair black to fight at Shino-wara, visits the local temple in the form of an old rustic. When the priest has heard something of his story and prays for him, Sanemori appears in the form of a warrior to tell and dance his last battle and to attain salvation. In the second Kiyotsune's retainer visits his wife to give her a lock of Kiyotsune's hair found after he committed suicide. Hurt and angry that he died without her, the wife refuses the lock of hair. As she sleeps his ghost appears. He and his wife each reproach the other for cruelty, and he tries in vain to placate her by explaining his situation and the reason for his suicide. After a description of his suffering in the warriors' hell he attains salvation. The former play is analyzed as having a double jo-ha-kyū structure; the latter is said to have a single jo-ha-kyū structure. How well does this display the structure of these two plays?

Sanemori opens with a speech by a kyōgen actor, which intro-duces the waki, a priest staying at Shinowara. It is curious because its suggestion that the priest's words and conduct are strange is never referred to again, and because, brief and unusual though it is, it is treated as the jo section of the first part of the play. The waki then enters with his attendants and sings an opening sashi (rather than a shidai or issei but serving the same function), and after brief chanted exchanges with the attendants, concludes this dan with an age-uta in unison. The shite, an old man, enters, also singing a sashi, followed by a prose passage which serves as a sort of nanori, and then a song which concludes the dan. These two dan make up the ha, or intensi-fication section, an unusually brief and simple one.

The kyū section is the fourth dan, made up of exchanges which are not called mondō but serve as a mondō between the waki and shite, and closing with an age-uta which the chorus joins. The shite has identified himself as the ghost of the hero Sanemori and leaves to change costume for the second part of the play. This is scarcely "climactic" or "conclusive" as kyū is usually understood. In fact, the jo-ha-kyū labelling is a misnomer for what is a fairly standard opening for Noh plays: usually these dan would be called the jo and the first and second part of the ha section.

After the ai-kyōgen, in which Sanemori's story is retold by the kyōgen actor, the second act of the play begins. The waki and his attendants are sitting at the waki pillar while waiting for the shite to return, and as they wait they sing the machi-utai. The shite enters, now magnificently dressed as the warrior Sanemori. He sings and after the song exchanges lines with the chorus. These two dan make up the jo section of the second act.

In the third, fourth, and fifth dan, labelled the ha section, the shite and chorus sing together or in response such varied forms as the age-uta, kuri, sashi, and kuse. There is a prose katari immediately after the sashi, and the kuse is a maikuse or danced kuse, so this is a rich and varied section. The play concludes with a kyū section made up of a rongi between shite and chorus, who then sing a description of the battle in which Sanemori died as he mimes the scene.

This second half of the play is fine and rich but in terms of analysis might just as well have been taken to be the third part of the ha section plus the kyū section, Nogami's more frequent analysis.

Kiyotsune begins with the waki, Kiyotsune's retainer Awazu-no-Saburō, singing a shidai, chanting a prose nanori, and then singing a michiyuki or travel song. This is the jo section. The ha begins with a mondō between the waki and the tsure, Kiyotsune's wife. She chants a kudoki, or song of sorrow, on being told of her husband's death, and the chorus sings her grief in a sage-uta and an age-uta. The second dan continues with a prose speech by the waki, a second kudoki by the wife, and ends with a sage-uta by the chorus. Still part of the ha (but not named as first, middle, or final parts of the ha, Nogami's usual terms which are taken from Zeami), the third dan brings the shite, the ghost of Kiyotsune, on stage. He sings a sashi, then exchanges chanted lines with his wife. The fourth dan

has another sashi, a kakeai, and then a sashi leading into the magnificent kusemai in the fifth dan. The sixth dan, containing the wife'
kudoki and Kiyotsune's reply, closes the ha section. The kyū section
is the seventh dan, in which a description of the eternal warfare in
the Asura world, the warriors' hell, is sung by the chorus and mime
by the shite.

In terms of plot and of forms used, this is a clear and cogent
analysis of the play's structure. It would be applicable to Sanemori
and the other warrior plays.

What of the woman-plays? Does the double jo-ha-kyū analysis
fit any better the twenty-seven plays so analyzed? Tōboku[18] is a
charming play about Lady Izumi, a Heian poetess of great beauty
and passion. The "Plum-tree-by-the-Eaves" which she planted still
blooms, and she herself has gained enlightenment by hearing the
Lotus Sutra and writing poetry about it. The play opens with the
waki and companions entering the stage, singing a shidai followed
by a brief prose nanori, then the michiyuki and arrival. This is
the first dan, and a conversation between the monk-waki and the
kyōgen actor make up the second; these two make up the jo section.
The ha section is the third dan, a conversation between the waki and
shite, ending in an age-uta sung by the chorus. Equally brief is the
single-dan kyū section in which there is a rongi between the shite and
chorus, followed by the naka-iri, the shite's return backstage to chan
costume in preparation for the second part of the play. The ai-kyōge
is a conversation between the waki and kyōgen actor which retells the
basic plot of the play. After the machi-utai of the waki and attendant
which constitutes the jo section, in the second dan, which starts the
ha section, the waki and shite discuss the "Burning House" parable,
and the chorus closes with an age-uta. The third dan is the kuri,
sashi, and kuse sequence, with its accompanying dance. The ha section closes with the jo-no-mai and a brief exchange of verses between
the shite and chorus. The shite continues to dance in the fifth dan,
the kyū section, as the chorus takes up her song about salvation.

This outline reveals at once that the structure is really the sam
as that of Hagoromo, Matsukaze, and other plays of the third group,
which are usually treated in the analysis as Zeami suggested: jo of
one dan, ha of three, and kyū of one dan. The basic elements of
waki entrance, shite entrance, development of relationship of waki
and shite through conversation and song, the kuri-sashi-kuse sequence
and the final song are all here with relatively little expansion to dema

the changed analysis. What has changed is that the _shite_ has returned backstage briefly, while the _ai-kyōgen_ retells the plot, before appearing in "true character," in the second half of the play (which ordinarily does not affect the analysis). In fact, the second half is considerably more than half so far as the poetic text and the dance are concerned. Conversely, the first part of the play, in most of these third group plays treated as having a double _jo-ha-kyū_ stucture, is far too slight to bear such an analysis. To do so renders the very terms meaningless since the _ha_, for example, is not an intensification at all but is instead a very brief exchange, and the _kyū_ is in no sense a fast close. Moreover, this analysis misrepresents the over-all structure of the plays.

There are "problem" plays, however, in the sense that they do not fit into the simpler analysis. Ōhara Goko, for example, is divided into three acts in Nogami's analysis and arranged in the double _jo-ha-kyū_ structure. It is somewhat longer and, in terms of characters on stage, is a more complex play. [19] It tells how the _shite_, the former empress Kenreimon-in, lives now as a nun at Jakkō-in with two attendants who were formerly court ladies. She is visited by the retired emperor Go-Shirakawa, a _tsure_ of the second part of the play, and his attendant courtiers to inquire of her spiritual state as well as of the last moments of the former emperor. Nogami has apparently felt it necessary to take each set of characters as they appear in different combinations and each place in which the action occurs as a different act. The opening scene between the _waki-zure_ and _kyōgen_ actor who is his attendant is so brief and relatively unimportant that it hardly justifies being called an act. The same might almost be said of the two _dan_, called _ha_ and _kyū_, making up the second act; still, the conversation and exchange of _uta_ between the _shite_ and her ladies, though brief, are important in idea and mood. The greatest problems lie in the second half of the play. While it is possible to say that it follows the general form of the Noh play, since it has _rongi_, _kuri-sashi-kuse_, and a _katari_ as central and basic features, it has more. The "more" can be thought of in terms of characters: the retired emperor Go-Shirakawa has a role far more important that a _tsure_; the second _waki_ is an unusual role since the same _waki_ usually continues from the first to the second act, but it is a small role; and the roles of the two ladies in waiting, both _shite-zure_, are longer than usual for _tsure_. Or the "more" may be thought of in terms of speeches and songs, which are more extensive than in most plays. However, they may be considered to be a slight diversification as well as intensification of feeling. Unlike Funa Benkei, there is no double action in Ōhara Goko. The empress is the shite of both parts and the emphasis of the plot--and text--is on her recollection of the fall of the Heike, particularly the death of the young emperor Antoku. Bursting at the seams it may be, but the play could not be divided into two, as might conceivably happen to Funa Benkei. Yoshino Shizuka likewise is analyzed by Nogami as having three acts, but since the shite and waki are the same in all three parts, the structural problems are not too difficult.

Zeami's Nishikigi[20] and Semimaru[21] may serve to represent the plays of the fourth group. Nogami treated the one as a double jo-ha-kyū structure, and the second as having a single jo-ha-kyū base. Both begin with the waki entering the stage, singing the shidai followed by a nanori, and michiyuki. In Nishikigi the waki and tsure are priests; in Semimaru the waki and companions are courtiers and what serves as the travel song is called an age-uta.

The shite enters next in the first play, a man accompanied by the tsure, the woman he loved in vain, and they sing a shidai, sashi, sage-uta, and age-uta before beginning their mondō with the waki in the third dan, called the ha section. The fourth dan or kyū section then gives the shite a chance to tell his story, the chorus to sing about the burial mound, and the shite and tsure then to disappear.

In Semimaru the waki and shite-zure, the courtier and Prince Semimaru, discuss the latter's sad fate in their mondō, which completed the jo section, and then continue talking as the courtier gives Semimaru suitable clothes for the hut in which he is to be abandoned, and then leaves. After a brief speech by the kyōgen actor, a retainer who offers to serve the abandoned prince, the ha section starts with the entrance of the shite, the prince's sister, Sakagami, singing an issei and dancing a kakeri, continuing with the chorus's age-uta. The second ha section begins as he describes his playing on the lute, while his sister listens; she recognizes him, and in the kakeai they greet and discuss their situations. The ha section contains the kuri-sashi-kuse sequence (this time an iguse, not a danced kuse). The play concludes with a kyū section which is made up of a rongi and their chanted farewells in which the prince urges his half-mad sister to visit him again, and they separate weeping. Different as it is, the scene has something of the strange power of Ophelia's mad-scene and the scene at the graveside. The performance I saw last summer was one of the most moving theatrical experiences I have ever had.

Nishikigi is as remarkable a play, but the double jo-ha-kyū
analysis seems to me unsatisfactory. What has been described above
as the opening of the play seems too slight to bear the labels jo-ha-
kyū, and what follows--described below--is clearly the end of the
intensification and the complete kyū or rapid close, rather than the
cycle of jo-ha-kyū. What follows is a brief ai-kyōgen, after which
the priests sing the machi-utai, called the jo of the second part of
the play. Then, in the ha section, the shite speaks from the burial
mound and the tsure from the shite pillar; they discuss their plight
and feelings with the waki, then re-enact their ill-fated love in
the kuri-sashi-kuse sequence, concluding with a haya-mai or rapid
dance. In the kyū section the dance continues and the chorus sings
a kiri or fast song, describing their fate. Rearrangement of the play
into the same general pattern as Semimaru would better represent the
essential structure.

Funa Benkei,[22] Ikari Katsuki,[23] Eboshi Ori,[24] and Taniko,[25]
among the fifth group of plays, are almost two plays, though only
the first two have been analyzed by Nogami as double jo-ha-kyū in
structure. In all four plays the shite of the first and second parts
are totally different persons. They are related by plot and performed
by the same shite actor, but they are not represented as "temporary"
and "true" forms of the chief character, as is usually the case.
Structurally the first part of the play is a complete dramatic action
with dancing or mimed action, sufficient to be a Noh play in its own
right or needing little development to become one; the second half
could be similarly treated. They are late plays or have usually been
assigned to the later period, author and dates unknown. Although
they use the elements regularly used to make up a Noh play, they
seem to be breaking out and groping beyond, becoming almost a
different genre.

For the most part, however, the forty-nine plays in the fifth
group are simple and regular in structure. Most are two-act or two-
part plays involving the change in the shite from a "temporary" to a
"true" form, and Nogami regularly puts the second act in the kyū
section. In Kurama Tengu,[26] for example, the shite is a wandering
priest who announces his arrival at the Kurama Temple to view the
flowers. In the second dan, the first part of ha, he is a spectator
only, while a kyōgen actor delivers an invitation to the waki, the
priest of the temple, to go view flowers; he does, taking along the
children who are students at the temple, including Ushiwaka (the young
Yoshitsune, played by a kokata). In the third dan, which is the second

in the <u>ha</u> section, the <u>kyōgen</u> actor urges that the <u>shite</u> be sent from the scene. The <u>waki</u> suggests instead leaving the scene to the <u>shite</u> and departs with all the children except the <u>kokata</u>. In the fourth <u>dan</u>, the <u>shite</u> and <u>kokata</u> talk together in the <u>mondō</u> form, and the chorus closes the second part of the <u>ha</u> section with a song in praise of hospitality and the <u>shite</u>'s love for the <u>kokata</u>. In the fifth and sixth <u>dan</u> the <u>shite</u> and <u>kokata</u> continue to discuss the situation in prose and song, the former revealing himself as the chief of the <u>tengu</u>, the latter as the scion of the Minamoto family currently studying in the temple.
The second act begins with the <u>kokata</u> awaiting the return of the <u>shite</u> in his true form, though not actually singing a <u>machi-utai</u>. The <u>shite</u> enters and announces himself, but not in the <u>shidai</u> or <u>issei</u> form; he continues his exchanges with the <u>kokata</u> and chorus in prose and song, the high point being a <u>katari</u> or prose narration accompanied by miming. In a dance called the <u>hataraki</u>, the <u>shite</u> completes his promised teaching of military secrets to the young Yoshitsune, and the chorus in the final <u>kiri</u>, or fast song, expresses the <u>shite</u>'s promise that the Minamoto clan will be triumphant, and he will protect the young hero.

Other plays, like <u>Momiji-gari</u>,[27] utilize the standard elements: the entrance of the <u>waki</u> with the <u>michiyuki</u>; the entrance of the <u>shite</u> with prose and song which set the theme of the play; the development of the relationship of <u>waki</u> and <u>shite</u> through varied prose and verse forms and with the aid of the chorus; the <u>kuri-sashi-kusemai</u> sequence which brings the play to its highest point of verse, dramatic, and dance expression; and the closing rapid dance and song which bring the play to its fast close. Although the interruption caused by the <u>naka-iri</u> and the changed form of the <u>shite</u> cause the term "act" to be used--and in one play, <u>Take no Yuki</u>,[28] Nogami has divided the whole into seven acts!--the basic structure does not change. In most of Zeami's plays, the five sections referred to above (basically those Zeami himself suggested), are defined by the song and/or prose forms used. Most clearly, the third <u>ha</u> section is the spot for the <u>kuri-sash</u> <u>kusemai</u> sequence of song and dance. Professor Bohner has pointed out some twenty-three variations of this sequence, depending on what forms are omitted or included and who sings various parts, and even the fact that fifty-seven plays have no <u>kuse</u>.[29] However, even when later writers--or Zeami himself--do not use these precise forms, substitutes functioning in the same way are used. Thus a basic structure may be clearly discerned.

The basic structure is a lyric one, which is made clearer, I believe, by translating <u>jo</u>, <u>ha</u>, and <u>kyū</u> as I have done in most instance above as "introduction," "intensification," and "rapid close." The usual translation, "introduction," "development," and "climax," suggests a more intellectualized, Aristotelian understanding of the structure. It seems to me that the lengthy series of analyses above, even though largely formal in nature, illustrate this point. These are lyric plays whose single impulse is lyric, an intensification of the central emotion by enhancing the poetry, music and dance until the whole comes to a rapid close. The enhancement of verse can be seen in the texts themselves, in the almost baroque decoration, the complexity of rhetorical devices used, whereas the enhancement of the music and dance must be felt in the performance. Another way to say this, perhaps, is to point out that no new facet or change of character is revealed; no new argument or general understanding of the play demands a reversal. Zeami specified from the beginning that the materials of the plays should be familiar. Background of character and plot must already be understood by the audience. Modern viewers of Noh plays discover this in reverse (unconsciously at least) when they see a Noh play for the first time. Elaborate background information in the printed program or provided by friends leads one to expect grand and complex events on stage, but, comparatively speaking, nothing happens. On inquiry one finds that most of it happened before the play started; it is all "understood"; the viewer is seeing a quintessentialized emotion, recollected in tranquility. This is less true of group four plays, but the generalization may stand.

However, it is not easy to see why the Chinese character _ha_ meaning "break," "tear," and the like, should have the meaning here of "intensification." Zeami uses it as a matter of course, without explanation. Yokomichi and Omote more or less neglect the term in favor of a different sort of analysis--purely serial. Nogami, who so consistently uses the term in his analysis, gives only a sort of etymological interpretation, which helps but little. Sanari Kentarō in his seven volume _Yōkyoku Taikan_ (A Complete Collection of Noh Plays) identifies song types but does not analyze the plays into _jo-ha-kyū_ structure and simply quotes Zeami. It is necessary, then, to go back to Zeami, who in the second section of the _Nōsakushō_ merely says, "The first _dan_ of the _ha_ section consists of the appearance of the _shite_, from the _issei_ through one song."[30]

This is in fact a clue, but at several removes. The term _ha_ comes from, or to be more circumspect, seems possibly to be related to, a term used in the analysis of the Chinese _ta-ch'ü_ or "long songs" popular in the Sung dynasty in China. The term used there is _ju-p'o_, which may be read <u>ire-ha</u> in Japanese. In the Sung entertainment for the term indicated "the entrance of the dancer," which is precisely Zeami's use of the term, the entrance of the <u>shite</u> or actor-dancer.

Feeling that there must be some relationship between the Japanese Noh drama and Chinese drama since the Japanese had borrowed so many of the entertainments of the Chinese court to use in their own, I was fascinated by Shichiri Zukei's <u>Yōkyoku to Genkyoku</u> (The Japanese Noh Play and Yüan Drama) which appeared in 1940 but gained no adherents among Japanese scholars. Shichiri's exhaustive listing of similarities between the Noh and Yüan drama showed more than mere coincidences, and his research into possible opportunities for borrowing from China showed they were ample. Nevertheless, the timing was not quite right, and there are too many and obvious differences between these two highly polished dramatic forms to permit direct borrowing.

Clearly, what was needed was some sort of intermediate form. Of course, various <u>t'ao-shu</u> or "song sets" existed, but they seemed too formless. The analysis of the <u>ta-ch'ü</u>[31] provides the form and its comparable use of the term ha an explanation of the use of it in the Noh drama. The ta-ch'ü are described and illustrated in books like Liu Yung-chi's <u>Sung-tai ko-wu chü-ch'ü lu-yao</u> (Essentials of the Song-Dance Drama of the Sung Dynasty)[32] and Wang Kuo-wei's <u>T'ang Sung ta-ch'ü k'ao</u> (Examination of T'ang and Sung <u>ta-ch'ü</u>),[33] but it is the former which gives an idealized chart of the form:

I. <u>San-hsü</u>, Japanese reading <u>sanjo</u>, has six parts but the beat is not introduced until the "head song" which begins the
II. <u>P'ai-p'ien</u>, which has ten parts, the ninth called <u>tien</u>, which acts as a bridge with ever increasing beats to the
III. <u>Ju-p'o</u>, the entrance of the dancers. Of the seven parts the third is called <u>ch'ien kun</u>, "first flowing" (as of water); the fourth is <u>shih ts'ui</u>, "real urgency" (quickness); the fifth is <u>chung kun</u>, "middle flowing" (suggesting accelerando); the sixth, <u>hsieh p'o</u>, "slow the beat"; and seventh, <u>sha kun</u>, "final flowing." Chang Yen, <u>Tz'u-yuan</u>, specifies that in <u>ch'ien kun</u> and <u>chung kun</u>, "first and middle flowing," there is one beat to six words, whereas in <u>sha kun</u>, "final flowing," there is one beat to three.[34] It is clear that from <u>ch'ien kun</u> on to the end of the entertainment there is the same effect as in the <u>kyū</u> section of the Noh drama, a rapid accelerando and fast close. The character <u>sha</u> slightly resembles <u>kyū</u> but seems not to be related to it in meaning; however, since <u>kyū</u> means swift and hurried, it suits

the function of the section.

Japanese visitors to Sung China could easily have brought back a clear idea of the ta-ch'ü, even if not the texts themselves, and the idea could have influenced the development of the Noh form in the Kamakura period. Perhaps even more important than these relationships is the fact that the Yüan plays, the Noh drama, and Peking Opera are similar in that the lyrics and lyric intensification are the primary elements in the play. Although Yüan plays and Peking Opera are larger and more complex forms than the Noh, their basic structure is similar.

FOOTNOTES

1. Nose Asaji, ed., <u>Zeami jūroku-bu shū hyōshaku</u> [Zeami's six-teen books, collected and annotated], 2 vols. Tokyo: Iwanami Shoten, 1940, I, 590. Referred to hereafter as ZJBS.

2. <u>ZJBS</u>, pp. 591-2.

3. <u>ZJBS</u>, pp. 596-7.

4. <u>ZJBS</u>, p. 601.

5. <u>ZJBS</u>, pp. 604-5. This is the source of statements in the pre-ceding four paragraphs.

6. Cf. Noël Péri, <u>Le Nō</u>. Tokyo: Maison Franco-Japonaise, 1944, and Donald Keene, <u>Nō, The Classical Theatre of Japan</u>. Tokyo and Palo Alto: Kodansha International, 1966. References to Bohner and Minagawa appear below.

7. Hermann Bohner, <u>Nō, Einführung</u>, "Mitteilungen" der Deutschen Gesellschaft fur Natur- und Völkerkunde Ostasiens, Supplement-band XXIV (Tokyo, 1959), pp. 211-12.

8. <u>Japanese Noh Drama, Ten Plays</u>. Tokyo: The Nippon Gakujutsu Shinkōkai, 1955, pp. 5-17.

9. Arthur Waley, <u>The Nō Plays of Japan</u>. London: George Allen and Unwin, 1921, p. 218.

10. <u>Ibid</u>., p. 224.

11. <u>Ibid</u>., p. 226.

12. Minagawa Tatsuo, "Japanese Noh Music," <u>The Journal of the American Musicological Society</u>, X, 3 (1957), 183-5.

13. Ezra Pound, <u>The Translations</u>. New York: New Directions Press, n.d., p. 256.

14. It was in fact both the first piece I studied and then translated, <u>Tsurukame</u>, "The Crane and the Tortoise," <u>The Husk</u> (May 1955).

15. Nogami Toyoichirō, Yōkyoku Zenshū [Comprehensive collection of Noh plays], 6 vols. Tokyo: Chuō Koron Sha, 1936, I, pp. 357-62.

16. Nogami, V. pp. 435-56; Yokomichi Mario and Omote Akira, Yōkyoku shū [Collection of Noh plays], 2 vols. Tokyo: Iwanami Shoten, 1960, II, pp. 150-61; Japanese Noh Drama, pp. 161-82.

17. Nogami, II, pp. 115-30 and pp. 175-88 respectively; Japanese Noh Drama, pp. 37-55 and pp. 57-73 respectively.

18. Nogami, II, pp. 235-46; Japanese Noh Drama, pp. 75-89.

19. Nogami, III, pp. 125-42; Donald Keene, ed., Twenty Plays of the Nō Theatre. New York and London: Columbia University Press, 1970, pp. 281-97.

20. Nogami, IV, pp. 217-32; Keene, Twenty Plays, pp. 81-97.

21. Nogami, III, pp. 393-406; Keene, Twenty Plays, pp. 99-114.

22. Cf. note 16.

23. Nogami, V, pp. 457-68.

24. Nogami, VI, pp. 247-72; Waley, pp. 102-114.

25. Nogami, V, pp. 567-88; Keene, Twenty Plays, pp. 315-331.

26. Nogami, VI, pp. 171-84; Gaston Renondeau, Nō, 2 vols. Tokyo: Maison Franco-Japonaise, 1954, II, pp. 449-75.

27. Nogami, V, pp. 487-98; Japanese Noh Drama, II. Tokyo: Nippon Gakujutsu Shinkōkai, 1959, pp. 141-56.

28. Nogami, IV, pp. 455-70.

29. Bohner, pp. 234-36.

30. Sanari Kentarō, Yōkyoku Taikan [A complete collection of Noh plays], 7 vols. Tokyo: Meiji Shoin, 1954, "Head" Volume, p. 229.

31. Cf. comparative chart in "Discussion of Roy Teele's Paper."

32. Liu Yung-chi, <u>Sung-tai ko-wu chü-ch'ü lu-yao</u> [Essentials of the song-dance drama of the Sung Dynasty], (Shanghai: 1957).

33. Wang Kuo-wei, <u>T'ang Sung ta-ch'ü k'ao</u> [Examination of T'ang and Sung <u>ta-ch'ü</u>]. Taipei: I-wen Printing Co., 1964.

34. Liu Yung-chi, pp. 23-25. I am grateful for notes from Steven West, Assistant Professor of Chinese, University of Arizona.

BIBLIOGRAPHY

Bohner, Hermann. No, Einführung, "Mitteilungen" der Deutschen Gesellschaft für Natur-und Völkerkunde Ostasiens, Supplementband XXIV. Tokyo, 1959.

Ichiri, Zukei. Yōkyoku to Genkyoku [The Japanese Noh play and Yüan drama]. 1940.

Japanese Noh Drama, II. Tokyo: Nippon Gakujutsu Shinkōkai, 1959.

Japanese Noh Drama, Ten Plays. Tokyo: Nippon Gakujutsu Shinkōkai, 1955.

Keene, Donald. Nō, The Classical Theatre of Japan. Tokyo and Palo Alto: Kodansha International, 1966.

————. Twenty Plays of the Nō Theatre. New York and London: Columbia University Press, 1970.

Liu, Yung-chi. Sung-tai ko-wu lu-yao [Essentials of the song-dance drama of the Sung Dynasty]. Shanghai, 1957.

Minagawa, Tatsuo. "Japanese Noh Music." The Journal of the American Musicological Society. Vol. X, no. 3, 1957.

Nogami, Toyoichirō. Yōkyoku Zenshū [Comprehensive collection of Noh plays]. Tokyo: Chuo Koron Sha, 6 vols., 1936.

Péri, Noël. Le Nō. Tokyo: Maison Franco-Japonaise, 1944.

Pian, R. C. Sonq Dynasty Musical Sources and Their Interpretation. Cambridge: Harvard University Press, 1967.

Pound, Ezra. The Translations. New York: New Directions Press.

Renondeau, Gaston. Nō. Tokyo: Maison Franco-Japonaise, 2 vols., 1954.

Sanari, Kentarō. Yōkyoku taikan [A complete collection of Noh plays]. Tokyo: Meiji Shoin, 7 vols, 1954.

Tsurukame. "The Crane and the Tortoise," trans. by Roy E. Teele.
    The Husk. May 1955.

Waley, Arthur. The Nō Plays of Japan. London: George Allen and
    Unwin, 1921.

Wang, Kuo-wei. T'ang Sung ta-ch'ü k'ao [Examination of T'ang and
    Sung ta-ch'ü]. Taipei: I-wen Printing Company, 1964.

Yokomichi, Mario and Omote, Akira. Yōkyoku shū [Collection of Noh
    plays]. Tokyo: Iwanami Shoten, 2 vols., 1960.

Zeami jūroku-bu shū hyōshaku [Zeami's sixteen books, collected and
    annotated], ed. by Nose Asaji. Tokyo: Iwanami Shoten, 1940.

DISCUSSION OF ROY E. TEELE'S PAPER

Teele: I didn't do what I really intended. I intended to start where I ended. Bothered with problems of structure (the jo-ha-kyū mold has never completely convinced me), I found myself going through play after play which culminated in a huge stack of analysis. Eventually I decided this approach was wrong and I threw out the translation of jo-ha-kyū as "introduction, development and conclusion." I now feel that "introduction and expansion" is a better description. Kyū isn't a conclusion of a climax; it is nearer to a close. The formal Aristotelian concept of beginning, middle and end is really not compatible with the Noh form.

Sesar: I felt the same way. The form has to be interpreted in several senses. If you think of jo-ha-kyū in terms of the play, in some sense you can think of introduction, development and climax. But since they are musical terms, there ought to be a way of defining them textually, as we did with Yüan Drama. I think they represent shifting musical moods.

Malm: I don't think that they were originally musical terms. They were related to the bugaku dance, so they bear a choreographic relationship too.

Sesar: But the dance was never performed without gagaku accompaniment.

Crump: To what does the kyū part refer--in either the music or in the dance?

Sesar: Well, the concept of beginning, middle and end arises with the musical shift from jo which is quiet and slow. That is to say, I have noticed that every play seems to intensify gradually and that is consistent with the rough pattern of the play. In this respect jo-ha-kyū, viewed musically, may represent a shifting from one mood to another. The kyū is dramatically short and musically swift.

Crump: The kyū or "fast" must refer to something other than the content.

Sesar: The jo-ha-kyū can be viewed as a literary structure as
            well as a musical one. In that sense jo-ha-kyū repre-
            sents a beginning, middle and a close; it does conform
            to the Aristotelian concept and does give the play a log-
            ical structure.

Teele: We must take care that the ha section does not become
            confused with a sense of development. It is an intensi-
            fication of mood and does not increase the complexity of
            the play. Intensification occurs probably in both the mood
            and the music. In many, many plays the kyū section is
            very short, in some cases as short as twenty or twenty-
            five lines.

Crump: Isn't the ha section the only place that you can undertake
            lengthening, if you are intent on doing so?

Pian: It's an easier place to stretch.

Crump: Then "extension" still holds true as a description of ha.

Pian: As I read your paper I think of the ritual songs of Chiang
            K'uei. [1] The beginning is a welcoming of the gods, followed
            by the traveling and then the sending off at the close.

Crump: Are the songs tz'u?

Pian: Chiang is imitating local customs.

Crump: What does he call the forms?

Pian: I can't recall at the moment.

Crump: Are they included in his tz'u collection?

Pian: Yes, they are there; they are called ceremonial songs.
            The sequence he uses is strongly reminiscent of what we
            are dealing with in the Noh.

Teele: Structurally speaking, it certainly could apply.

Pian: The building up of ritualistic dances to a flurry at the
            close seems to be a universal characteristic.

Teele: Well, there are many different kinds of dances, and the feeling evoked by them varies from play to play.

Sesar: The Noh as a ritual would be an interesting pursuit. Particular plays are performed for special occasions even today. This is true, too, in regional Noh. <u>Tsuru-kame</u> is part of the New Year's festivities every year. Rituals are theatrical anyway.

Teele: I'm not denying that, but I would point out that this is theatre in which the religious element is relatively slight.

Sesar: I feel that theatre is essentially ceremonial. Modern theatre has lost this quality today. Plays today are performed according to production schedules. The time in which a drama was produced is important too. Consider the slapstick and farcical varieties of plays; their contents were not religious, but they were usually performed on ceremonial occasions nonetheless.

Crump: That's the fiesta component of dramatic shows.

Sesar: Just because theatre has become a diffused art today shouldn't influence the way we talk about it. I think the distinctions between theatre and drama have arisen only in the past 100 years.

Pian: This is precisely the problem in analyzing Peking Opera. Take a story like <u>K'ung Cheng Chi</u>: in the end, after K'ung-ming has executed Ma Su (someone he is very fond of for unclear reasons), he is very sad. At the end of the play General Chao Yün asks him why he is sad. K'ung-ming has to lie. He says he is sad because he is thinking of Liu Pei, who gave him instructions he did not follow. Against Liu Pei's advice he trusted Ma Su. The opera ends with a great banquet in honor of General Chao Yün, which spoils the whole drama. The only reason I can think of for ending the play in this way is the habit of ending the drama with a theatrical bang and a flourish of pageantry. You can't end with a man in tears.

Crump: The same is true of Yüan drama, but not for the Noh. In Yüan drama the peak of excitement comes in the third act and then slides downhill in ceremonial trivia. This corresponds fully with the Wayang Kulit[2] of Southeast Asia. Whether you have the height of ecstasy or the depths of despair, the violent emotions must come before the end and there must be a reaffirmation or a coasting downhill to a calm close. That, I think, may be the vestigial remains of ritual. People shouldn't leave the theatre with charged-up emotional batteries; too much could happen.

Sesar: If we judge a Noh play by its text, generally speaking the performance ends on a high note; but in terms of the performance itself, the actor leaves the stage in the same slow fashion he uses to enter. This serves the function of calming. I can't recall whether or not music continues after he departs.

Malm: It doesn't. There is total silence.

Teele: Many plays actually end in the suffix "-keri" signifying that an affair has been completed. Dale and I were talking last evening about another facet that fascinated me, the structure of the ta-ch'ü. I had been looking for some way to indicate that the Japanese might have been influenced by Chinese entertainments. In the Sung ta-ch'ü the terms jo-ha-kyū are used. There is a set of songs with forms that appear similar to the sashi/kuri/kusemai in unmeasured meter, followed by the dance. I feel that the ta-ch'ü is, in some fashion, a crucial turning point. Japanese travelers in China might have witnessed these performances and carried them back to Japan where they found their way into the Noh. Of course, it would be naive to say this is the prototype, but I have been looking for something like this for a long time and discovered it last evening. This chart makes my trip here a success. (laughter) (See Chart I)

Sesar: From hearing the comments made yesterday on Vietnamese music,[3] I feel that something of this nature may be characteristic of all Asian drama. The basic roots may not be possible to uncover, but the overwhelming similarity points to something which became really widespread.

CHART 1

	unmeasured or slow	meter begins	tempo accelerates →	high point of dramatic tension	meter breaks down	return of rapid tempo
Sung ta-ch'ü	hsü san-hsü (unmeasured)	p'ai-p'ien (meter begins)	p'o ju-p'o kun — dancer enters — tremolos begin — tempo acceleration?	hsieh-p'ai	meter closes	sha-kun a closing tremolo? — rapid tempo?
Noh drama	jo waki enters (perhaps unmeasured)	ha shite enters (meter begins) — 1st dan — 2nd dan	question and answer section — tempo acceleration? — 3rd dan	high point of the drama — 4th dan	(meter closes)	kyū closes in a fast piece — kiri — 5th dan
Yüan drama: "Nine Turns on the Peddler" suite	Huo-lang-erh Chiu Chuan (perhaps unmeasured)	Turns 2 and 3 slow arias	Turns 4 and 5 ? — tempo acceleration?	Turn 6 fastest tempo reached	Turn 7 begins to slow in tempo	Turn 8 ? — Turn 9 after phrase 3 music is unmeasured... last 4 phrases accelerate to a flurry — Coda ?
Peking Opera	tao-pan the interjective aria free and rhapsodic	man-pan the lyric aria slow, ornate melody in 4/4 time	yüan-pan the narrative aria medium-paced with less ornamentation 2/4 time	erh-liu (acceleration) a lyric, unornamented aria that accelerates toward the close but ends in a free, unmeasured section		liu-shui-pan a fast animated aria where tempo builds to a breaking point after which the "breaking loose" occurs and tempo disintegrates

As the chart implies, there seem to be structural similarities between the Sung ta-ch'ü and the Noh drama that go beyond the borrowing of the terms jo-ha-kyū and that can be extended to Yüan drama suites and even to Peking Opera. The example from Peking Opera is not one that can be found in every drama, but Professor Pian confirms that this general framework is not misleading. We know that there were tempo changes in Yüan drama suites and that the first aria (or the first two) in the suite were unmeasured. What we observe in the suite "Nine Turns on the Peddler" is encouraging.

Crump: The ta-ch'ü is in the right place at the right time. Japanese travelers were there and the ta-ch'ü was at its height.

Pian: What about gagaku that was transported to Japan much earlier?

Teele: This is the court tradition of China, ya-yüeh.

Sesar: I bought a copy of Yōkyoku to Genkyoku,[4] and in looking over the bibliography I discerned that it was an academic wrangle. In Japan there is a controversy which maintains that Zeami regarded Noh as a purely Japanese art. Discussion of influences, therefore, always signals to the Japanese that their claim to originality has been snatched away again. I think the answer is quite simple: I believe that there were some influences, and if they can be traced, all well and good. But it should be kept in proper perspective; in terms of the Noh art, it doesn't count in large measure.

Crump: To link it to Yüan Drama is not plausible because the dates are wrong, but the time for borrowing comes out just right for the Sung period.

Sesar: It may be that terms only were borrowed after the forms were set and the tradition was established.

Teele: My teacher, Konishi, studied this extensively and wrote a well-known article on the subject. He discovered in the archives that the masks which grace the theatre of today are all elegant and beautiful. He further discovered that in the early period some very realistic masks were used, faces of men who really looked like fishermen, women who looked like ordinary women, etc. In light of this, the question of origins is really one which should be reopened.

Sesar: Speaking from the point of view of comparative literature, there is a vast difference between the Noh play Yō Ki-hi and the Yüan drama Wu-t'ung Yü. However, since one act in the Yüan version deals with the spirit journey, I think some interesting comparisons could be made between these two versions.

Crump: There has also been a lot of loose talk about the Noh mask
          and Chinese theatrical make-up. The Chinese stage face
          has never been anything but make-up. There is only one
          exception and that is the god. Gods had masks with jew-
          eled eyes and gilt faces.

Pian: And the T'iao-chia-kuan is purely ritualistic. He is the
          god who comes on stage before all performances with
          small flags acknowledging rich patrons, important person-
          ages, and the audience in general; this is all completely
          outside the drama. He wears a mask. Of course, in to-
          day's Peking Opera even the faces of gods are painted.

Malm: My question, stimulated by all these remarks, is how much
          can we trust the neat, clean theory and nomenclature of the
          Noh? If you search around in the writings of Zeami, you
          will encounter a few of these terms, but I wonder if terms
          like age-uta and sage-uta were the original names of these
          sections?

Pian: Are you asking if these terms were originally used by
          Zeami himself?

Malm: I have not personally consulted the oldest surviving Noh
          drama texts to be able to answer that. I hoped some of
          you Asian specialists who do the reading could answer that.

Teele: One problem I had in studying the texts of three major edi-
          tions (Nogami,[5] Sanari[6] and Yokomichi[7]) was that terms
          in the various texts vary considerably. There is a lack
          of consistency. Places where the dan sections are divided
          also vary.

Malm: It happens that the leader of the group now touring in the
          United States was my teacher. I took lessons in matsuri-
          bayashi with him. Since I had studied kabuki, I knew all
          the drum patterns, but I made a fatal error one day while
          playing. I encountered a pattern and asked what its name
          was. Later, when I asked how old the name was, he said:
          "Oh, I named it myself." He was aware that drum pat-
          terns in kabuki and Noh have names, so in keeping with
          the tradition he made up names for his patterns, and they
          were christened as recently as 1968. So, in using mate-

rials one must be cautious. It is difficult to say sometimes how much is historically traceable and how much
has been added.

Crump: Roy, you have done a great deal of collating and combining
through these texts. In the final analysis do you find your
results are convincing?

Teele: Yes. The Noh texts available to us are all late texts.
Konishi points out that many manuscripts, particularly
those in the Kanze Archives, have never been published.
There isn't enough money to collate them. Konishi has
shown how many texts have been cleaned up and polished
in a linguistic and literary sense. In this respect we
can't really go all the way back to the early times to
assess the changes that have occurred, and many things
have happened to the plays in the course of time.

Johnson: I think that there is another possible and important missing
link and that is Korea. A Korean expert should have been
a member of our group. I know about and I have seen one
performance of an entertainment that was pretty well stamp
out during the Japanese occupation: a mask dance entertain
ment that resembles what we see in ta-ch'ü, with dancing,
singing and spoken dialogue. There were two or three people performing at one time, no more than three and I don't
know if any texts survive . . .

Sesar: Donald Keene mentioned the same thing. He thinks that
one of the important sources is Korea.

Johnson: These entertainments may be as old as the Noh and Korea
is the normal course of transmission.

Sesar: What you point out very clearly is that there has been considerable variation of form and that variation seems to be
a kind of attempt to break out of fixed forms. Zeami himself indicates in his prescriptions, although not in rigid detail, that he had a sense of a general formal pattern. This
is clear in his classification of the plays. The first three
classifications fit that general pattern. The fifth group also
conforms to it, but in the fourth group you can see an attempt to branch out of it.

Teele: These are problems of analysis.   One play in the Nogami
          text has seven acts.

Crump: Do trilogies or suites ever occur?   Constellations?

Sesar: None that I can think of that were related thematically.

Teele: Zeami did specify that there should be comic farces
          (kyōgen) between plays.   In this respect he was aware of
          the need for humor sandwiched in between the lyric plays.
          There is an example of the play of the stone boat followed
          by the kyōgen farce about the stone god, which could con-
          ceivably be put together.   I would like to examine old pro-
          grams to see what plays were combined in performance.
          Without a thorough examination I can't reach any conclu-
          sions.   It was the mode to perform five Noh plays at one
          time.

Pian: Your comment about kyōgen becoming more and more a
          part of the story is interesting.

Teele: But this happens in only one or two plays.   I deliberately
          selected Tsuru-kame because it was an extreme example
          of a purely nondramatic dance-play and Funa Benkei too,
          because it is about as far as one can go in this direction.
          Are there any that are more dramatic than that?

Sesar: It may well be that the first three classes of plays were
          used as openers and the kyōgen was introduced later.   I
          think that the main part of the program is over after the
          first three plays: the religious play, the god-play, fol-
          lowed by the woman- or warrior-plays, which are the most
          moving.   The comic interlude follows, then a nice genzai-
          mono in turn, with a ghost-play at the end for those who
          want to remain for the whole program.

Teele: I have speculated that Zeami recognized the need for the
          comic element and in addition, sometimes a suite of plays
          were analyzed into jo-ha-kyū: the god-play is the jo, the
          next three plays are the ha and the kiri-nō[8] is the conclu-
          sion, or the kyū.

Pian: Another fact that struck me was that the description of a past event is dominant in these themes. The narration of events gone by seems to be so important. Miming is also a way of describing something that occurred in the past. It is more like a narrative of past events than it is the acting out of a drama, a story unfolding. I am suggesting by this that the origins of Noh were narrative origins.

Sesar: Zeami described this <u>kusemai</u> as music arising from both words and deeds. In other words he felt that it was suitable not only for relating a tale but for dramatic purposes as well. The origins of the <u>kusemai</u> were not only in the narrative, but the dance as well. It was a kind of dance-narrative.

Teele: <u>Katari</u> is a special prose-narrative form which I did not mention. It is a <u>kotoba</u>, a heightened speech form. In this case the emphasis is on the lyric aspect and not the narrative. In the Noh play the distinction between the two is felt. Pure narrative takes one form; lyric moments take another.

Pian: Well, even lyric moments (i.e., arias) bring the drama to a temporary halt.

Teele: But the primary element in the Noh is the lyric moment. The narration serves like a mounting for a stone.

Johnson: The same is true of Yüan drama. The aria is the opportunity to burst into the lyric moment. The plot never advances.

Crump: This can become a fault. In the Ming drama, where word play, puns and literary alliteration become the whole excuse for the drama, you have the most threadbare arrangement of bodies on the stage imaginable.

Sesar: You mention on page 196 that the Nogami text contains a brief opening speech by a <u>kyōgen</u> actor, which is unusual. There are several of these, though admittedly few in number. The interesting aspect is that most plays which open with a <u>kyōgen</u> deal with Chinese subjects: they are <u>karagoto</u>. This is my point.

Seiobo and Tōbōsaku open with a kyōgen. Tsuru-kame
opens with one too. Kantan, Kanyōkyū, Kōtei and Sanshō
all begin with a kyōgen speech. The waki opens with a
nanori section in prose in place of singing, similar to the
kyōgen opening in the following plays: Kappo, Shōjō, Taihei
(all karagoto plays). It is obvious that in plays dealing with
Chinese subjects it was deemed suitable to open the play in
this way. This is why I felt that these kinds of plays were
being handled in special ways.

Pian: Your structural scheme amazes me in how similar it is
to Peking Opera. The shidai in fixed rhythm is like the
ting-ch'ang shih. This is described by the term free-
rhythm. This is just like the yin-tzu in Peking Opera,
one lone line which is drawn out. Then there follows a
nanori, a self-introduction, which is parallel to the pao-
ming of Peking Opera. The entire sequence is the same.

Crump: Then we run into trouble. Travel songs don't show up.

Pian: Yes, they do. The tao-pan which is sung off stage is
perfect. The tao-pan is sung even when an actor travels
back from a fainting spell.

Crump: I was going to say that Yüan drama is an excuse not only
for establishing a series of lyrical peaks, but perhaps
most common, most elaborate, most lavish and most lively
pieces of all are the song journeys.

Johnson: Can you ever write tao-pan with the character which means
road?

Pian: Yes, and people argue all the time about it . . . wait . . .
no! that is a word in the fourth tone. The real word is a
third tone. It is interchangeable with "upside-down tao,"
which proves that it is a third tone.

You mentioned chanted prose, speech and recitation. How
do they differ?

Teele: I was careless. They all refer to the same style. It is
a kind of chant that never bursts into a melodic line. I'm
speaking of kotoba.

Pian: In performance I note that the stress is all evened out, and something approaching a monotone is reached in terms of stress.

Crump: Well, how does heightened speech sound?

Pian: Well, suddenly my mind goes all blank.

Johnson: Is it this: <u>hao-t'ien-ch'i yeh</u>! (mimics a female line from k'un-ch'ü)

Pian: That's really just a signal to the orchestra to begin the aria. It is called <u>chiao-pan</u>, "to call the <u>pan</u>."

There are really three kinds of delivery. Recitation of a verse at the beginning of the play when the actor appears on stage is one of them. The final syllables are elongated into a melismatic passage. Then there is prose style, by which the character reports who he is. Finally, heightened or elevated speech, which for me is a very general term that could include all these kinds of delivery, including some types of arias.

Sesar: Some verses in the Noh acquire their names because of the kind of music to which they are sung. <u>Issei</u> is one example. Isn't there something equivalent to <u>issei no hayashi</u>? The music therefore is important in determining the manner of delivery.

Pian: How about speech with instrumental background? Does this occur?

Teele: Well, even the <u>katari</u> is normally delivered without background.

Crump: Is there a clapper or a drum used for punctuation? Iris, don't we have speech in Peking Opera which is accented by percussion from time to time?

Pian: Yes, there are different kinds. Most of them are punctuating; some are formulaeic. Take the <u>chiao-t'ou</u> (the cry) for example. It opens with a gong pattern that sounds like this: <u>ch'ing-k'uang-ts'ai-ts'ai-ts'ai</u>. The actor cries out

"Heaven!" and the gongs repeat ch'ing-k'uang-ts'ai-ts'ai-ts'ai, after which the actor cries "Heaven!" again. There can be any number of repeats this way. When it concludes, the percussion punctuates with k'uang-k'uang-ch'ing-k'uang. Speech then follows. This entire sequence is a pattern. When the audience hears the gongs play the opening pattern, it knows the actor is about to call out to Heaven, to his father, etc.

Teele: In the Noh there is something called kakeai but it doesn't have any percussive background. I would call it basically a kotoba, but it does have the term kakeai attached to it. It begins with an extended no, no and then becomes a kotoba. It means to call or greet. I don't know whether Zeami used it or not. That would be valuable to determine.

Pian: You often talk about 5- and 7-syllable lines. Are they stretchable? Can you add extra syllables?

Malm: Yes, as I noted in my example when the beat was delayed.

Pian: That's musical and not verbal.

Malm: You will remember last evening in the lecture that one line was extended to nine and ten beats.

Pian: But isn't that melodic stretching? I'm talking about adding extra words, not nonsense syllables.

Teele: You mean seven becoming eight or nine? That is rare, it is planned in the music.

Pian: Then it is very different from what I'm thinking about.

Crump: Iris means, does the verse hold strictly to five or seven syllables?

Malm: The verse sections? No, they don't.

Johnson: Ch'en-tzu is what we are driving at here. Are there padding words in the texts?

Pian: That's exactly what I mean.

Crump: Well, Japanese is a polysyllabic word language, whereas
            Chinese is a monosyllabic word language, or at least it
            tends in that direction to an overwhelming degree. In
            Chinese we tend to count syllables instead of words.

Sesar: In Japanese, vowels are held over too, so some syllables
            are multiplied by extension.

Malm: Look in my text on page 116. There I have added up all
            the syllables for your comparison.

Pian: But that's peanuts compared to our problems in Yüan dram
            (laughter)

Crump: I'll say. You add two syllables and we add five words.

Malm: (Sings a line from his text, demonstrating a line extended
            to nine beats).

Pian: That is very subtle and you have demonstrated a valuable
            point, that it is being used for dramatic reasons.

Teele: It would be interesting to examine the literary text to see
            if there were textual reasons for extending that line. We
            now have the musical analysis; to have the textual analysis
            would be very useful at this point.

Malm: That is precisely the usefulness of this conference: to cal
            together both musicians and experts in Asian letters to
            share knowledge on these kinds of issues. Here we are
            really being interdisciplinary.

Pian: On page 208 you make comparisons between the Noh and
            Yüan drama. It is interesting that the points you bring
            out--song-dance forms, travel songs, lyric shidai, issei
            forms, self-introductions, poems, etc.--are all the less
            dramatic elements. All the comparable aspects are mostly
            formal or ritualistic and are the less dramatic aspects.

Sesar: But in terms of the Noh they are not less dramatic. Com
            pared to more lively things, they only appear that way. I

relative terms, however, they are equally dramatically powerful.

Pian: You deal with a very skillful manipulation of these patterns in your paper, Carl, for a dramatic purpose. I agree, they are very unusual. It is true of Peking Opera as well, but my point is that in the places where they are comparable . . .

Teele: We have something like the ji-utai, the chorus.

Crump: There are no choruses in Yüan times, but there is in kao-ch'iang of the Szechwan theatre.

Pian: The chorus is interesting. In this spot, it seems to be making a commentary.

Teele: It is always hard to define. Sometimes the Noh chorus is singing what the actor is thinking about or thinking of doing. It is rarely commentary.

Johnson: Where did the Szechwan chorus come from?

Crump: It is obviously heavily dependent on Ming dynasty thematic materials. It is an indigenous form in Szechwan.

Pian: It is simply the Szechwan style.

Malm: You will recall in the historical section in my chapter that I made frequent reference to many instruments which are obviously not just Chinese, but which have Central Asian origins. Lawrence Picken claims to have located Chinese ceremonial (ya-yüeh) tunes as far away as Central Asia.

Crump: I don't recall any leader in the ta-ch'ü or san-ch'ü, but there is one in the Wu-ch'ü and he is called Mr. Bamboo Staff (Chu-kan-tzu). He is the leader of the dance.

Johnson: There were troops of dancers too, both male and female.

Pian: There is no chorus in the Peking Opera. Well, perhaps there is a remnant. I remember one instance where the main character does something which is not quite correct, and the soldiers moan in unison. This happens in the "Ruse of the Empty City" (K'ung Ch'eng Chi). K'ung-ming is trying to think of ways to pardon Ma Su. Each time he goes beyond accepted behavior, the soldiers moan in unison. In "The Trial of Su San," the courtesan, who is being tried for murder (the judge is her former lover), makes an attempt to catch the judge's attention at the close of the trial to see if he recognizes her. He really wants to acknowledge her, but at that moment the guards of the court moan in unison in protest.

Malm: We should recognize that the chorus in the Noh really has its origins in courtly entertainments and originally had nothing to do with theatre at all. In the gagaku, and we all know that gagaku was the football marching band of the T'ang dynasty, they even made formations much like football half time shows of today. I once caught hell for making that comparison in a book. The chorus was the big thing in the court performances and you can find this evidence in illustrations. It didn't come to Japan from Chinese drama, it came from the court.

Crump: But be careful. If Roy is worrying about borrowing from the full-fledged drama, maybe he shouldn't. Perhaps he should go all the way back to what you suggest.

Teele: Well, that's what I would like to do. As you pointed out, these things in Noh had to have origins earlier than Yüan drama because of the time sequence.

Pian: You were discussing the fact that acting roles became numerous in Chinese drama . . .

Teele: I was thinking of all the various types of tan, sheng,[9] etc.

Pian: Actually, it is still limited to the basic roles. Why is the emperor played by the kokata in the Noh drama?

Teele: An exalted personnage should not appear on the stage. But in Tsuru-kame the emperor is played by a shite or a waki--I can't remember clearly.

Sesar: Yes, but he is a foreign emperor. That doesn't count.

Pian: What is the pre-Noh dance that appears on page 196; (quoting) "kuse: a name borrowed from a pre-Noh dance?"

Teele: It was for a popular entertainment at the court. O'Neill makes much of it in his book. There were many kinds of dances that pre-date the Noh, imayō . . .

Sesar: The Kagura[10] dances, the shrine dances . . .

Teele: It is like Iris' lecture yesterday demonstrating all the forms that were incorporated into Peking Opera. Is that correct?

Crump: I don't think Iris meant it quite that way. Peking Opera is probably the end product of that sort of thing, but I wouldn't describe it quite that way . . .

Pian: No. I wasn't trying to show Peking Opera as an end product, but rather to illustrate the kinds of forms from which Peking Opera could borrow.

Malm: Well, kyōgen was incorporated into Noh and that was strictly Buddhist. It is all pantomime, all masked and the music is totally different--one flute and a gong. There is only one melody and everything is sung to it.

Teele: I identified the name kuse as being incorporated into Noh but not necessarily anything else. I could have mentioned kouta, which means a small song.

Pian: In speaking of the role of the author, you state that the author must be careful to use suitable music. What is meant by "suitable music?"

Teele: This is a paraphrase. It means simply that the author must be acquainted with all the possible forms and know when they are appropriate.

Malm: Although my specialty is not Noh, in other Japanese traditions the man who composes the text does not write the music.

Pian: Well, this statement is interesting: "the first stage is to know the materials to use, divide it into sections and set it to music as a final process." (p. 189) The process is the same in Peking Opera, but, does this suggest that the melody already existed?

Malm: I don't know, and I don't even know that about <u>naga-uta</u>, my real specialty. I have asked many times whether the text or the tune came first, but I have never received a satisfactory answer. Quite often a text is selected and worked out with a singer and a <u>shamisen</u> player; a drummer is then found to join them and the drummer's task is to tell the flute player when to come in. It is really a joint composition. This isn't the process followed for Peking Opera, is it?

Pian: Well, in Peking Opera the melody not only already exists, it is already labeled. One possible way to compose a Peking Opera is to find someone to compose a text compatible with the Peking Opera style. The places where particular arias are to be used are even specified. All the parts can be labeled by someone unable to hum a single note. Then it is given to a professional opera singer (this happened in Taiwan at any rate) who hums it. And what I can't tell you is whether or not the melody is fixed at that point! The singer then consults a more literate person who may recommend changes here and there.

Crump: Changes in the words or the . . .

Pian: I don't know! Anyway, the literatus serves this basic function. This is as far into the process as I was able to penetrate. One important process is the change of a line into a 7-syllable line (223) or a 10-syllable line (334). Then it can be sung. I have watched my husband sing to entries in a telephone book. As long as the syllables are distributed correctly he can do it. Of course this would be the dullest possible opera and one could turn out hundreds of operas in this way. In a multiform melody system you choose the right section of melody to fit the word-tone. Usually there are only the two divisions to worry about: the level and the oblique. After you have done this, however, the melody may not sound nice. If it happens to contain too many even-tone words, the melody may have too many high notes. A sensitive person would then make changes. These are musical considerations. One may then decide to bring out a particular word in the line. Perhaps it is a name which should be emphasized clearly so that everyone understands it. The name is set according to its tone in a literal imitation of the word. Finally, it may be noted that the text describes bees flying up and down. Imitation of this may be desired, so it is reshuffled again. In using a pre-existing multiform melody there are many levels of consideration in setting a word and I refer to a careful setting.

Johnson: Is it possible to set down a basic skeletal structure for a multiform melody?

Pian: In a paper which will be published this spring I have taken twenty-five animated arias from "The Trial of Su San" and cut them up. I have aligned all the same slots so that a comparison can be made. In the Noh is there a composer of this type or is he more of the Western type? Are there existing melodies at the disposal of the Noh composer?

Teele: Well, we can't say about Zeami, but to use a modern example, a minister in a church where I worked wrote a Noh play about missionaries coming to Japan. He composed the music himself and it was sung in church.

Sesar: I have a certain feeling about Zeami. Both Zeami and his father were actors and worked in a troupe. I assume this included musicians and players all traveling together. I think most of the playwrights were performers as well. This tells us a great deal. It must have been a collaborative effort. A style was developed by a single troupe, which suggests different styles among different troupes.

Teele: I have a feeling about the Noh drama in contrast with Yüan drama: I don't think there were definite arias types. I think that, like Wagner, once the music gets going it continues on its own. Therefore, the composing process is quite different.

FOOTNOTES

1. For Chiang K'uei's seventeen songs see: Rulan Chao Pian, <u>Sonq Dynasty Musical Sources and Their Interpretation</u>. Cambridge: Harvard University Press, 1967, particularly pp. 83-9 <u>passim</u>, and the transcriptions and notes pp. 99-129.

2. <u>Wayang Kulit</u>: the puppet theatre of Indonesia.

3. Mr. Addiss' comments from the floor indicated possible influences on Vietnamese music-theatre by Yüan drama. Similarities in problems of setting tonal language texts to music were also introduced.

4. A work by Zukei Shichiri.

5. Nogami Toyoichiro, <u>Yōkyoku Zenshū</u>, Tokyo: Chūō Kōron Sha, 1936, 6 volumes.

6. Sanari Kentarō, <u>Yōkyoku Taikan</u>, Tokyo: Meiji Shoin (1st ed. 1953), 7 volumes.

7. Yokomichi Mario and Omote Akira, <u>Yōkyoku shū</u>, Tokyo: Iwana Shoten (1st ed. 1960), 7 volumes.

8. <u>Kiri-nō</u>: the fast plays which close the program. They are usually plays about demons or the supernatural.

9. <u>Tan</u>: a general term for female roles; <u>sheng</u>: a general term for male roles.

10. <u>Kagura</u>: entertainments performed before the gods.

age　上

awase kariginu　袷狩衣

age-uta　上歌

Awazu-no-Saburō　粟津の三郎

age suteru　上捨てる

bachi　撥

ageyori　上より

banshiki　盤渉

ageyori suteru　上より捨てる

Bashō　芭蕉

Ai-kyōgen　間狂言

Benkei　辨慶

Aki　安藝

binsasara　編木

Amaterasu　天照

biwa　琵琶

Antoku　安德

bugaku　舞樂

Aoki　青木

Cha Mei An　鍘美案

Aoki-ga-hara　あおきが原

Chan Huang-p'ao　斬黃袍

Ariwara no Narihira　在原の業平

Ch'ang-hen Ko　長恨歌

Ariso　荒磯

"Ch'ang-k'ung Wan-li"
　長空萬里

Ashitaka　愛鷹

Ch'ang-pan Hill　長坂坡

Aso　阿蘇

Chang Po-ch'i (Feng-yi)
　張伯起（鳳翼）

Asura　阿修羅

atote　後手

ch'ang-san-le　唱散了

atsuita　厚板

ch'ang-yu　娼優

Atsuta　熱田

Chang yü-tz'u　張宇慈

Awaji　淡路

chango 杖鼓

Chao Shih Ku Erh 趙氏孤兒

Ch'ao T'ien-tzu 朝天子

Chao Tzu-ang 趙子昂

Chao Yün 趙雲

chappa ちゃっぱ

che-che-che-che 這

chen ching-shen 真精神

Ch'en Hou-chu 陳後主

Ch'en Kung 陳宮

Ch'en Shih-mei 陳世美

Ch'en Shu-pao 陳叔寶

ch'en-tzu 襯字

cheng 箏

Cheng Ch'ien 鄭騫

Cheng Ch'ing-mao 鄭清茂

Cheng Jo-yung 鄭若庸

Cheng-yin P'u （太和）正音譜

Ch'eng Ying 程嬰

chi ㄔ

chi-ch'ü 集曲

Ch'i Ju-shan 齊如山

Chi Pen 季本

Chi San Ch'iang 急三槍

chia 甲

Chia Kuei 賈貴

Chiang K'uei 姜夔

Ch'iao Meng-fu 喬孟符

chiao-pan 叫板

chiao-t'ou 叫頭

ch'ien-ch'iang 前腔

ch'ien kun 前袞

chih-ch'iung . . . che 至窮…者

chih, hu, che, yeh 之乎者也

Chih Sun 志孫

chih yü yi ch'ü . . . che
　　　　至于一曲…者

Chin 晉

ch'in 琴

Ch'in Hsiang-lien 秦香蓮

Ch'in Kan-lo 秦甘羅

Chin Sheng-t'an 金聖嘆

Chin Wei 金唯

ching 淨

ch'ü-p'u 曲譜

<u>Chü ta kang</u> 鋸大缸

<u>Ch'ü-tsao</u> 曲藻

chū u 中ラ

chū uki 中うき

ch'uan-ch'i 傳奇

"Ch'un Chiang Hua Yüeh Yeh" 春江花月夜

<u>Chung-hua Huo-yeh Wen-hsüan</u> 中華活葉文選

chung kun 中袞

<u>Chung-kuo Ku-tien Hsi-ch'ü Lun-chu Chi-ch'eng</u> 中國古典戲曲論著集成

Chung Ssu-ch'eng 鍾嗣成

<u>Chung-wen Ta Tz'u-tien</u> 中文大辭典

<u>Chung-yüan Yin-yün</u> 中原音韵

daijin-eboshi 大臣烏帽子

daijin-waki 大臣脇

dan 段

deha 出端

dengaku 田樂

dōbyōshi 銅拍子

<u>Eboshi Ori</u> 烏帽子折

eikyoku 宴曲

ennen 延年

<u>Erh Chin Kung</u> 二進宮

erh-huang 二黄

Erh-huang man-pan 二黄漫板

erh-liu 二六

Etsu 越

<u>Fa Men Ssu</u> 法門寺

Fan Erh-huang 反二黄

Fan Hsi-p'i 反西皮

Fan Hsi-p'i man-pan 反西皮漫板

Feng Huan Ch'ao 鳳還巢

Feng Meng-lung 馮夢龍

fu 賦

fu-mo 副末

<u>Fu-pao T'ang Chi</u> 頁苞堂集

<u>Fuji</u> 富士

<u>Fuji-san</u> 富士山

Fujiwara no Moronaga 藤原 師長

fumi 文

Funa Benkei 般辨慶

furi 振

fushi 節

gagaku 雅樂

gaku 樂

gaku-mono 樂物

ge 下

ge no chū 下の中

ge no kuzu 下の崩

ge osae 下押え

Gekkyūden 月宮殿

Gen Zatsugeki Kenkyū
元雜劇研究

Genji 源氏

Genjō 絃上 or 玄上 or 玄象

Gennin Zatsugeki Josetsu
元人雜劇序説

genzai-mono 現在物

gigaku 伎樂

Go-Shirakawa 後白河

Gorō Tokimune 五郎時致

ha 破

ha-no-ichidan 破の一段

ha-no-nidan 破の二段

ha-no-sandan 破の三段

Hagoromo 羽衣

Haku Rakuten 白樂天

Hakushi monjū 白氏文集

Han-hsü Tzu 涵虚子

han-kaiko 半開口

han kizami 半刻み

Han Rei 范蠡

Han-tan (Chi) 邯鄲記

Han Wu-ti 漢武帝

"hana no Miyako mo, haru no sora"
花の都も，春の空

hane 撥ね

hang-chia 行家

hang-chia sheng-huo 行家生活

hao t'ien-ch'i yeh! 好天氣也

haru 張

hashigakari 橋懸

hataraki はたらき

hataraki-goto はたらき事

hataraki-mono はたらき物

haya-fue 早笛

haya-mai 早舞

haya-tsuzumi 早鼓

hayabushi 早ぶし

hayashi 囃子

Heike Monogatari 平家物語

"hi no moto" 日の本

hichiriki 篳篥

hikae 控え

hira nori 平乗り

hito ga mashi ya na na mo naki
    mono nari
    人がましや字名も字き者
ho なり
    ほ

Ho Liang-chün 何良俊

Ho Wei 何為

hon-yuri ほんゆり

Hou Han Shu 後漢書

hsi-ch'ü 戲曲

"Hsi-ch'ü Ch'ang-ch'iang
    Ch'uang-tso yen-chiu"
    戲曲唱腔創作研究

Hsi Chü Pao 戲劇報

Hsi-ch'ü Tz'u-tien 戲曲辞典

Hsi-ch'ü Yin-yüeh Lun-wen Hsüan
    戲曲音樂論文選

Hsi-ch'ü Yin-yüeh Yen-chiu
    戲曲音樂研究

Hsi-hsiang Chi 西廂記

Hsi Hsüeh Hui K'ao 戲學彙考

Hsi K'ao 戲考

hsi-p'i 西皮

Hsia-jo Village 下若里

Hsia Yeh 夏野

Hsiang Sheng Chi Chin 相聲集錦

Hsiang Yü 項羽

Hsiao Ch'ang-hua 蕭長華

Hsiao Ch'ang-hua Yen-ch'u Chü-pen
    Hsüan Chi
    蕭長華演出劇本選集

Hsiao-kua-fu shang-fen 小寡婦上墳

hsiang-chan 响餞

hsiao-huang-men 小黃門

Hsiao Shu-lan 蕭淑蘭

hsieh-lü 協律

hsieh-p'ai 歇拍

hsieh-tzu 楔子

hsien 限

Hsien yu wen; hou yu tse 先有文；後有則

hsien-yün 險韻

Hsin Ch'ü-yüan 新曲苑

hsin ti ch'ao-jan 心地超然

Hsü 序

Hsü Chih-hao 許志豪

Hsü Fu-tso 徐復柞

Hsü Ta-ch'un 徐大椿

Hsü Wei 徐渭

Hsüan-ho (Sung) 宣和

Hsüan-ho Yi-shih 宣和遺事

Hsüan-tsung, Emperor 玄宗

Hua-mei Hsü 畫眉序

hua-pu 花部

Huan-sha (Chi) 浣紗記

Huang-chou Fu 黃州府

huang-men 黃門

Huang Ying-erh 黃鶯兒

Hui-lai 回來

Hui-lung 迴龍

Hung-fu Chi 紅拂記

Hung Tsung Lieh Ma 紅鬃烈馬

Hung-yang Tung 洪羊洞

Huo-lang-erh Chiu Chuan 貨郎兒九轉

Huo-yeh 活葉

iguse 居曲

Ikari Katsuki 碇潛

Iki 生

imayō 今樣

ire-ha 入れ 破

iri 入

iro-ōkuchi 色大口

Ise 伊勢

issei 一聲

issei no hayashi 一聲の囃子

itsuko 壹鼓

Itsukushima 嚴島

Iwanami 岩波

Iwashimizu 石清水

Izumi, Lady 泉式部

Jakkō-in 寂光院

Jen Na 任訥

ji 地

ji-utai 地謡

Jien 慈圓

jo 序

jō 上

jō-gami 尉髪

jo-ha-kyū 序破急

Jo-hsia village 若下里

jō ko osae 上小押え

jo-no-mai 序の舞

jō osae 上押え

jō u 上う

jō uki 上うき

juan-hsien (yüeh-ch'in)
阮咸（月琴）

ju-p'o 入破

ju-sheng 入聲

kabuki 歌舞伎

Kadensho 花傳書

kagura 神樂

kaiko 開口

kaiko 揩鼓

kakari かかり

kakeai 掛け合

kakegoe 掛け声

kakeri 翔

kami-mai-mono 神舞物

kami-mono 神物

kamikaze 神風

Kamo 賀茂

Kan 漢

kan mitsuji 甲三地

Kanami Kiyotsugu 觀阿彌清次

kane 鐘

Kantan 邯鄲

Kantan-otoko 邯鄲男

Kanyōkyū 咸陽宮

Kanze Kan-ami Kiyotsugu
観世観阿彌清次

kao-ch'iang 高腔

Kao Ming 高明

Kao-t'ang, Mt. 高堂

Kappo 合浦

Kara Monogatari 唐物語

karagoto 唐事

karagoto-mono 唐事物

kasanekashira 重頭

Kashima 鹿島

kashira 頭

kashira suritsuki 頭すりつき

Kasuga Myōjin 春日明神

Kasuga Ryūjin 春日龍神

Kasuga Shrine 春日神社

katari 語

Kayoi Komachi 通い小町

kazura-mono 鬘物

Kenreimon-in 建礼門院

keyaki 欅

Ki no Tsurayuki 紀貫之

kiri 切り

kiri-mono 切り物

kiri-nō 切り能

kiribyōshi 切り拍子

Kiyotsune 清経

kizami 刻み

kizami otoshi 刻落し

ko-lü p'ai 格律派

ko tsuzumi 小鼓

Kōdanshō 江談抄

kōguri 甲ぐり

koiai こい合

kokata 子方

Kōken, Emperor 孝謙

Kokinshū 古今集

Komachi 小町

Komagaku 高麗楽

Konishi 小西甚一

kōryo 高呂

Kōtei 皇帝

kotoba 詞

kotoba 言葉

kouji-jō 小牛尉

kouta 小唄

Kōwaka mai 幸若舞

ku-cheng 古箏

Ku Ch'in Ch'ü Chi 古琴曲集

Ku-chin Ming-chü Ho-hsüan 古今名劇合選

Ku-ch'ü Tsa-yen 顧曲雜言

Ku-ch'ü Ch'en-t'an 古曲塵談

Ku-tien Hsi-ch'ü Sheng-yüeh Lun-chu Ts'ung-pien 古典戲曲聲樂論著叢編

k'u-t'ou 哭頭

ku-wen 古文

k'uai-pan 快板

Kuan Han-ch'ing 關漢卿

Kuan Yü 關羽

K'uang Ku-shih 狂鼓史

k'uang-k'uang-ch'ing-k'uang 匡匡傾匡

kudoki 口説き

kun 袞

k'un-ch'ü 崑曲

kun-pan 滾板

k'un-pu 崑部

kung 宮

kung-ch'e 工尺

K'ung Ch'eng Chi 空城計

K'ung-ming 孔明

kung-tiao 宮調

Kuo Wu Kuan 過五關

Kurama Tengu 鞍馬天狗

kure tsuzumi 腰(呉)鼓

kuri 繰り

kuri/sashi/kusemai 繰り/差し/曲舞

kuse 曲

kusemai 曲舞

Kwanze 観世

Kwanze Kojirō Nobumitsu 観世小次郎信光

kyōgen 狂言

kyōgen kuchi-ake 狂言口開

kyū 急

Lei-chiang Chi 酹江集

Lei-chün 類儁

Li Hou-chu (Yü) 李後主(煜)

li-chia pa-hsi 庋家把戲

Li Po 李白

Liang Ch'en-yü 梁辰魚

Liang-chou Hsü 梁州序

Liang Yü-sheng 梁玉繩

Liao 遼

Lii Kwei Fuh Jing 李逵負荆

Lin-ch'uan 臨川

Lin Ch'ung Yeh Pen 林冲夜奔

Lin Lu 林綠

Ling Shan-ch'ing 凌善清

Liu Chi-tien 劉吉典

Liu-chih 柳枝

Liu Hung-sheng 劉鴻聲

liu-li 流麗

Liu Pei 劉備

Liu-shih-chung Ch'ü 六十种曲

liu-shui 流水

liu-shui-pan 流水板

Liu Yen-po 劉延伯

Liu Yung-chi 劉永濟

Lo River 洛川

Lo Chin-t'ang 羅錦堂

Lü (version) 呂

Lu Hsün 魯迅

Lu-kuei Pu 錄鬼簿

Lü Po-she 呂伯奢

Lu Sheng-k'uei 盧勝奎

Lui Tsun-yuen 呂振原

Ma Chih-yüan 馬知遠

Ma Su 馬謖

machi-utai 待謠

mae-jite 前ジテ

maete 前手

mai 舞

man-pan 慢板

Manyōshū 萬葉集

Mao Chin 毛晉

Mao K'un (Lu-men) 茅昆 (鹿門)

mashi bushi 增節

matsuri bayashi 祭囃子

Matsura 松浦

Matsukaze 松風

mawashi 迴し

Mei Ting-tso 梅鼎祚

Meishō 名生

Mekari 和布刈

Meng Ch'eng-shun 孟稱舜

Mi Shih 麋氏

michiyuki 道行き

mijikaji 短地

miko 巫女

Mimashi 味摩之

Mindai Gekisakka Kenkyū

明代劇作家研究

ming-chia 名家

Ming-feng 鳴鳳

Ming-shih 明史

Mishima 三島

Mio 三保

mitsuji 三地

Miyako 都

mizugoromo 水衣

Momiji-gari 紅葉狩

mondō 問答

mono no aware 物のあわれ

Mu-k'e Fort 穆柯 (寨)

Mu-tan T'ing (Huan-hun Chi)
牡丹亭 (還魂記)

Murakami, Emperor 村上

Murasaki, Lady 紫 (式部)

Na ni ga na ni shi te na ni to ya ra
何が何して何とやら

nagaji 長地

nagaji kaeshi 長地返し

naga-uta 長歌

naka-iri 中入

nan-ch'ü chüeh wu ts'ai-ch'ing
南曲絶無才情

nan-hsi 南戲

Nan-k'o (Chi) 南柯 (記)

nan-lü-kung 南呂宮

nan-lü-tiao 南呂調

Nan-pang-tzu 南梆子

Nan-tz'u Hsü-lu 南詞敍錄

Nan-tz'u Hsü-lu T'i-yao
南詞敍錄提要

nanori 名宣

nanori 名乘

nanori-bue 名乘笛

Nara Ehon Yokohon
奈良絵本横本

Naruo 鳴尾

Nashitsubo, Lady 梨壺

ni-ni-ni-ni 你

ni no tsuzumi 二の鼓

Ni Heng 襧衡

nien kan-pan 念乾板

Nien Nu-chiao 念奴嬌

Nien Nu-chiao Hsü 念奴嬌序

Nihon Koten Zenshū 日本古典全集

Nihon Shoki 日本書記

Ning-hsien Wang 寧獻王

ningen rashii 人間らしい

Nishikigi 錦木

nochi-jite 後仕手

Nogami (Toyoichirō) 野上豊一郎

Noh 能

nōkan 能管

nomi 呑

nori-ji のり地

Nōsakusho 能作書

Nü Ch'i Chieh 女起解

nyūwa 柔和

ō nori 大乗

ō tsuzumi 大鼓

Ōbeshi 大癋

odorite 踊手

Ōhara Gokō 大原御幸

okuri 送リ

Omote 表章

Ono no Komachi 小野小町

oroshi 下ろし

oroshi makuri 下し捲リ

Otomo no Kuronushi 大伴黒主

Pa I T'u 八義圖

pa-ku-wen 八股文

Pai Ling Chi 白綾計

Pai Ma P'o 白馬坡

P'ai-p'ien 排遍

Pai-t'u Chi 白兔記

p'ai-tzu 牌子

Pai-yüeh (T'ing) 拜月(亭)

pan-ch'iang 板腔

pao-ming 報名

Pao-yü 寶玉

pei-ch'ü 北曲

pen-se 本色

pen-se yü 本色語

pen we kung-tiao 本無宮調

p'i-pa 琵琶

P'i-pa (Chi) 琵琶（記）

P'ieh-chi 甓記

Pin-pai 賓白

p'ing 平

P'ing-kuei Pieh Yao 平貴別窰

p'o 破

Po Chü-yi 白居易

po-lan 波瀾

pon ぽん

P'u An Chou 普庵咒

p'u-shih 朴實

P'u Teng Erh 撲燈兒

rai-jo らい序

rankei 鸞鏡

Rinyūgaku 林邑樂

ritsu 律

rōei 朗詠

Rokkasen 六歌仙

rongi 論様

Rosei 盧生

ryūteki 龍笛

ryo 呂

Ryōko 龍虎

sagariha 下端

sage-uta 下歌

Sakagami 逆髮

San Chi Chang 三擊掌

san-ch'ü 散曲

San hsü 散序

san no tsuzumi 三の鼓

san-pan 散板

san-sheng 三聲

san-yüeh 散樂

Sanari Kentarō 佐成謙太郎

sandō 三道

Sanemori 実盛

sangaku 散樂

Sanjo 散序

Sanshō 三笑

Sao-t'ou 掃頭

sarugaku 猿樂

sarugaku no Noh 猿樂の能

sashi 差し

sashi jō さし上

sashi nanori さし名乗

Seiōbō 西王母

Semimaru 蟬丸

serifu 台詞

Sha-kou 殺狗記

sha kun 煞衰

Shakatsura 娑竭羅

Shakkyō 石橋

shamisen 三味線

Shao-hsing Hsi 紹興戲

Shen Te-fu 沈德符

Shen Yüeh 沈約

sheng (musical instruments) 笙

sheng (male roles) 生

Sheng-ming Tsa-chü 盛明雜劇

shibui 澁い

Shichiri Zukei 七理重惠

shidai 次第

Shiga 志賀

shih 詩

Shih Ching-t'ang 石敬塘

shih-erh-k'o 十二科

Shih Hui 施惠

"Shih-huo Chih" 食貨志

shih ts'ui 實催

shih-wen p'ai 時文派

shike-mizugoromo 絓水衣

shiko 四鼓

shin-jo-no-mai-mono 真序之舞物

shin-no issei-no-hayashi 真の一聲の囃子

Shinowara 篠原

Shinzei Kogakuzu 信西古樂図

shirabyōshi 白拍子

shiro-ōkuchi 白大口

shiro-tare 白垂

shite 仕手

shite-zure 仕手連

shiwa-jō 皺尉

Shizuka Gozen 静御前

shō 笙

Shō yō mei chō rai Fu sō
   gen ben sei
   初陽每朝來 不遣還本栖

shobamme-mono 初番目物

shōban 鉦盤

shodō 初同

Shōjō 猩々

Shōki 鐘馗

Shōkun 昭君

shōmyō 聲明

Shōnagon (清) 少納言

Shōsōin 正倉院

shūnen-mono 執念物

shu-lai-pao 數來寶

shu-pan 數板

shūgen 祝言

Shūgyoku-shū 拾玉集

Shui-hu Chuan 水滸傳

Shui-tiao Ko-t'ou 水調歌頭

shuo-pai 說白

shuramono 修羅物

Soga Monogatari 曾我物語

Ssu Lang 四郎

Ssu Lang T'an Mu 四郎探母

Ssu-ma Ch'ien 司馬遷

Ssu-ma Yi 司馬懿

ssu-p'ing 四平

Ssu-p'ing-tiao 四平調

ssu-sheng 四聲

Ssu-sheng Yüan 四聲猿

Ssu-yu Chai Ch'ü-shuo
   四友齋曲說

Su San 蘇三

Su Tung-p'o 蘇東坡

Sui Shu-sen 隋樹森

Suiko, Empress 推古

Sumidagawa 隅田川

Suminoye 住の江

Sumiyoshi 住吉

Sung Chiang 宋江

Sung-jen P'ing-hua Ssu-chung
宋人評話四種

Sung-tai ko-wu chü-ch'ü lu-yao
宋代歌舞劇曲錄要

Suwa 諏訪

ta-ch'ü 大曲

Ta-p'eng 大鵬

Ta-ya T'ang Tsa-chü Ssu-chung
大雅堂雜劇四种

Ta Yü Sha Chia 打漁殺家

Taihei 太平

Taihei Shōjō 大瓶猩々

T'ai-ho Cheng-yin P'u
太和正音譜

T'ai-ning 太寧

taiko 太鼓

takakizami 高刻

takakizamikiri 高刻切り

takakizamisuteru 高刻捨てる

Takasago 高砂

Take no Yuki 竹雪

Tama-no-i 玉井

Tamura 田村

tan 旦

"T'an Chia Kuei Nien Chuang"
談賈貴念狀

Tan-ch'iu Hsien-sheng, Han-hsü tzu
丹邱先生涵虚子

Tan-hsien P'ai-tzu Ch'ü
單絃牌子曲

T'an-hua Chi 曇花記

T'ang Shun-chih 唐順之

t'an-tz'u 彈詞

tang-chia 當家

tang-hang 當行

Tanikō 谷行

T'ang Hsien-tsu 湯顯祖

T'ang Hsien-tsu Chi 湯顯祖集

T'ang Sung ta-ch'ü k'ao
唐宗大曲孝

tao (upside down) 倒

t'ao 套

T'ao [Ch'ien] P'eng-tse
陶(潛)彭澤

T'ao Chün-ch'i 陶君起

tao-pan 倒板 or 導板

t'ao-shu 套述

T'ao Tsung-yi 陶宗儀

te　手

tegumi　手組

teiryo　低呂

tengu　天狗

Tenko　天鼓

ti　笛

tiao　調

T'iao-chia-kuan　跳加宮

Tiao-ch'ung Kuan　彫蟲館

T'ien Tan Chiu Chu　田單救主

T'ien tso pao lai ti tso pao
天做保来地做保

t'ien-tz'u　填詞

Ti-liu Tzu　滴溜子

ting-ch'ang shih　定場詩

Ting Ping-sui　丁炳燧

tō-kammuri　唐冠

to-pan　塌板

tō-uchiwa　唐團扇

Tōboku　東北

Tōbōsaku　東方朔

Tōdaiji　東大寺

Tomomori　知盛

Tomonari　友成

tori　取リ

tori kashira　取頭

tori kizami　取刻

toro tsuzumi　答臘鼓

Tōryō　棟梁

Tōsen　唐船

tsa-chü　雜劇

"Tsa-men t'ai-shang chien"
咱們台上見

ts'ai　材

Tsang Mou-hsün (T. Chin-shu)
臧懋循 (晉叔)

Ts'ao Ts'ao　曹操

tse　則

tse　仄

Tseng P'ao Tz'u Ma　贈袍賜馬

Tso-Tz'u Shih-fa　作詞十法

Tsu Yü-lin　簇御林

tsuki serifu　着也リふ

Tsukushi　筑紫

tsukusuma　つくすま

Tsung-pao 宗保

tsure つれ

Tsurukame 鶴龜

tsuyo 強

tsuyogin 強吟

tsuzuke 続け

tsuzumi 鼓

tsuzumi (early form) 豆美

T'u Lung 屠隆

t'ung-ch'iang 同腔

Tung Chieh-yüan 董解元

t'ung-fang 通方

t'ung-pai-tzu 銅拍子

tz'u 詞

Tzu-ch'ai Chi 紫釵記

Tzu-ch'ai Ssu-chi 紫釵四記

Tzu-hsiao Chi 紫簫記

uchikaeshi kashira 打返頭

uchikomi 打込み

ui-kammuri 初冠

uke nakakashira うけ中頭

uke nakakashira suritsuke

うけ中頭 すりつけ

Ushiwaka 牛若

uta 歌

utai-bon 謡本

waka 和歌

waki 脇

waki-issei 脇一聲

waki-nō 脇能

waki-zuri 脇連

Wan-li 萬利

Wang Chi-te (Po-liang)

王驥德 (伯良)

Wang Kuo-wei 王國維

Wang P'ei-lun 王沛綸

Wang Po-liang 王伯良

Wang Shih-chen (T. Yüan-mei)

王世真 (元美)

Wang Tao-k'un 汪道昆

warai-jō 笑尉

Wei Liang-fu 魏良輔

Wei Lung-hao 魏龍豪

wen 文

Yōkyoku to Genkyoku 謡曲と元曲

Yoshino shizuka 吉野静

Yoshitsune 義經

yowa 弱

yowa kuzushi 弱くずし

yowa sashi 弱差し

yowagin 弱吟

Yü, Lady 虞氏

Yü Ch'an-shih 玉禪士

Yü-chüeh Chi 玉玦記

Yü-ho Chi 玉盒記

Yu-kuei Chi 幽閨記

Yu-meng 優孟

Yü-ming T'ang 玉茗堂

Yü-ming T'ang Ch'uan-ch'i 玉茗堂傳奇

Yü-ming T'ang Ssu-meng 玉茗堂四夢

Yü T'ang Ch'un 玉堂春

"Yü T'ang Ch'un han pei lei mang wang ch'ien chin" 玉堂春含悲淚忙望前進

"Yü T'ang Ch'un lo-nan feng fu" 玉堂春落難逢夫

Yü-t'ung 玉通

Yüan-ch'ü Hsüan 元曲選

Yüan-jen Pai-chung Ch'ü 元人百种曲

Yüan k'un-ch'ü 元崑曲

Yüan-men Chan Tzu 轅門斬子

Yüan, Ming, Ch'ing Hsi-ch'ü Yen-chiu-lun-wen Chi 元明清戲曲研究論文記

yüan-pan 原板

Yüan-yang 鴛鴦

yüeh-fu 樂府

Yüeh-fu Ch'uan Sheng 樂府傳聲

yūgen 幽玄

yün 韵

Yung-chia 永嘉

yuri 搖り

Yuya 熊野

Zeami Motokiyo 世阿彌元清

Zegai 善界 or 是界 or 是我意

Zenchiku 禪竹

MICHIGAN PAPERS IN CHINESE STUDIES

No. 1. The Chinese Economy, 1912-1949, by Albert Feuerwerker.

No. 2. The Cultural Revolution: 1967 in Review, four essays by Michel Oksenberg, Carl Riskin, Robert Scalapino, and Ezra Vogel.

No. 3. Two Studies in Chinese Literature: "One Aspect of Form in the Arias of Yüan Opera" by Dale Johnson; and "Hsü K'o's Huang Shan Travel Diaries" translated by Li Chi, with an introduction, commentary, notes, and bibliography by Chun-shu Chang.

No. 4. Early Communist China: Two Studies: "The Fu-t'ien Incident" by Ronald Suleski; and "Agrarian Reform in Kwangtung, 1950-1953" by Daniel Bays.

No. 5. The Chinese Economy, ca. 1870-1911, by Albert Feuerwerker.

No. 6. Chinese Paintings in Chinese Publications, 1956-1968: An Annotated Bibliography and An Index to the Paintings, by E. J. Laing.

No. 7. The Treaty Ports and China's Modernization: What Went Wrong? by Rhoads Murphey.

No. 8. Two Twelfth Century Texts on Chinese Painting, "Shan-shui ch'un-ch'üan chi" by Han Cho, and chapters nine and ten of "Hua-chi" by Teng Ch'un, translated by Robert J. Maeda.

No. 9. The Economy of Communist China, 1949-1969, by Chu-yuan Cheng.

No. 10. Educated Youth and the Cultural Revolution in China by Martin Singer.

No. 11. Premodern China: A Bibliographical Introduction, by Chun-shu Chang.

No. 12. Two Studies on Ming History, by Charles O. Hucker.

No. 13. Nineteenth Century China: Five Imperialist Perspectives, selected by Dilip Basu, edited with an introduction by Rhoads Murphey.

No. 14. <u>Modern China, 1840-1972: An Introduction to Sources and Research Aids</u>, by Andrew J. Nathan.

No. 15. <u>Women in China: Studies in Social Change and Feminism</u>, edited with an introduction by Marilyn B. Young.

No. 16. <u>An Annotated Bibliography of Chinese Painting Catalogues and Related Texts</u>, by Hin-cheung Lovell.

No. 17. <u>China's Allocation of Fixed Capital Investment, 1952-57</u>, by Chu-yuan Cheng.

No. 18. <u>Health, Conflict, and the Chinese Political System</u>, by David M. Lampton.

No. 19. <u>Chinese and Japanese Music-Dramas</u>, edited by J. I. Crump and William P. Malm.

Price: $3.00 (US) each
except $4.00 for special issues #6, #15, and #19

Prepaid Orders Only

NON SERIES PUBLICATION

<u>Index to the "Chan-Kuo Ts'e"</u>, by Sharon Fidler and J. I. Crump. A companion volume to the <u>Chan-Kuo Ts'e</u> translated by J. I. Crump. (Oxford: Clarendon Press, 1970). $3.00

MICHIGAN ABSTRACTS OF CHINESE AND
JAPANESE WORKS ON CHINESE HISTORY

No. 1. The Ming Tribute Grain System by Hoshi Ayao, translated
by Mark Elvin.

No. 2. Commerce and Society in Sung China by Shiba Yoshinobu,
·translated by Mark Elvin.

No. 3. Transport in Transition: The Evolution of Traditional
Shipping in China, translations by Andrew Watson.

No. 4. Japanese Perspectives on China's Early Modernization: The
Self-Strengthening Movement, 1860-1895 by K. H. Kim.

Price: $4.00 (US) each

Prepaid Orders Only

Michigan Papers and Abstracts available from:
Center for Chinese Studies
University of Michigan
Lane Hall
Ann Arbor, Michigan 48104
USA